Soldier Spy

To 'THE POSH GEEK'

Great to meet you,
let's grab a beer
soon!

'TC' 06

Soldier Spy

TOM MARCUS

MICHAEL JOSEPH
an imprint of
PENGUIN BOOKS

MICHAEL JOSEPH

UK | USA | Canada | Ireland | Australia
India | New Zealand | South Africa

Michael Joseph is part of the Penguin Random House group of companies
whose addresses can be found at global.penguinrandomhouse.com

First published 2016
001

Set in 13.75/16.25 pt Garamond MT Std
Typeset by Jouve (UK), Milton Keynes
Printed in Great Britain by Clays Ltd, St Ives plc

A CIP catalogue record for this book is available from the British Library

HARDBACK ISBN: 978–0–718–18484–1
TRADE PAPERBACK ISBN: 978–0–718–18485–8

This book is dedicated to my wife.
Without you, I would have been lost a long time ago.
My one true constant. *Semper Vigilat*

Chapter One

As I pulled my clothes out of the double-sealed bag, the smell of piss hit me. Taking a minute to avoid being sick, I had to partly hold my breath to be able to wear them. Then they become a part of me. When people think of spies in the cinema or in their nice homes, they don't imagine me.

My covert radio was in full flow as I was receiving constant updates about our target. Changing into my ripped old trainers and twenty-year-old piss-covered combat bottoms, I could hear the words I'd been waiting for: 'STAND BY, STAND BY!'

The Operations Centre had a covert camera outside the target's house. Our target was now out in the open, presumably on his way to last prayers at the mosque. I knew I had about twenty minutes to get into position. I needed to be able to watch our target enter the mosque without him noticing me, and give the team the alert when he came out.

Leaving the back of the van dressed as a homeless man, stinking, I now looked like I'd been living on the streets of North London for the last ten years. Armed with my fingerless woollen gloves and soggy cardboard, I sat on the pavement and waited.

From my position I could see the main gates of the

mosque and I knew roughly the direction our young male target would be coming from and I could see all the faces entering and leaving the mosque. Our target should exit and then turn away from me as I discreetly alerted the team.

Holding an old coffee cup, asking for change, I bowed my head slightly and prepared to transmit on my covert radio or 'net' as the operators called it. 'Zero Six has the mosque entrance,' I murmured, giving the appearance that I was just a tramp muttering to himself.

'Roger that, Zero Six. Target is running free towards the area of the mosque now, light grey shalwar kameez, full beard as of yesterday, tan open-toed sandals.'

Having the team leader give me the description is essential. It allows me to lock on to him naturally without looking as if I'm studying the hundreds of males walking into the mosque, which is really difficult to do given how dark and wet this night is.

'From Zero Six, target walking north on St Thomas Road, I have control.' Letting the team know I could see the target was vital: it meant I could keep them out of the area as long as I could see him, saving our team for later if they needed to get close to him.

The target was self-radicalized; his parents were both doctors. We'd known about him for a number of years, and that he'd travelled to West Africa to fight with Boko Haram. Recently he had returned home. I'd noticed over the past few weeks that a bruise had started to appear in the centre of his forehead, indicating he was praying far harder.

We knew from his emails and text messages that he wanted to commit mass murder at a local school. We didn't know which one or when. But it was in the next few days. Maybe tomorrow.

This type of attack planning wasn't the work of the usual extremists we fight every day. My suspicions that our target was getting help to move around the globe freely were eating away at me.

We differ from the police in a lot of ways. Firstly, our levels of compromise are much lower, because of our skill sets, tactics and the resources available to us. Put simply, the people we hunt never know we're there, and even when they end up in court they still don't know how they got caught.

The police like to arrest quickly, to remove the threat to the public as soon as possible. But that doesn't defeat the problem, it merely takes away one of the foot soldiers. We want the whole infrastructure. By letting our targets go about their daily lives and progress their attack-planning stages all the way to their endgame, whether that is a suicide bombing, hostage-taking or mass murder, it lets us see their cell and develop what we call an intelligence picture.

We light it up from the inside, seeing their methods, financial backing, recruiting procedures, planning, hierarchy and known associates. It's not about taking this one particular attack out of the equation, it's about using this one to identify, and stop, ten others.

As the crowd of worshippers descended on the mosque, I made a mental note of how few females were entering compared to the hundreds of males.

'Zero Six, do you read? Base.'

'Yes. Yes, go ahead.' Just at this point a very kind if slightly uptight woman dropped some change into my cup, but I could tell from her face that she was repulsed by the smell of my clothes.

So with twenty-seven pence in my tattered Starbucks cup, the Operations Centre told me that our target had been spotted on local CCTV near the area. This was great news, I knew I had the right guy, but it was always nice having a fresh set of eyes confirm you had control of the right target.

'All stations from Zero Six,' I responded. 'Target IN, IN to the mosque. I can give a standby on exit but CAN'T go with!'

I hated the technical silence of our radios when we were waiting for a standby to wake the whole team up. It's isolating, the lack of chatter over the radio. My legs had gone numb and the cold from the pavement was creeping into my hip joints. Moving my toes in my ripped trainers, I was trying to force blood around my body while quietly asking for any spare change from the passers-by, who by now, as it started to rain and the temperature dropped, weren't lifting their heads up to look at me. Even the local police foot patrol ignored me. I was living my cover and it was working perfectly.

'All stations, Zero Six!' I whispered urgently into my covert radio. 'People coming en masse out of the mosque.'

Only the women came out first, most in full abaya worn over normal clothes. Sixteen left the mosque, all talking together apart from two straggling behind. I had

4

counted fourteen women into the mosque earlier. Had I got it wrong? I was sure I hadn't.

'Team leader, do you read? Zero Six.'

'Go ahead.'

'Can all stations keep an eye out for the target, please? He may have changed appearance.'

I wasn't 100 per cent sure, but needed the team to be open to the possibility that our target had changed his clothing inside the mosque.

As the male worshippers started to leave the mosque, I couldn't see our target. I knew something wasn't right. 'From Zero Six, all stations cover the exits out of the area, mass exit from the mosque.'

The majority of males were leaving south, away from me as planned, which was good for my cover but meant I couldn't see our target at all.

Most of the women travelled south, away from the mosque too, apart from the two stragglers who were dressed in full burkhas and walked directly past me, their long garments soaking up the heavy rain.

Just as the two women from the mosque walked past me, I got a message on the radio from one of my team. 'A good possible for the target now walking south of the mosque, approximately 150 metres out and still moving. Same clothes as described entering the mosque. Can't see his face yet.'

Fuck me, how had I missed him? I was scanning the area constantly, and I've never missed anyone leaving before. Just as I began to reply, I caught a glimpse of one of the two women in burkhas. As the burkha rose up on the stride, I noticed one of them was wearing tan open-toed sandals.

'ALL STATIONS, ZERO SIX! Target could be walking northbound dressed as a woman, full black burkha, open-toed tan sandals, five foot, six inches, alongside another of similar description. Base, acknowledge!'

'Roger that, Zero Six. The team is still following this good possible walking SOUTH away from the mosque.'

As the team still hadn't called a visual recognition of the target's face, I knew I had to do something. Yet if I stood up from this soaking-wet pavement, I risked drawing the attention of anyone providing counter-surveillance.

'From Zero Six, does your possible have the same sandals on as earlier?'

'Can't see at this distance.'

I was very aware that, if this was our target now dressed as a woman, he was going to great lengths to slip out of the area without being watched. This was a classic operational mindset. If someone like this, so close to their endgame in the attack-planning stage, was going to such lengths to evade people like us, it meant he was about to carry out an attack or go into hiding prior to the attack. Either way, it was bad.

The target would likely have people helping him watch for surveillance, so I had to be careful how I moved away and got control of what I was pretty sure were two men in full burkhas. The radio was completely frantic with the Ops room constantly asking for updates and with team members calling and then discounting 'possibles' – people bearing a resemblance to our target.

6

There was an off-licence over the road from me. Slowly and awkwardly clambering to my feet, I peered into my tattered coffee cup, shaking the change I had, and headed over to the shop front. The two burkha-clad people were still walking away from me, about thirty metres distant now and moving at a faster than normal pace as they navigated the other pedestrians. I needed to be quick here.

Looking through the shop window, I acted out a scenario in which I pretended I was checking the prices of the super-cheap alcohol and realizing I didn't have enough money. Dejected, I turned to walk north to follow the two burkhas, who were now a good fifty metres in front of me. I was starting to lose control of them.

'Base, Zero Six. I'm sticking with these two possibles, now heading north.'

'Roger that, Zero Six, you're on your own until confirmed either way.'

At this point I thought I'd lost the support and confidence of my team and senior figures in the Operations Centre. I'd had an important job outside the mosque and for whatever reason I'd missed him. In reality I knew the team trusted me as a seasoned operator, but it was hard not to feel like you'd dropped a bollock with someone so close to carrying out an attack.

The challenge for me now was to change my profile quickly from homeless tramp to a normal bloke on his way home and close the increasing gap between me and the two dark figures, who were disappearing fast.

Changing the way you look on the street, on the move, is hard to do without drawing attention to yourself.

Luckily for me it was bin day, the streets lined with bin-bags and wheelie bins. Staying on the opposite side of the street behind the two figures, I walked close to a group of people who had been drinking heavily and were clearly still under the impression that they were in the pub. Quickly unzipping my disgusting combat jacket, I dropped it into my right hand as I walked past a bin. I lifted the lid quickly but quietly, dropping the jacket in and cushioning the lid so as not to startle my new drunken friends.

Moving straight over the road away from the staggering group, I ducked behind a moving bus and threw my woollen gloves to the floor. As daft as it sounds, I remember thinking: *Fuck me, I've had these clothes for years, this better be the right target!*

I still needed to get out of the combat bottoms. I just had to go for it and risk it. As I'd closed the gap slightly, I could afford ten seconds or so. I turned into a dark alleyway on my right and started pulling them off. As I struggled to get my feet out of the legs, I noticed a homeless guy under some cardboard, trying to keep warm and dry. His pupils were clear white despite his dirty face and long greasy hair.

I muttered, 'Fuckers pissed on me!' in my best drunken voice – he bought my story and I left my twenty-year-old combats on the floor. Time to get control of those two burkhas.

I caught a glimpse of one dark figure turning right and east down the next street, a good 100 metres away now. Quickening my pace but without looking odd, I could still hear the chatter on the radio getting more and more chaotic. Still no sign of the target, despite the team now checking a vehicle that had driven off with someone who looked like our target, now miles away from our location.

I needed to cross the road again, taking care to avoid the possibility of being ambushed by following him around a blind corner.

As I got alongside the street I looked down it from the other side of the road. There was only one figure wearing a burkha now, but I could tell by the height compared to the height of the cars that this was one of the two I was following. Where the fuck was the second one?

This was a nightmare situation; I needed support here. Just as I was about to transmit I heard a house door slam shut behind me. Resisting the urge to turn around straight away, I pretended that I'd stepped in dog shit and used the edge of the pavement to scrape it off the bottom of my trainers. It gave me just enough of a glance back to try to see who'd slammed it.

I could see a male entering a car. Five foot six to eight inches tall, same slim build as our target and definitely of Somali origin, but clean-shaven. I couldn't be 100 per cent sure this was our target.

'Base, Zero Six, possible for the target, now clean-shaven, entering a green Toyota Yaris, partial VRN to follow.'

When you do this game for a long time, you develop an acute awareness of how target demeanour changes. We missed our target coming out of the mosque, I believe, because he changed his appearance. Now in the area where he has become unsighted I've seen another Somali male of a similar height but clean-shaven. This close to his endgame, it would make me think he's about to carry out an attack; he's cleansing his body.

'From Zero Six, partial VRN YANKEE SIX NINE SIX OSCAR TANGO. Base, acknowledge.'

'Base, roger that, all stations full VRN YANKEE SIX NINE SIX OSCAR TANGO YANKEE. This vehicle belongs to the uncle of the target!'

'Zero Six, roger, vehicle now running free west and last seen indicating right and north.'

The Operations Centre were thinking the same as me: this was highly likely our target, using a high degree of operational security in a vehicle we hadn't seen him drive before.

Normally I'd casually walk a natural route through the local area back towards my vehicle or arrange a vehicle pick-up, but the radio was still constant with my team acknowledging my suspicions and searching the area for this vehicle. I needed to get on the hunt for the target and quick.

'Any station pick me up? Zero Six.'

'Yeah, TC, go to the main. I'm swinging through now.'

Even though our communications were encrypted to Top Secret level and would take even the best hackers from China roughly ten years to crack, we hardly ever used our names on the net, almost always our service numbers.

I could sense the urgency in everyone's voices now and

rightly so; if we didn't get hold of this vehicle or the target we could have a massacre at a school any day now.

Seeing our team car moving fast through the traffic, I knew this one was my pick-up. Jumping in the passenger seat, I gave a very quick confirmation to the Operations Centre that I was now in a team vehicle rather than on foot.

'Zero Six, complete Charlie Nine.'

'All Stations, the vehicle is westbound on the A110 Enfield at the junction of Silver Street.'

The target must have been driving at a serious speed to make it that far north so quickly. He obviously wanted to avoid any chance of him being followed. The team swarmed into the area searching for this vehicle. I could hear everyone calling up the areas they were checking:

'Checking north on Silver Street towards the police station.'

'I've got westbound on the A110 towards the McDonald's.'

'Checking south London Road towards Argos.'

Shouting out visual markers as well as compass directions on a map is absolutely the quickest way to ring-fence the whole area. The trick here is to avoid looking like a police/Special Forces unit swarming the area searching for people about to do evil. We still need to blend in, while seeking to find our target vehicle as quickly as possible.

And then I spotted it. 'From Charlie Nine. Vehicle is parked on Willow Road on the west side, facing south opposite the junction of Peartree Road. One up, driver's side.'

Being the one to find a vehicle that was previously

running free or getting control of a target that's not been under control is a great feeling; you get the instant acknowledgements from your team.

'Base, roger, Charlie Nine – can you keep control?'

I remained in the car, which is why Base was now referring to me as Charlie Nine.

'Yes. Yes!'

'Base, roger, EXECUTIVE ACTION figures THREE!'

The senior officers obviously didn't like this and called for Executive Action to come and arrest the occupant of this vehicle. Executive Action is usually carried out by armed police of SO19 Counter Terrorism Unit, but at this response time it would more than likely be Special Forces embedded with it our teams. They aim to arrest but are authorized to kill if they face resistance.

'Charlie Nine. Roger, no change.'

Those three minutes felt like a lifetime. No radio chatter at all; everyone keeping quiet in case Base needed to update or more importantly if I had to relay the disastrous news that the vehicle had moved away or the target had got out on foot.

I caught a glimpse of the first Range Rover as it came screaming down the street side-on to the target vehicle, no lights on, smashing straight into the side of the Toyota Yaris. Just as it landed back on the pavement, two other Range Rovers, lights on full beam, came screaming in north and south to pin the car into position, but to be fair the Yaris was now a crumpled mess on the pavement, leaking all sorts of fluids, the airbags inside inflated.

As smooth as clockwork, the strike team smashed and pulled back the windscreen on the car – you can tell they practise this a lot – and like a rag doll the man was dragged through the windowless front and thrown onto the bonnet of one of the Range Rovers by two massive blokes in typical undercover SAS clothing: civilian but utilitarian combat trousers, sturdy hill-walking-type boots, pistol thigh-fits on their legs. As the two huge men zip-tied his hands, another, who had appeared from nowhere, placed a black hood over his head, bundling him into the back of a windowless Transit van.

As the Transit van drove away, the Range Rovers reversed out of position to follow it as it transported the prisoner to Paddington Green police station, used to hold and question high-profile terror suspects.

'Charlie Nine, Base, do you read?'

'Charlie Nine, yes, yes.'

Operations Centre told us that we needed to stay in the area until SO19 and Special Branch could retrieve the crumpled Toyota Yaris. Within minutes armed police arrived alongside typical plain-clothed Special Branch, and shortly after that an unmarked recovery vehicle arrived, as did the local residents who had heard a crash but luckily hadn't witnessed the dramatic arrest.

'All stations from Base, CEASE and WITHDRAW, acknowledge down the list.'

Leaving the area, I was dropped off at my van and travelled back to the debriefing room in the Operations Centre. Still smelling faintly of old tramp, I was running the last couple of hours through my head. This had to be our target. But what if it wasn't? If he didn't change his appearance, how did I miss him? Who was that person in the other burkha? Could this be the one who had been helping our target? I wanted answers and I was fairly sure I wasn't about to get them.

I walked through the one-way glass doors and I saw my whole team, the Lead Operations Officer and two senior officers whom we usually only see if we've fucked up and someone has been shot in a case of mistaken identity.

As the debrief unfolded, we learned that our target was in that Toyota Yaris; he HAD shaved his beard. In the boot were six homemade pipe bombs, all linked to detonate at the same time from a single call on a brand-new pay-as-you-go phone found on the target. Special Branch also found Chinese Type 56 assault rifles with eight full magazines of ammunition. His target was a local school. He planned to attack two coaches of teenagers returning home after a school trip to France. Approximately sixty children, their accompanying teachers and their waiting parents. He was going to kill them all.

The senior suits left the room, and our Operations Officer briefed us for our job the following day: a high-profile IRA member was flying over to Glasgow to meet other senior members in a pub. It was anticipated they would be discussing members of the Police Service of Northern Ireland whom they planned to kill to disrupt the peace process.

And that was another day done, no praise, no handshakes, no thanks and certainly no medals.

We don't do this for recognition or commendations from the Queen.

Some people join the service out of a sense of duty, some out of wanting to do some good by removing the evil.

I do it because it's all I know. I'm a hunter of people and I'm damn good at it.

Chapter Two

As a kid, I didn't have any family. Not in the traditional sense of the word. My dad was an abusive alcoholic, which eventually took his life. His dependency on booze was spawned from his time in the army as an infantry soldier. My mum, for whatever reason, detached herself from the situation of poverty and abuse, which ultimately meant I raised myself from the age of about six. Growing up on the harsh streets of a sprawling northern city, sometimes staying in squats, taking myself to school, I knew even then there had to be more to life. I had to be able to make something out of this pile of shit.

I remember one morning on my way to school, seeing a shiny blue Ford Cortina. At the age of eight, unaware of the danger of talking to strange men, I asked the driver what he did to have the money to be able to drive a car like that. His reply made me determined to get out of this situation one day: 'Ha, I do something that is way beyond someone like you. Enjoy your walk to school!'

I was never academic, nor physically the strongest at school. I was the dirty unkempt kid in the corner of the class, the one no one spoke to. The one that didn't get bullied but wasn't included either. The outcast. But the driver of that Ford Cortina did me a favour that day, when he assumed I would always be poor and never amount to anything. If a stranger made that snap decision about me, then it was more than likely everyone was thinking the same. If I wanted to be able to afford to wash my clothes at the laundrette round the corner, I needed to go after the money myself.

I stole a bucket from a local building site and, first thing next morning, started washing cars, near my school so no one knew where I lived in case they told my dad. I didn't bother knocking on any doors; my plan was to wash all the cars on the street before people got up for work in the hope that they would noticed how nice their cars looked and come and give me some money for it. Using the outside tap on the playground of my school, I hauled the cold water and washed the cars with my hands. I was doing a reasonable job and I was sure I'd end up with enough money to buy something better than beans on toast for tea.

On my third car I noticed a really fat guy coming towards me with the knuckles of his hands facing forward, walking in a waddle due to his size, wearing a hi-vis jacket and dirty jeans. This was it, I thought, my first payment for washing his car, but I carried on cleaning the one I was doing even more enthusiastically, so he knew I wasn't just a kid, I was serious about my new business. Unfortunately, I didn't get any money; he was the owner of the building company I'd stolen the bucket from and he had recognized the logo on the side of it.

'Listen, my property, my rules.' And with that he kicked over the bucket so it lay on its side and drove his heavy boot straight through it, shattering it into dozens of pieces all over the pavement.

Watching his fat arse waddling away from me, I learned another valuable lesson: there will always be a bigger dog with sharper teeth, but mongrels have a way of surviving. In order to live on the streets and keep going, however, I needed to see the threats before they got to me. That bucket he stamped on could quite as easily have been my head. I was alone as a kid but that didn't mean I had to just take what life threw at me, there was an opportunity out there for me somewhere and I wouldn't stop until I found it.

Joining the army wasn't a way out for me; I didn't see it as a last option. It was my choice. I wanted to be part of a family, part of something that was fighting for good.

I walked into the army careers office on a rainy day. An infantry soldier, a bit overweight, sat behind a desk and welcomed me through the door.

'Son, how old are you?'

'Fifteen, I'm fifteen. I want to be a soldier.'

I knew he didn't think I had it in me; I could tell by the slight smirk on his face and the pause before he offered me a seat as he shared a smile with one of his colleagues.

He started describing what the British army did, the various trades and entry requirements, but I could tell he was just going through the motions, he wasn't actually trying to recruit me.

'Have you ever lived on the streets?' My voice broke into a slightly higher pitch as I interrupted his half-arsed sales pitch.

'Son, I fought in the Falklands War! Living on the streets is a piece of cake to people like us.'

Shifting in my seat, I felt myself grow a few inches taller.

'War, with all your soldier friends to help you? All your food in your backpacks? I know I'm young and you don't want me, but I've raised myself up till now. I'll be good. I just need a chance.'

He looked across the office to his colleague, dumbfounded that a kid like me had managed to speak up for himself. You could read the thought process on his face.

Passing me a leaflet for the Royal Engineers, he went on to explain what I had to do next.

'You need four GCSEs to be a mechanic – the army is short of grease monkeys who can fix the TCBs at the moment. You will travel the world, son, and listen to me here . . .' He leaned forward just enough so that I could smell the stale smell of cigarettes and coffee on his breath. 'If you don't get these exams, I'm not taking you. So if you aren't clever enough, CHEAT!'

As I walked the five miles back home I held on to that leaflet so tightly it was hardly readable that night in bed. So I did exactly that. I cheated in my exams and made it into the British army's apprenticeship scheme at sixteen years old. I wasn't old enough to vote, drink or see an adult movie.

After completing my trade training as a Plant Operator Mechanic, I was posted to Germany. At the time mine was the biggest regiment in the British army, with

1,500 troops in one camp. It became quickly apparent that I wasn't a good mechanic. In fact I was absolutely fucking shit at it. But I could run, I was fast and fit.

The major in charge of our workshop pulled me into his office. 'Marcus, this isn't for you. You are going on the army's Physical Training Instructor course and will move to work in the gym.'

Training every day? The responsibility of being one of only five PTIs in a unit of 1,500 soldiers? This was great news.

Passing the course was easy: you put 100 per cent effort in at all times, you learn what is being taught and before you know it you're wearing the coveted Crossed Swords PTI badge and are training troops.

Twice a year we had a basic fitness assessment, which consisted of press-ups and sit-ups within a two-minute period and a 1.5-mile run. Our commanding officer, who was new to the unit, having returned from a tour with Special Operations, was cheating on his sit-ups by bucking his hips up to help him sit up rather than using his core strength. Walking up and down the mats, I was looking for cheating like this and reminded him that his repetitions didn't count.

As the test came to an end, I read out a list of names who'd failed and would be required to attend remedial training, starting on the parade square at 0530hrs every morning in the run-up to Christmas before being retested. The commanding officer, a colonel, was on that list.

The next two weeks, prior to Christmas leave, were

interesting. The regimental sergeant major, who was in charge of discipline in the camp, wanted my head on a stick!

He threatened me with jail on a daily basis for embarrassing the CO, and the officer in charge of the gym often had to protect me from it. A former SAS officer himself, he listened to my reasoning. I wasn't trying to make a name for myself, this was basic soldiering.

'If he is going to ask his soldiers to do something, he must be able to do it himself. He has to lead by example.'

Every morning I would face the stare of the colonel as I thrashed everyone to get them fit enough to pass the retest, until finally it was time for our Christmas leave parade briefing.

Every year we had a briefing on the parade square by the CO and RSM prior to going home. It was always the same format: what to expect next year, the achievements of this year and don't get arrested. This year's briefing was slightly different, though, due to the attacks on the World Trade Center on September 11th only a few months before. Above all, make sure you come back!

Out of nowhere the atmosphere changed, the CO screaming at the top of his voice, 'RSM!'

The man mountain marched over to me; as he got closer I felt like I was actually getting smaller. Slamming to attention, the RSM's chest was touching my nose. Instantly I thought I was going to jail, I was going to be fast-marched off to the guard house and that would be my Christmas. Would I even get Christmas dinner? Man, this was shit.

The commanding officer then went on to explain how

a 'Little Hitler' had decided he would make a mockery of the rank structure in this camp, how I showed no respect for senior officers and how that had to stop.

I could still feel the RSM breathing down on me, I was ready to be whisked away, but refused to let the fear of the unknown show on my face. I had to stand by my actions.

All of a sudden the RSM took a side step to my left, his right. I could feel the earth shake as his size 14 boots impacted the ground. I had a clear view of the CO walking towards me with his slightly longer than normal hair, hands behind his back and the quirky way he wore his uniform. It always looked out of place, probably because of his previous undercover role.

Refusing to back down, I looked the colonel straight in the eyes. Now in touching distance, he directed his words straight at me while speaking loudly enough for the whole parade to hear. 'This is for having the biggest balls in the regiment!'

Producing from behind his back a bottle of champagne, he handed it to me and leaned right in to talk privately in my ear. 'Enjoy your Christmas leave, but you're not coming back. You start Special Operations selection in the New Year. Now fuck off!'

While the other guys patted me on the shoulder in congratulation, all I could think was: *What is Special Operations? What do they do?*

New Year's Day came and I was sitting on the platform at the train station that I'd been told to report to. I still had no clue what I was about to do, what the unit did or whether I'd pass. One of the course instructors approached me in civilian walking gear.

'Are you on a course?' he asked, checking his clipboard of ID card photos against my face.

I nodded and was directed on to a nearby coach. This was alien to me: no uniforms, no rank and no military vehicles. As the coach filled with other anxious soldiers left the train station, I realized I was the youngest by far. If I wanted to be a part of this unit, despite the fact that I still didn't know what 'they' did, I knew I would have to give everything to get through.

That first night in the large huts, surrounded by senior ranking non-commissioned officers, I felt like a young baby chick in a room full of virile cocks. As we were screamed at to get outside for more 'phys', I could tell the other guys on the course didn't think I deserved to be there. In their eyes I was from the wrong background for Special Operations, not coming from a strong soldiering unit like the Parachute Regiment or Royal Marines, and then there was the issue of my age.

After being thrashed for nearly two hours in the pitch darkness, we went through pass-or-fail vehicle recognition in a red-hot dark room designed to increase the effect our lack of sleep was having. This was going to be easy for me; I'd always loved cars, and never being able to afford one added to the obsession. A constant stream of photographs was fired at us, everything from a side profile of a Ford Orion to the tail light of a Transit van. I was in my element and, without volunteering the answers too frequently, I was nicknamed 'the boy racer'.

To seal my fate, one instructor, trying to emphasize the importance of noticing details, asked the room: 'You all recognize where the 70mph indication line is on the speedo, but how many of you know what that is in kph? It's nearly always on the speedo next to the 70mph in a smaller font.'

Without thinking, I fired my hand into the air. I knew it was 110.

'Hand down, boy racer, I don't require another answer.'

The three instructors in the room looked at one another as I lowered my hand in shame; it was then I got the sense they knew I focused on the tiny details.

One of the hardest things during selection wasn't the weapons training with the SAS or even the lack of sleep, it was the essay writing. Three nights in a row during camp one, which is the sleep deprivation and physical torture stage, we were taken in the middle of the night to a very hot room and told to sit at a desk and watch a video. As the video on Burma tribes starts playing, the instructors walk out of the room switching the lights off. It's a battle just to stay awake, never mind remember the details of what you're watching on the huge TV screen. An hour later, just as the credits start rolling down the screen at the end of the documentary, the instructors burst in, turn the lights on, and give you another hour to write an essay of exactly what you have just watched.

As you desperately try to scribble as much as you can quickly without it becoming illegible, the hour ends and everyone files out of the room, handing their efforts to the instructor, who then shreds everything in front of you all without even reading it.

The next night, same again, 0300hrs straight into the same room, this time a documentary video on how different plastics are made, lights off and some people take this opportunity to sleep. Having only had two hours to close your eyes over the past forty-eight hours, it was really tempting. But I had to prove I was eligible to join this unit, which I still didn't know anything about. Biting my lips and the insides of my cheeks to stay awake, I was drawing blood but it worked. Just as the documentary ended, in came the instructors again, an hour to write what we had seen and file out of the room, once again met with the sound of the shredder without even a glance at our efforts.

The third night hit us slightly earlier at 0230hrs. I was knackered and my eyes felt like they were actually bleeding at this point. The video started playing and the heating was turned up as the lights were switched off and the instructors left us to watch a video on 'Wire Rope and Cordage'. It's without doubt the most pointless and boring video I've ever seen. It was hideous. After two hours of watching how wire rope is made and the uses of cord in industry we were given thirty minutes to write as much as we could. I was one of four who managed to stay awake during the film. My writing had become almost childlike by this point; I very nearly asked for a crayon to make it a bit neater!

As we all piled out of the room for the third time, I couldn't hear the shredder kicking into action, instead the papers were being read and assessed by the instructors. You could sense the fear in people who'd used this opportunity to sleep, expecting it to be like the last two nights. The next day there was a massive cull of volunteers as the instructors weeded out those who they didn't want to work with in their unit.

Those of us that remained were given new 'known as names' and allowed to remove our candidate numbers. It's affectionately called Baptism. No one is allowed to know our real names so we are given new ones. The training major couldn't decide on a name for me.

'What are the initials of your full name, 211?'

'TCM.'

'Right, well you can't be named TM because the lads would call you trademark for ever, and despite what you think, I'm not that cruel. TC it is then. No longer number 211.'

After six months of brutal training I became one of the youngest people ever to pass selection to become part of a deeply secretive, deniable covert counter-terrorism unit in Northern Ireland.

I excelled. Growing up on the streets, I was comfortable being around danger; it was like wearing my watch. Without it I felt naked and isolated but with it on my wrist I felt normal, at home, peaceful. People just don't get how you can be calm and content sitting among the most dangerous terrorists and mass murderers, but for me it became my world. Working in the Falls Road in Belfast, surrounded by the murals reminding you of the threat you faced if caught, didn't faze me. We were armed with our pistols and always had Heckler and Koch rifles in the cars. It's one of the very few places in the world where you can travel from the most stunning landscapes, turn a corner and be faced with traffic lights that are surrounded by armour casings to stop them being broken during the constant riots.

I owe Northern Ireland a lot, especially the Special Ops unit. Twice a year we receive new arrivals, the handful of volunteers who pass the selection course. This latest course was the first in a few years I didn't return to Hereford to train, as I was needed as a commander on a large operation. I think a decision was also made to change our approach in the selection process, to tone down some of the situation-awareness training. I was quite often called in to play the aggressive hostile local, but with no guidelines or parameters it became difficult to assess when the exercise was going too far. If I could see one of the volunteers was not dealing with the situation or driving out of the roadblock as they should, I'd start smashing the car up with a crowbar and, if I sensed they were crippled by fear, I'd keep going and drag them out of the vehicle through the windows. It wasn't a case of not being able to switch off my aggression; I just fell into the role and made it as realistic as possible. Sometimes that would cause the volunteers on selection to shoot me with a blank 9mm loaded in their pistols, or they'd end up in a crying mess having shat themselves.

One cold night just before Christmas, a couple of years

after I'd joined the unit, we deployed up to RAF Alder-grove to provide armed protection for our SF Hercules landing with the latest successful volunteers. After no sleep for the last seventy-two hours, they were completely exhausted, but one of them instantly stood out: Lucy, who would become my wife.

She is one of the very few women to have ever passed the course, which offers zero dispensation for females, who have to do everything the men do. As the training team walked off the plane ramp in front of the recruits, I held my HK53 rifle slightly tighter, desperately wanting to look more professional without appearing as if I was trying to impress her. It was love at first sight. Having spoken to the training team before they returned to Northern Ireland, I knew she was an incredible shot on the ranges. I was sold hook, line and sinker.

A few days later we had our Christmas party. As we were a deniable unit, the detachment officer in charge, a major, didn't want us drinking on the streets of Belfast through fear of being caught, so we had our own bar within our secure compound. Every year we'd all buy the 'bar' a Christmas present, and my present that year was a bottle of absinthe, which I managed to share with Lucy. The warrant officer in charge of security within the unit joined us for a few glasses, but stopped after he started hallucinating!

It was clear Lucy and I just 'got' each other. I loved how she took the piss out of me while being interested in what I had to say. Up till then I had thought that love was utter bollocks and people were lying about how they really felt about their partners. It was at that point I found my soulmate, someone who made me think of life outside this covert world, someone who made me want to go and eat ice cream while walking round Giant's Causeway. Ultimately this woman, who was matching me glass for glass from the bottle of absinthe, made me think I was more than just a covert operator.

Within days of that amazing night at the unit bar in which Lucy and I got absolutely smashed on the contents of that green bottle, we had decided to get married. Four months later we managed to get five days' leave at the same time and got married at a small town hall. From that point on we become known as Mr and Mrs Smith, and while I'll never be as good-looking as Brad Pitt, Lucy will always surpass Angelina. Being married to someone who was trained to kill in the Special Forces training ground of Hereford is the perfect recipe for happiness.

As my experience grew I was given more responsibility by the MI5 officers who handled my covert operations on a day-to-day basis. Soon I was recruited directly into the service. At the time applications for the Security Service/MI5 were close to 100,000 a year, so they really had no need to tap people on the shoulder any more.

My handler, a senior intelligence officer who'd been with MI5 for over ten years, brought me in for a debrief while I was in the gun cage reloading magazines for my Sig Sauer 228 pistol. As I placed my weapon on his desk, he spoke in quieter than normal tones, aware of the other intelligence officers and admin support who shared the same open-plan office.

'What you do for me on the ground is perfect, but I need more from you. I want you to officially join the service,' he said.

This was unexpected, but I was beaming with pride inside. Poker face on, I let him continue; these intelligence officer types always had an angle they were working. 'The Islamic extremists are out of control on the UK mainland, we have the Russians and Chinese doing whatever they want, and the recruitment teams are hell-bent on bringing in posh cunts with degrees. We need you on the ground. You're comfortable on the streets.'

As I desperately tried to conceal a smile that I could feel emerging on my face, Ian hit me with more good news, 'And obviously while the pay isn't huge, you'll make more than you do with the army here. Sound good?'

Sensing this could be the best career move I ever made, and could potentially give me the chance to escape the hole of debt I was struggling to get out of, I barely let Ian finish his sentence. 'Roger that, boss, when do I start?'

That was the day my covert career stepped up yet another gear, and soon after the 7/7 attacks on London I officially became part of MI5 after working under their direction unofficially for years. My world was dark, no colour, no right or wrong and no back-up. People like me exist to fight those no one dares face. I wasn't the last resort; I was the only option.

Chapter Three

Even though I was tapped on the shoulder to join MI5 by my handler, I still had to go through the majority of the surveillance training everyone else has to do. Of the staff who join the Security Service with a view to joining an operational team, whether that be agent handlers, method of entry teams, technical installations or surveillance, 99.9 per cent will have applied via the traditional methods, either by responding to an advert in the paper or through the MI5 website. Nearly everyone coming through the system, therefore, will be trained in exactly the same way, hence the reason I went through most of the training too, so I could understand the surveillance team's methodology, how they move together, etc. The truth is, surveillance officers from MI5 are unquestionably the best in the world. It was a nice feeling when I was recruited to know that I was going to be further trained to become the best I could possibly be.

Because I didn't live in London at the time I started training for the surveillance team, I was allowed to stay in one of the service's safe houses in North London. It was the first time I'd lived in the capital. I obviously knew where Thames House was, and most people these days recognize the building; you only have to look at the armed police who patrol outside of it twenty-four hours a day and the security bollards on the pavement to realize this is a sensitive building. When I received my instructions detailing the date and time I was to go to Thames House, I wasn't surprised to read that I was required to enter via a more discreet door rather than the main row of front doors at the centre of the building. The side entrance was a heavy, bomb-proof door leading straight into a tiny security room lined with thick ballistic glass. Inside was a team of very alert security staff, who immediately looked at me with suspicion as I walked in, beckoning me over to the intercom.

I gave my real name and the reference number from my paperwork, and was directed to put my bag and jacket through the X-ray scanner, which was exactly like the ones you get at airports.

'Photo ID, please.'

Responding to the metallic voice, I handed my passport into a small hatch that snapped shut as soon as I dropped it in. No more than thirty seconds had passed when another door behind the scanner opened up and a security guard appeared with a metal detecting wand, ready to scan me.

'Shoes off, please, sir. Do you have any metal objects in your body, surgical pins, etc.?'

Even though they were calling me 'sir', I still got the feeling they didn't fully trust I was who I said I was. I'd take that as a compliment because of how I looked and acted; if people in a posh building like this thought I looked out of place then I'd look right at home on the streets.

Once the scanning and body search were over, I put my shoes back on. I hated wearing shoes and smart clothes at the best of times, and I felt slightly awkward kneeling down on the marble tiles tying my shoelaces, while the security guard towered over me. As I stood upright the guard handed me back my bag and knocked on the window to signal one of the other security team to make a call for someone to collect me.

Surveillance training lasts months and is followed by a year on probation. It's probably one of the longest training courses of its type in the world, definitely the most intense, and is broken down into very distinct blocks of skill sets. Every course usually starts with five or six 'candidates' who attend a Security Service induction on the first day, in which you go through basic administration like having your pass issued; for those who are operational you sign for your service credit card and alias address details, and of course for the thousandth time you sign Section one of the Official Secrets Act.

After an hour or so of initial general Thames House briefings, the induction is then split off into different branches, or departments as they are known within Thames. B Branch, for example, comprises all the administration and security roles, everything from pay to discipline; G Branch all the international counter-terrorist roles. The surveillance teams come under A Branch, specifically A4. Those in the intelligence community, not just in the UK but the whole world, who knew of A4, knew it was the home of the most effective surveillance operators in existence.

We were led up to the fourth-floor training room, walking past the 'tubes'. Every single MI5 employee will have walked through these tubes at some point; they are the security pods that you slide open once you activate them with your unique pass code. Once you step inside, it assesses your weight and height to determine if it's only you inside the tube and you're not being held at gunpoint. When the tube is happy you're not a threat or under duress, it closes the door behind you and slides open the other half of the tube in front, allowing you to walk into the building. That's your door into work.

The service has a strict no-phones policy inside the building, so once you've passed through the security tubes there are thousands of tiny lockers for employees to place their phones in. The woman leading us towards the A4 surveillance training room explained that the lockers were for Thames staff. 'Operators don't have to use these, so don't worry about them,' she said.

It was already starting to become obvious that surveillance officers were treated differently here, and I liked that. In the awkward silence as the six of us entered the lift, I sensed that the other candidates on this course were nervous. Leaving the lift, the woman guiding us through this maze walked alongside me, guessing I was uncomfortable in a suit. 'Don't worry, tomorrow you won't have to wear that monkey suit!'

When we were herded into the training room, I stayed quiet, found a chair and sat down. The chief instructor, Darren, wasn't there yet. The room was a fairly typical briefing, instruction-type layout with a few differences, namely it had key historical artefacts from A4's surveil-lance history: old radios, the first pin-hole cameras and so on. The others on the course, three guys and one woman, were nervous, and you could tell they didn't know what to expect. I was sure that the woman was ex-military, due to the way she held herself: petite but strong.

Eventually Darren walked in and started the introductions, going round the room, asking our first names and shaking everyone's hand.

I was last to be welcomed by him. 'TC, you're Ian's boy, right?' he asked.

I was relieved that Ian had told the training team about me, and the fact that he'd told Darren my known-as name out there made me relax about the whole thing. From that point on I knew this was no longer a pass-or-fail course for me, it was about learning the service's way of operating compared to the military methodology.

Darren was a cockney, and couldn't look less like an officer in Her Majesty's Security Service: earrings, long shaggy hair, gold rings, tattoos, basically everything you would imagine from a London wide boy doing dodgy deals on the streets. I liked him. He explained that he'd been in A4 for years, having come from an undercover police drugs team. Continuing his introduction to the course, he told us we'd meet the rest of the training team soon, who would be with us day in day out for the next six months.

'Before I bring the rest of the training team in, I just want to wish you the best of luck in passing this course. Not everyone does, but you've done the hard bit by passing the application process; 47,000 people applied for the seat you're sitting on. Take pride in that.'

I saw a hint of a smile from two of the guys when Darren said that. The woman whom I suspected was RAF glanced at me with a knowing look; she was proud she'd made it this far but was determined not to show it.

'That said, be mindful of the fact that one, maybe two, will fail this. Statistically some of you won't pass. Now, being potential surveillance officers you will have noticed that TC there is known to us. He was recruited, so if you start to struggle and you don't feel you want to talk to us about it then for fuck's sake use him.'

As Darren opened the door the training team piled in, fifteen serving surveillance officers and three Met police advanced driving instructors from the Advanced Driving Unit (ADU). It was a free-for-all of handshakes welcoming us to the service. As we all got acquainted, I noticed Darren in the corner of the room talking to the head of the ADU, and the guy who I presumed was the most experienced surveillance operator in the corner of the room near the door. He'd clearly mentioned me to them as they both looked over at me at the same time. I was either in for an easy time, or the pressure would be ramped up to push me to my limits and see what I was really capable of.

A good ten minutes of introductions and camaraderie had passed when Darren shouted up and asked the training team to leave so the driving instructors could give us a briefing. The first phase of the surveillance training is advanced driving, where candidates are taught how to drive at speed and move through red lights safely.

'Right, what we're going to do is teach you how to drive. Get rid of those bad habits and get you driving in a way that is progressive and safe. You WILL learn police commentary, the police safe system of handling and driving at speed.'

The driving instructors weren't surveillance operators. You could tell a mile off these guys were Met police, and their specialism was driving. Stressing certain words, they wanted to let us know that if we didn't pass the driving phases, we couldn't continue with the rest of the course; a typical power play from people who felt inadequate so needed to assert their position despite not being operators.

'IF you pass the different driving phases we have for you and you are assessed to be of the same standard as police advanced instructor level, then you will be trained to forget everything you know . . . Why is that, TC?'

As the other guys on the course looked at me for an answer to the instructor's question, I maintained my posture and didn't shift. I needed to let the instructors know I was respectful of their position but that I wasn't intimidated by this first day on the course.

'Because where we are going to be working, no one drives like a police officer. Undercover police look like undercover police and it stands out a mile if you've got your hands at the ten and two position on the steering wheel in the middle of Bradford.'

The instructors all gave a slight smile at my answer; they knew I was having a little dig at undercover police, but thankfully they respected that and didn't take it the wrong way. The other guys on the course didn't even recognize that I was having a bit of banter with them.

'Right, shall we get out of here then and go and see the cars you'll be driving for the next few weeks?'

The head driving instructor apparently had a reputation for failing people on their driving assessments – he noticed absolutely everything. Ian had warned me about him before I started my course; he'd fail people if their gear changes weren't smooth enough or if they weren't making enough progress in the corners. So it was sod's law that, as we walked into the car park, he told me and the ex-military woman I now knew as Emma that he'd be our instructor, and it came with a warning, 'TC, you'll be with me. If Emma doesn't pass, neither will you. Got it?'

'Got it. We'll both do you proud.'

I knew Emma would have a good degree of driving ability, having been in the military, and she seemed switched on, but that the pressure would be on for me to help the others pass the course.

Following the instructors to three gleaming white saloon cars, I tried to lighten the mood with my new driving partner, Emma: 'Hope our team cars don't look like these police ones!'

They were a Mercedes C-Class, a VW Golf R and a Jaguar STR with accompanying extra mirrors so the instructors could see all around the cars while sat in the passenger seat with us tearing round the country.

'You'll be driving these cars and we'll swap them around every few days so you get used to the different capabilities of each vehicle. They are designed to look like police cars. Remember you're in training and we have to do this safely. You'll be driving in excess of 120mph every day across the country, so the more official we look the less likely we'll get pulled over by the police, giving you more driving time.'

Walking to the front of the cars, I knew what was coming next because I'd done driver training similar to this with the Special Ops unit in Northern Ireland. The instructors were about to start taking us through 'first checks'; before you get into that car every day you're meant to check all the basics – oil, brake fluid, tyre damage, the whole thing. The instructors went into quite a lot of depth initially, though, describing the power to weight ratio of each vehicle; the way the engine was laid out, which gave you a good indication as to which end the drive was directed to, either the front or the back wheels, and so on.

To be honest with you, all I wanted to do was get in and fucking drive. I loved driving fast safely. It's a real art to be able to move through traffic and across country at speed without upsetting anyone or over-using your brakes.

After an hour or so, we had a quick toilet break, and once everyone was back at the cars we were handed our packed lunches in brown paper bags and separated into two teams of two with a one-to-one instructor for one of the guys, who I assumed didn't have much driving ex-perience. Obviously I was with Emma and the chief instructor.

'Right, TC, you're going to go first. All I want today is to iron out any bad habits you've picked up since your previous training. I don't want any progressive driving, just pure basics, OK?'

Nice and relaxed first afternoon of driving, then. Sliding into the driver's seat, I went through all the adjustments I needed to make – mirrors, seat and steering position – while Emma got into the back and the instructor started filling in his paperwork. He had his own mirrors, one on top of each wing mirror and two rear-view mirrors. One was angled so he could see behind us and another one so he could see my eyes; he needed to know that, if I wasn't turning my head, I was at least using my eyes to look and maintain observation all around the car at all times.

As I dipped the clutch and started the engine, I reached for the open door to close it. The instructor stopped his paperwork. 'Aha, TC, yes, I remember now, your open door policy when starting the engine has just reminded me.'

Opening the glove box, he pulled out a small roll of Sellotape and a drawing pin. I knew what was coming. 'Please tell Emma what I'm doing.'

As he placed the upturned pin on top of the gear stick and put two lengths of tape over the sharp pin, holding it in place, I half-turned to Emma in the back.

'If I get lazy with my control of the car and rest my hand on the gear stick, he'll hit my hand, slamming it on to the pin. It makes sure I don't get lazy, but change gear properly and hold the steering wheel with both hands when I'm not changing gear.'

'That's right, and I know from the training you've had previously that you'll remember how much this hurts, so don't get lazy.'

Our Merc was the first vehicle to leave the car park, as the other guys were still receiving instruction. Waiting for the barriers to open to let us out of the rear exit of Thames House, I held the car on the handbrake, playing the game. Usually on a ramp like this I'd hold it with the clutch, but I wanted an easy driving phase so I did exactly what the instructor wanted to see. Out and right on to Horseferry Road and over the bridge, I followed the instructor's directions through London. He'd only say it once, as we'd be expected to be able to follow simple commands.

Apart from giving directions, the instructor was completely silent throughout, although he would be watching my eyes in his mirror like a hawk. I knew he was assessing whether I'd seen certain road signs, speed limits, what other vehicles and pedestrians were likely doing around the car and if I was pre-empting light changes, how smooth my braking and accelerating were: in other words, how safe and aware I was. All standard basic stuff you'd expect an advanced driver to be doing.

After nearly two hours of trouble-free driving and no pin punctures in my left hand it was time to change with Emma. The instructor's posture and teaching style changed when she got into the driving seat – much softer and calmer, more nurturing – and it was nice to see this side of him.

'Right, let's get rid of this pin, shall we? I'm sure you

won't be needing this, Emma; we'll reserve the pain for the army boy in the back seat.'

Laughing, Emma relaxed a bit. I didn't mind being made fun of if it lightened the mood in there. As the car began moving back through London again, Emma was driving really well, but cautiously. It was all the instructor was after at this stage. He started to quiz her on the road signs we were passing, and gently guided her out of the bad habits she'd picked up over the years, namely resting her foot on the clutch and wrapping her thumbs around the steering wheel instead of laying them flat. It's only stuff everyone does but we we're being trained to a high standard to allow us to move through standstill traffic at high speeds, so all these little things help us be safer and quicker drivers.

As the weeks progressed, the other candidates' driving got sharper and smoother, except for one of the guys. He could make ground and drive safely at high speeds but he couldn't give commentary at the same time. For him the amount of concentration it took to drive at 140mph through Bala in Wales meant he had absolutely no more brain capacity to give a full talking commentary on what he could see and what the vehicle was doing, which for a potential surveillance officer wasn't good at all. Prior to the final assessment, the instructors, who were desperate to get him to pass, put him in the same car as Emma and me while I was doing my high-speed intercept assessment, which is where we drive as fast as we can from London to Glasgow with the focus on safety.

If the instructor has to step in at any point to say slow

down, speed up, or point anything out regarding safety, then you fail. It's a long drive and made even more intense by the constant commentary you have to give. 'I'm travelling north on the Mike One at 135 miles per hour, in lane three of three. The weather is mild and dry with clear skies. White Ford in lane two of three ahead and watching to see if he is looking to move into my lane, covering my horn and lights to act as a hazard warning. Past the white Ford now, accelerating to 140 miles per hour, check of my rear-view mirror and near-side mirror, no vehicles coming up behind me and nothing in lane two of two, indicating to my near-side, checking rear-view and wing mirror again with a confident look over my left shoulder to check my blind spot. All clear, moving into lane two of three, going past the one-mile marker board and gantry for Junction 31 of the Mike One.'

This commentary has to be fluid and constant without breaks; there is always something to talk about. Unfortunately, Emma and I were the only two in our car to pass the intercept assessment and we were now down to four candidates.

We progressed on to urban driving methods, in which we look to be able to move through London traffic at speed, making use of the bus lanes, driving through red lights, one-way streets, bumping half of the car up pavements to squeeze through tight spots and ultimately trying to be as quick across the city of London as the Tube.

On the last day of the driving phase we all sat down with Darren, the chief instructor and the driver trainers who'd been assessing us over the past weeks. It's all very relaxed, around a table in the training room. It's pass or fail. They tell each of you first if you have passed or failed and, if you have passed, what to work on going into the surveillance phase of training.

The comments were quite fair really. The other two guys got passes and were told they needed to concentrate on not getting lazy once they started the surveillance vehicle follows. It's incredibly easy to fall into bad habits once you become target orientated.

'When people in your team die, it will more than likely be from a crash. Be careful.'

Darren had that look in his eyes, he's dealt with death a lot. He wasn't big-timing it. Emma was next. She passed too which I was incredibly pleased about. She'd worked very hard and actually got top marks on the written assessments on the police roadcraft test we did prior to this meeting. I was given extra time on the test because Darren made the point that the words 'would be dancing around like a fucker' for me.

'TC, fail.'

The other guys looked stunned and the frown on my face said it all, I didn't believe it for a second.

'Only joking, yeah, fine, no issues.'

And that was it, no other feedback, which I took as a compliment. I was starting to learn the service was a lot like the Military Special Ops unit in Northern Ireland. No feedback was good. Darren gave me a small smile out of the corner of his mouth and a nod in acknowledgement. After we shook hands with the driving instructors,

Darren ushered them out and shut the training-room door.

'Right, congratulations. Fun bit over. Unfortunately after all that driving, you're not actually going to drive a car for about a month, while we teach you foot surveillance.'

I always found this approach a bit arse about face really. I can see the argument as you go straight from foot surveillance into vehicle follows but a month away from driving for some of these guys is a huge amount of time.

'Get yourself back to the safe houses, you start early tomorrow morning. If you're not used to walking mega miles, tape your feet up. You'll be averaging around twenty miles a day for the next month. See you in the morning. No drinking tonight.'

I didn't celebrate that night. I got some Chinese food as I left the Tube, walked back to the house and prepped my kit for the next day. Twenty miles a day sounds a lot for most people, especially in the world we live in now with transport taking us everywhere, and electronic meetings, lifts in the office, etc. But it's a sneaky way for the service to put in physical standards without actually saying people have to be of a set fitness level. If they can't follow a target throughout the day due to their lack of endurance, they fail the course instantly. Simple.

The next morning I woke up at 0430hrs for my morning run. If my body remained sharp, my mind would find everything a bit easier. I loved running around North London at that time in the morning, everything is quiet just before the daily madness starts of heavy traffic and everyone rushing to get the Tube with their caffeine fix in hand. The only people up at this time were delivery drivers going to the depots and the homeless adjusting their positions, trying to stay warm.

When I got back to the safe house I was still the only one up and I jumped in the shower. As I left the bathroom in just a towel to return to my small bedroom, Dave stumbled out of his bedroom in his pants, carrying his fags and coughing as if he was dying of lung cancer already.

'Dude, the fuck??'

'Been for a run, mate, you want some breakfast putting on?'

'TC, I can't eat first thing in the morning, you know that. What are you running for, you bell end!?'

I loved Dave already, he was like a comedy TV character, never downbeat, honest about his slightly chubby build and, despite having absolutely no security or investigations experience, he was picking this stuff up quickly. Dave's best quality was how fucking funny and positive he was. Always made me laugh.

I've always been an early riser and a light sleeper so the early starts on this course weren't an issue for me. I would not have any problems with the endurance aspect of the foot surveillance phase, but I needed to keep on top of my admin and fuel my body. Even the fittest people in the world would fail this if they didn't eat. The easier your body finds it, the fewer demands you will put your mind under, and when you're being asked to remember virtually everything it pays to make life easy for yourself.

I would always leave the safe house before everyone else; they travelled together but I knew we were still at risk even though we weren't officially MI5 officers yet. To think an MI5 safe house is actually 'safe' is a mistake. Yes, it has all sorts of cover and protection around it, people doing back searches on the property, and it has state-of-the-art locks and alarm systems, but the house is still in a street accessible by anyone. Travelling to and from it as a group makes you a huge target.

Leaving and arriving at Thames House was an operation in itself for me. I would vary my routes in and out every day, I'd change my profile by taking a different coloured top in a small bag; I'd even turn my phone off at different points in my journey. I had spent nearly all my adult career so far staying in the shadows, hiding from the terrorist organizations hunting them down. A lot of my awareness came from my days in Northern Ireland. The threat to our life out there was so great that not only were we armed 24/7, we also had a little covert LED that could be seen on the dash as we approached our cars. If it was flashing we would know instantly that our cars had been booby-trapped with an improvised explosive device.

The threat wasn't only from people wanting to kill us, we faced a bigger threat from hostile intelligence agencies. The building behind Thames House was owned by the fashion company Burberry. The issue I had with that was that it overlooked the rear entrance to our building and crucially the vehicle exit from our underground garage. If I was a Russian intelligence officer looking to recruit and blackmail MI5 officers, the perfect place to place a covert camera would be in that Burberry building. I trusted no one.

Grabbing a coffee from a local shop near Thames House, I circled my route back towards the River Thames and Horseferry Road. I had time to kill and wanted to make sure a woman I'd spotted near the London Eye across Lambeth Bridge wasn't following me. Stopping at a shop window, I forced her to go past me as she walked towards the Channel 4 building. Satisfied she was no longer a threat, I made my way back towards St John's Gardens, taking a seat to finish my coffee. It was calm there, which I always found strange. One of the calmest places in London was this tiny little well-kept park just fifty metres from the Thorney Street back entrance of MI5, the world's best intelligence agency. It was a nice contrast to think of this little patch of green as the light before going into the building that dealt with only darkness.

The rest of the guys were already in the training room laughing and joking nervously as they waited for Darren and the other instructors.

'Get lost?' Dave was already cracking jokes, which meant he was probably the most nervous out of us all.

'Nah, was having a coffee with your mum.'

'Prick.'

As the laughter grew at our banter, the instructors walked in.

'Right, you can't learn surveillance in a classroom, so grab your stuff and we're going to split you off one to one with an instructor and take you out all day. You'll be back here in about eight hours.'

My instructor was ex-military too; he wasn't staying in A4 for much longer though, as he was transferring to G Branch.

'Right, you look like undercover military, you're not fucking Jack Bauer, listen to everything I say. I don't care how good you think you are, if I don't pass you, Darren will fuck you off,' he said to me. He'd obviously been briefed on me and was keen to knock me down and show me I wasn't an 'official' MI5 officer just yet. What a prick.

Funny that, because my hair was long and I wasn't clean-shaven like this cunt. Darren had just told me my profile today was spot on. I had to swallow his bullshit because it was likely designed to trigger a reaction in me to make me fuck up. Most ex-military who apply for the security service do so for the wrong reasons and they don't make good operators.

'I'll do everything you say,' I said, trying to be as humble as possible. He relaxed his positioning with me. I wasn't on a pass or fail like the other candidates on this course but I still wanted to make life as easy as possible. Plus arriving with my new team would be hard if the training team forewarned them of some cocky arrogant Northern bastard.

That day was easy, even though the instructor tried to push me harder than most, walking at a faster than normal pace, asking me constant questions throughout: what was the registration number of the vehicle we'd just passed, how old would I estimate the person walking by us carrying an umbrella was, what were the names of the last three streets we'd been down. I finally earned the instructor's respect and we eventually made it back to Thames House with the others for daily debrief.

Darren was explaining how important it was to have the ability to combine memory recall with a 'shit filter': 'Remembering everything is useless. You need to pick out the key points to remember and develop the sense of noticing what is out of place and what's not. This morning before you deployed, for example, how many people were in this room, including instructors?'

Everyone went quiet and I saw some of the instructors smiling, including the hard arse who'd been trying to beast me all day. It was simple memory recall and could be worked out by attaching trainers to candidates, etc., amazingly though, only Emma shouted out the right answer as I stayed quiet, trying to fly under the radar in case I came across as too confident.

'Eight. Eight people.'

'Easy, right? When I let the instructors in there was a young woman who followed roughly ten seconds later. Dave, give me an A-H of her.'

An A-H is the way we describe how someone looks: Age, Build, Colour, Distinguishing Features (clothing or carrying a large red bag, etc.), Elevation, Face, Gait, Hair.

Dave got most of the details about her, enough to recognize her anyway.

'She gave me a piece of paper which I purposely placed

on the table in front of you. What was written on that paper?'

The smiles of the instructors grew even wider and my instructor became particularly smug. Darren could see my eyes flickering and lips twitching as I muttered to myself what was written. The room went quiet as Emma also noticed I was thinking about the question.

'You know, don't you?'

Wanting to keep out of the limelight I looked at my instructor. He'd stopped smiling, straightened his body upright and developed a frown.

'Er, no, no, was just thinking that's all,' I said.

Darren took a step towards the desk inquisitively, wanting to know more.

'TC, you don't have a photographic memory. I can tell you took notice of that paper. Don't be embarrassed, mate, if you did try to remember it.'

The room was now quiet as my instructor spoke up from behind Darren.

'He's got good awareness; TC, do you remember that note put on the desk?'

Nodding, I knew that if I answered I was setting myself up here. I wanted an easy course. By telling these guys what was on the note placed on the desk now nearly ten hours ago and that I had sight of for about fifteen seconds, I knew if I didn't notice absolutely everything from that point on, it would be noticed more than if one of the candidates didn't notice something. Fuck. Darren pushed a bit harder: 'TC, I can see it in your eyes you are trying to be humble, but don't lie to me. I can forgive you wanting to be the grey man, but don't fucking lie to me.'

'Emily, 1 6 8 9 8 0 4 7 x.'

The room went still as Darren took half a pace back and offered his hand out as if to say, tell everyone the method you used.

'It's simple visual association, matching words and numbers with a visual image to make a story up that's easy to remember. Emily the Elephant is a massive big fat thing with tiny ears.'

A few laughs started to ripple around. Darren turned half towards the smirking instructors. He didn't need to say anything, his body language was telling them to shut up.

'And the numbers . . .?'

'One is a dagger, six is a golf club, eight is a massive pair of tits, nine is a meat hook, zero is a cake, four is the sail on a boat, seven is a cliff edge. Whole thing becomes "Emily a massive fat elephant with tiny ears picks up a dagger and steals a golf club from a woman with massive tits and ginger hair who falls on to a meat hook spilling blood everywhere. She grabs her tits and pushes them together to catch a cream cake oozing with jam, while sailing across the ocean on a sail boat straight off a cliff edge on to an X marks the spot."'

I could feel myself getting embarrassed, and started to feel a bit flushed. I hated standing out like this. It made me feel like I was a freak. Darren took the piece of paper out of his pocket and passed it around the candidates. I felt daft about my memory method, but it had always worked for me; the more graphic and insane the story, the easier it is to remember.

Thankfully, Darren lightened the mood. 'Right, tomorrow we'll build on the skills you've been taught today, same time, similar distance. TC, you're seeing the shrink because your story about Emily and cake is disturbing!'

The laughs returned and I didn't feel I was standing out any more. I wanted to belong. I didn't want to be thought of as different. Shuffling my chair out I grabbed my kit and we all made our way out of the training room. My instructor was waiting for me with Darren as I left the room with the candidates. 'TC, a word, please.'

Dave called out that they would catch me at home as they made their way to the lift.

'TC, that was good. I'm giving you a hard time on purpose. The other guys will likely pass this course and make good operators. You're not special and you're not destined to be a part of a deniable team working overseas and if I'm honest you make me nervous, you can be too keen.'

'What he's trying to say, TC, is Ian told me you'd be a good operator. And you are. You notice the right things, you live on the street very well, but talking from experience you're wound tight. Your psychological profile suggests you don't switch off. Listening to the instructor feedback from the candidates today, you move and travel differently from them to and from here,' Darren added.

This felt really strange. I was worried about being highlighted for remembering that piece of paper because

I didn't want to be expected to remember absolutely everything, yet here I was being told I was too switched on, too aware. This was the only way I knew how to be. When my son was about to fall over, I was there before he hit the floor because I could see it happening; I knew when a glass was about to be knocked over, and I knew what information I had to remember. If someone or something looked out of place, I would question it endlessly to anticipate the threat.

'Just be mindful of being a lit firework. Everyone wants the desired effect, but unless you have a solid grounding, a base, no one can tell what direction you are going to fly or where you're going to explode. Look at the teams, and your old team in the military. Not many old guys, are there? If you want a career with us, learn to breathe.'

That evening the walk home to the Tube across Lambeth Bridge was really isolating. Was I doing a good job or not? I just wanted to belong and here I was again not fitting in. It was my nature to notice everything and the instructors were training the candidates to notice and question what they saw, yet I was apparently doing it too much. Maybe I was wound too tight, but as far as I was concerned this nation needed oddballs like me to see and do things no one would think to do.

The rest of the foot phase of surveillance training went well apart from the last day in Brixton. It was test day for the candidates. You have to follow an operator from one of the teams through London, on and off Tubes, in and out of museums, shops, housing estates, open parks without the experienced operator flagging anything out of the ordinary. In reality you'd never follow one person everywhere yourself but it's a way of cramming in tons of pressure in a training environment to allow the instructors to assess your skill set.

I was halfway through my test day when the follow took me to a crossroads in Brixton. My 'target' had walked towards a block of flats. My instructor was behind me observing my natural behaviour and decision-making process. As I crossed the road I was presented with a problem in the form of an aggressive Jamaican asking for spare change. Last thing I needed. I knew this wasn't a role player.

'Any change, my man?'

'Sorry, mate, I'm skint.'

I tried to continue my walk, but he presented his large, slightly fat frame in front of me, blocking my path.

'Let me borrow your phone then.'

It wasn't a request, he was demanding I hand over my stuff. It was broad daylight and my instructor was some way behind me, I couldn't tell where.

'Ain't got a phone,' I said.

He'd stopped me in my tracks now as he took another pace towards me. I could smell the sweet aroma of cannabis masking a stench of stale alcohol and knew this wasn't going to end well. Fucking hell, I didn't need this.

'I'll cut you up, hand it all over NOW!'

Enough. I had to take this fucker out and I knew I had to be quick, otherwise I'd lose sight of the operator I was meant to be following. This guy was taller and a lot heavier than me, but if I took the advantage I would be able to put him down and run before he had a chance to react.

Spitting in someone's face nearly always gets them to take a step back briefly, unless you're dealing with someone who is used to fighting. Everyone hates being spat on in the face, especially if you get the aim right in their eyes or mouth. As my spit hit his right eye and his nose, I hooked my right foot behind his legs, grabbing a handful of his coat on his chest, and kept the momentum going to get away from him. Forcing his bulky frame over my leg, I slammed him into the floor, his right shoulder hitting the pavement first.

'Fuck off, you cunt,' I shouted.

Spitting in his face again, I let go of his chest and yanked my foot from under his hip before running across the road towards some flats. I couldn't see the operator I was meant to be following, but he couldn't have got very far. I was running, which made me stand out, and a quick glance behind me as I neared some flats told me the Jamaican was picking himself up off the floor, wiping his face. Hopefully he wouldn't start running after me and I could get on with this final foot surveillance test.

When I made it to the other side of the flats, I could see my target continuing towards a bus stop. I'd got control again. Stopping to read a billboard ad, I looked behind me again. Still no sign of the guy who'd tried to rob me seconds ago. Time to change my profile again. Taking off my black sports jacket, I replaced it with a dark blue hoody, hood up. The rest of the follow went without a hitch and we were soon back in the comfort of Thames House.

In the training room the other candidates, having passed this phase, had already been sent back to the safe house for the day, ready to start vehicle surveillance tomorrow. It was just me, the operator I had been following all day, Darren and my instructor.

Darren started the debrief.

'OK, tell me what went on with the guy in Brixton.'

So my instructor had seen it. Why the fuck didn't he back me up? I could tell by the operator's face that he didn't see or know what had happened.

'Big Jamaican guy came at me near the flats, tried to turn me over, I put him on the floor and ran. I didn't engage in a fight, it was self-defence.'

'OK, take a look at this pin-hole camera footage. Admittedly the image is shaky, but just explain what's happening here.'

My instructor was carrying a pin-hole camera and had caught the last few seconds of me dealing with the Jamaican. You could only just make out me throwing him to the ground and running.

'This is the very last of it. He wanted money and my phone, threatened to cut me up and blocked my path. You can't see it here, but the guy would have fucked me up. I spat in his face, threw him to the ground, swore at him and ran. I didn't hit him or anything, I was merely protecting myself.'

Darren looked at the other two and nodded in agreement; he knew I'd done the right thing.

'Happy with that, mate. Are you OK?'

'Yeah, fine, no dramas. I was more concerned about losing the target.'

The operator I'd been following all day laughed. 'I didn't see you all day, good follow.'

Darren wrapped the debrief up and asked the operator and my instructor to leave.

'OK, guys, thanks. Well done, TC, vehicle surveillance tomorrow. Let's just go over some admin, then we'll get you away.'

He waited for the others to leave the training room. When the door closed and it was just us two, he said, 'TC, you did the right thing with that twat today, but me to you, talking from experience I'm a little worried about you.'

Here we go again, for God's sake. This wasn't the world ending from some zombie apocalypse; some guy in a rough part of London tried to turn me over, I dealt with him and kept hold of the target, what was the big deal? Sensing that my deep breath in and out had become a sigh, Darren explained what he meant: 'Before the service I worked undercover with gangs, yeah? I know street kids when I see them, it's why Ian recruited you. But you look like you're dissociating life-threatening events while being hyper-vigilant to everything.'

'Isn't that what you need, though? Bad people doing evil need someone even worse to stop them.'

'Not quite, TC. I get what you mean, but we're an intelligent group of people, we act intelligently. Yes, we push the boundaries of what is acceptable, but I see little flashes in you that suggest you're on the edge of losing control or failing to recognize how dangerous things are.'

Darren could tell by the look on my face that I didn't agree with him.

'TC, on paper you're a grade A student, passing with flying colours, no problem. But experience is telling me that when handed potentially dangerous situations you're either going to not deal with them mentally or take your response too far.'

'I'm fine, Darren, honestly. If you need me to talk about my feelings to the shrink then I'll do it, but I honestly think I dealt with that guy properly.'

'The way you dealt with him was fine, it's just the speed at which you carried your focus on the follow. Most would have sought comfort or guidance from the instructor having dealt with something like that. I just don't want you to burn out.'

'It's fine, honestly. I get what you're saying, but there is no need to worry at all. I'm really grateful to be in this position.'

'OK, cool. Right, get yourself off, back in the cars tomorrow. Have a good evening.'

Lambeth Bridge was getting longer. For the second time in a month I walked across it feeling alone, as if I'd fucked up again. This course was easy, yet my personality was being brought into question. I think I would have preferred it if I was told it was my skill sets that needed tidying up, not my mental state.

As I lay in bed that night, I felt heavy, my arms lacked any energy. I was thankful that it was the driving phase the next day, although we'd be combining foot and vehicle surveillance, most of it initially would be sitting in a car. I think the number of miles we'd covered over the past month on foot – and the emotional rollercoaster of believing I was doing well on the course, only to sink to the depths by being held behind after class – had taken their toll. My eyes got too heavy to stay open.

BANG!

The noise of the bedroom door crashing shut brought my eyes wide open. I had somehow slammed into my door, having fallen asleep half-dressed. My bedroom curtains were still open and through them I could see the faint light from streetlights outside. My heart was thumping out of my chest. I'd just had a nightmare, but had no idea what it was about, I couldn't remember anything. The house was still and quiet, but I knew I'd probably just woken everyone up with the noise of my door. It was a good four feet from my bed; I didn't know how I'd ended up throwing myself out of bed into it as I struggled to slow my breathing down and to control my pulse rate.

My clothes were wet and I could smell my sweaty body odour. I needed a shower but would have to wait until the morning. Going into the bathroom would be a sure-fire way of waking the house up, if my door slamming hadn't done it already.

Sort yourself out, strip off, get into bed and relax, I thought. The beads of sweat were making me shiver as I climbed into bed, secretly hoping I wouldn't go straight back into the nightmare I couldn't remember.

The next morning, refreshed and in clean clothes, Dave came into the kitchen as I was having my morning porridge.

'Drop something last night, dude?'

'Oh yeah, fell out of bed, went with a right thump!' I couldn't bring myself to admit to another adult that I had a nightmare.

'Hahaha, you dick.'

He seemed to buy it.

The following months went by without a hitch. Everyone passed the vehicle surveillance phases, which combined our driving skills and surveillance knowledge built up in the foot phases, to be able to follow any vehicle across London and the entire country as a team.

The final test lasted a week, starting off with a simple 'pick-up'. Waiting for one target to leave an address in North London, it developed like a real operation from intelligence gained throughout the first day. Where the target's been, contacts they've met, new housing and vehicles and so on. Towards the end of the week you incorporated other agencies, such as the counter terrorism units of the police and SO19, Special Forces, GCHQ and MI6, as well as departments within MI5 itself. All designed to give candidates as much real world experience as possible before they join their new team.

On the final day of the surveillance course, you've already been told you have passed as you're asked to report suited and booted to Thames House for 'badging day'. I didn't own a suit and hated being in a shirt and tie, but I respected the seriousness of the day and made sure

I was clean-shaven that morning. The guys were on cloud nine; out of the five of us that had started this course, four of us passed, Emma, Dave, Chris a quiet Northerner and me. The other guy on the course, who was found unsuitable on the driving phase, had been offered a job in A2 watching our static surveillance cameras. The kick in the teeth for him was that these people watching the cameras are classed as 'support staff'. It's a low-level skill set, you're monitoring a bunch of cameras. That's it. Compared to the high skill set of A2A, who listen to the eavesdropping devices, it was an entry-level position, but he got a job out of it so he was happy. I don't think his heart was really in surveillance.

Dave and Emma were like little kids and Chris was his usual reserved self as we went to meet Director A to be given our Security Service IDs. His office was bare: just a desk, computer and secure telephone and four metal badges in front of him.

The director rambled on about operators being the tip of the intelligence sword. The nation depended on our reactions and judgement. I knew Dave wasn't listening, he just wanted his badge so he could go and celebrate in Leicester Square. Eventually, the director took the first badge and opened the black wallet up to see the photo of who it belonged to. It was Emma's. 'This is you then, the picture isn't ugly like the other three.' Classic old boys' women-are-the-fairer-sex type of comment from the director. Emma took it well, though. It was an important day. Dave, Chris and I got thrown our IDs and wished good luck as he ushered us out of his office.

Walking back down the stairs to have our photograph taken, we looked at our badges and each other's photos. It was before the badge and card were redesigned and to Dave's excitement the photo ID part still had a monogram of Vernon Kell, the service's founder, and the words 'On Her Majesty's Service' on it. The other side of the black folded wallet held a gold Security Service crest. In the real world, we'd hardly ever use these to identify ourselves. Only as a last resort and it would only be to the police to allow us to proceed or if we'd been arrested. Mine would remain hidden in a sports Tubigrip around my ankle.

I was now officially an officer with MI5, the Security Service of the United Kingdom, a defender of the realm. True to form, having our course photograph with my new team mates I looked like the runt of the litter. It was a proud day, but I just wanted to go home to my family, rather than the safe house.

Chapter Four

Walking with no back-up into a pub in Glasgow that's a known terrorist meeting place takes a certain amount of balls. You have to disregard any concerns you might have for your personal safety. Especially when you're an undercover MI5 operator and four of your targets are inside to talk about policemen they might potentially murder.

I'd worked against Irish terrorists for years. I preferred them to the Islamic extremists because they had a cause; they believed in what they were doing for the future of Northern Ireland. It became family duty. The self-radicalized Islamic guys just didn't have that, they just wanted to commit mass murder anywhere they could. It wasn't about religion or creating a caliphate. The leaders of these groups, particularly in Syria, Iraq and Africa, want power and control; they have merely used the lure of religion as a vehicle to drive that need, using people as pawns to carve out their own areas of control. At least when the IRA planted a car bomb, most of the time they would ring through a coded message to evacuate the area.

Preferring them didn't mean I liked them. They were far more dangerous to people like me. Their operational security and how they actively looked for us was better than any Russian intelligence officer. Irish paramilitaries like the IRA and UDA noticed the slightest detail out of place and they knew their surroundings extremely well. I was acutely mindful that they had caught people in the past.

As we drove close to the pub, I could hear over the radio my team taking up positions.

'Charlie Four, got the northern pedestrian route.'

'Charlie Five has eyes on the entrance to the pub and can give a standby.'

'One Eight has the south on foot.'

'Zero Six, do you read? Base.'

'Yes. Yes, go ahead.' This would be my last transmission on my body radio as I needed to remove it prior to going into the pub.

'Zero Six, be advised – the pub is extremely busy and all targets have left their phones at their home address. Roger so far?'

'Zero Six, roger.'

This wasn't good news. We didn't know what targets, if any, were already in the bar. It was mega-busy too, which would make it even more difficult to spot our targets. Basically, I would be going in blind.

'Further, the landlord's son is suspected in the murder of a known Loyalist paramilitary last week in Shankill, Belfast. Base out.'

Well, fuck me, let's just invite more hardline Republicans to the pub, in fact let's invite them all to Thames House for a tour of MI5 HQ and throw me to the fucking wolves.

'All stations from Zero Six, I'm in the area, will be into the pub figures five, ears out, ears out.'

I had to take my covert radio off and leave it in the van. The Irish paramilitaries were seriously good at outing undercover Special Forces and police. However, when high-profile targets like these came together only MI5 were allowed anywhere near them.

Our operating methods are different from those of other covert forces. Our profiles are all completely different. If you put us all in a room you'd never guess we were working together. Young, old, black, white, geeks, sheikhs, Muslims, men, women – the list is endless. Then we throw into the mix the way we dress – as builders, tramps, drunks, businessmen, pregnant mothers, OAPs . . . Even our vehicles have to match our profile. You can't be dressed as a tramp getting out of a brand-new Audi.

My current profile is a painter and decorator drowning his sorrows after losing his arse on the horses. As I remove my radio and place it in the glove box of the van, I memorize the map on the passenger seat. I need to know the local area in case it all goes to rat shit. How would I get to the main road as fast as possible to enable my team to pick me up?

I grab the paintbrush and pot of white emulsion I need to complete the look of a working decorator. I've done this so many times. Stepping out of the car in my white painter's coveralls splashed with various colours of paint and the odd splash of varnish, complete with my comfy paint-splattered trainers, I dip the paintbrush into the tin.

Just wearing the clothes won't do; you need to dispel any doubt in people's minds that you fit your profile, because when there is doubt, there is no doubt. Holding the brush over my left hand, I slide my right thumb over the bristles, flicking paint splatters over my hands and wrist, repeating on my right hand and hair, and I'm done. Tiny little paint spots cover my skin, as if I've just finished painting a ceiling in a local house. Then I throw the paint pot and brush into the back of my battered white van. I know I look the part; I am living my cover.

I quickly dart into the betting shop next to the target pub, as I need to remember a few of the races that afternoon and place a few bets. All this gives me reason to be in the area, provides talking points if I'm asked questions in the pub, and removes suspicion about me.

Making my way from the bookies to the pub, I scan the area subtly. I can't see any of our team cars. This is a good sign; if I can't see them, neither can anyone else. I am mainly trying to work out if the pub is being watched. The Irish are extremely good at identifying surveillance and security forces. It is their bread and butter.

OK, I know the meeting will happen now. Three hooded teenagers are sitting on a wall covering the main road past the pub; they can see everything, including all the vehicle movements in the area. I have to walk right past them. Betting slip in hand, I slow my pace down slightly, allowing my trainers to gently scuff the pavement as I walk past.

One of the group briefly turns his attention to me, but quickly discounts me as a threat. He obviously isn't looking for a scruffy painter down on his betting luck on his way to sit in the bottom of a beer or ten.

From inside the pub, I can hear the TVs blaring out the Celtic match. It's busy. Really busy. I count twelve men, all in Celtic football tops, smoking outside, but none of them take notice of me as they laugh and joke. Good start: no one watching outside on alert.

I'm hoping none of our targets are inside the pub yet; it will give me time to settle into the environment, choose my positioning and get to know the locals quickly. That said, you need to be aware of hostile teams already inside, making sure it's safe for their commanders to hold a meeting.

I squeeze through the packed crowd of men and the dense smoke to make my way straight to the bar. Choosing a drink in situations like this is always critical. You don't want to stand out by getting it wrong. Little things matter and that's why only the best operators from MI5 are allowed near these guys. You're in a pub, especially a rowdy lawless one like this – you have to fucking drink.

Quickly scanning the empties, I notice most people are on bottles of Budweiser. This is good news because the glass of the bottle is brown, so it allows me to control my rate of drinking and it's not easy to see how little I have drunk. The other advantage is, I can use it to crack someone's head open if this goes tits up.

There is a huge difference, often fatal, between a normal undercover operator and someone like me. You have to live your cover. Even when paying for a drink in a pub, I'm a down-on-my-luck, self-employed painter and decorator trying to pay next week's rent by betting on the horses. Handing a crisp £20 note to the landlord behind the bar wouldn't fit my profile. This landlord is probably looking out for people like me, given that his son was now an accomplished killer.

'Bottle of Bud, shot of JD.'

I put a handful of coins on the sticky wooden bar, picking out the £1 coins, and pay him in small change. At these prices I know the whiskey will have been watered down. The landlord turns to me: 'You look like you need a double.' I recognize the accent straight away: West Belfast. He raises the dirty glass to the whiskey optic to fill it, then turns to put the glass and bottle down in front of me.

Facing the bar and my drinks, with my back to the door, I am surrounded by cheering football fans, all offering their insights into how they would manage world-class players.

You have to wait and settle in situations like this, you can't take a position watching the door or trying to identify who is in the bar, because that would get you killed in a pub such as this one. I have no clue if our targets are here, and what's more I don't know who the hostile counter-surveillance team is and where they are.

The only thing I can control is how the landlord perceives me. Grabbing the change into my right fist, I return it to my pocket in a disgruntled shove. I throw my betting slip on the bar, pick up my glass of whiskey and in one seamless motion neck it.

I fucking hate whiskey, but it serves two purposes. It gives a strong smell of heavy alcohol on me and reduces suspicion from anyone who'd kill you if they even suspected you of being a member of the security forces, never mind MI5.

My empty glass doesn't have a chance to hit the bar before the landlord is over. I can barely hear him over the jeers and shouting; there must be close to a hundred people in the council-estate boozer, keeping a sure footing as drunks get bounced around, beer is spilled on the already-sticky floor, and every sentence includes at least one 'cunt', three 'fucks' and half a dozen 'twats'.

'Another one?'

The landlord is a bald, skinny wretch of a man. His appearance is typical: thin gold crucifix chain, sovereign ring on his right little finger, badly stained teeth to match his T-shirt, which states FUCK YOU in bold black lettering.

I lift my bottle of Bud and take a long swig of the warm beer and shake my head; he's sounding me out. I turn to watch the match on one of the many TVs, this one just to the left of the spirits rack, which is backed by mirrors, allowing me to keep my back to the door while having a fairly open view of the people around and behind me.

A good twenty minutes go by and I am on my second bottle. I haven't moved from my spot at the bar, but am now very slowly and briefly switching my focus from the TV to the mirrors, just for one or two seconds every couple of minutes. I need to build up a mental picture of who is in here. I know I'll have hours in debrief going through target-associate profiles so it's vital I remember who's in here and who they're talking to, how alert they are.

It's an art, being able to remember the smallest of details on a massive scale. A lot of people simply can't do it. Throw into the mix the fact that you need to do all this without getting caught, in a hostile environment surrounded by known killers who would love the kudos of taking out someone like me, and you're probably down to a handful of individuals in the whole world who can do this, day in day out.

That's why I was recruited. I am part of this community already, and without knowing it they accept me. Just as serving military can spot other soldiers on leave, killers recognize their own. I just hope I don't have to go that far today.

I haven't moved from this position for nearly an hour now. The match is over but the atmosphere is still filled with macho friendly aggression, everyone trying to be the alpha male without upsetting anyone else. I've identified nearly everyone in the pub via the mirrors and just as I pay for my third bottle of Bud the time has come. My targets are here.

Four senior players and the main Continuity IRA commander, who rose up the ranks in the Provisional IRA but didn't want the Good Friday Agreement to succeed, so he moved over to CIRA. The commander – 'the Shanker', as he's known to his soldiers, based on how many Loyalists he's personally killed in the Shankill area of Belfast – is deep in conversation with a guy I don't recognize: slim, well-dressed, with a short, neat beard, approximately six foot two to four inches tall.

As they move through the crowded pub the

atmosphere changes very subtly. I look towards the TV, taking a slow slug from my bottle and holding my betting slip in my hand; the races are on now. I need to live my cover, not watch the targets.

I recognize the four senior members with the Shanker, all of them counter-intelligence within CIRA, responsible for punishment and discipline within their own ranks if they suspect anyone of betraying them. They are animals: knee-cappings aren't their style. A bullet to the head is too quick. These guys enjoy torturing people.

Everyone in the pub obviously recognizes them and respects their positions, and only for a brief moment do the laughter and jeers quieten down before resuming full volume. All six move towards the back of the L-shaped pub. A group of tables immediately becomes vacant when the occupants realize who is walking towards them.

I have to quarter-turn my body towards them, away from the TV, to be able to see them properly, and there is absolutely no point in doing this. Other less experienced operators may try to do this but all you're going to do is highlight that your body language is interested in them, while gaining absolutely zero intelligence.

Remaining in position, I watch the races and think to myself how thankful I am that I ditched my radio in the van. It is far too crowded in here to move around freely, and someone would have felt it had I brushed past them at any point.

The landlord has disappeared, presumably upstairs to the pub's living area, and his son comes down and begins serving. Very cocky, early twenties, wet-look gel in his slicked-back hair, he has a look of a Kray twin about him. I tilt my bottle towards him and he does a straight swap for another lukewarm Budweiser. I pass him a crumpled £5 note, which gives me ample opportunity to look across at the target meeting while the landlord's son gets my change.

The four counter-intelligence players sit at tables either side of their boss and the skinny unknown, all very aware, looking towards the door at all times while assessing everyone in the pub. They aren't part of the meeting, they're bodyguards.

The intelligence on this job isn't fitting the picture I'm seeing: this isn't attack planning. This is a new contact, so I need to find out who this well-dressed, skinny man is. I need opportunity, and the team outside need to follow him once he leaves. The Shanker is no longer the priority.

Turning away from the group and looking back towards the TV gives me time to think while keeping an eye on the door. I am still in a very hostile environment, surrounded by some of the most dangerous terrorists in Europe, if not the world, and I'm being served booze by a known killer. This is the game I play, but you only lose once.

A good twenty or thirty minutes pass, the group have their drinks brought over to them, and now on my fifth bottle I am starting to feel the effects. I either need to eat something or slow my drinking down; neither easy in a place where people inhale their alcohol in seconds and the only food sold is in the form of crisps.

Fumbling my change to give the impression that I am far more drunk than I actually am, I buy two bags of crisps and use the opportunity to turn away from the bar and look back towards the door. Again the atmosphere changes, much more intimidating this time; everyone starts looking towards the entrance. Someone is here. Police.

Fuck me, what's a plain-clothes copper doing in here? Landlord's son.

Out of the corner of my eye, I notice the Shanker's protection detail signal two guys to the right of me. As the slightly dumpy young police officer worms his way through towards the bar, it is clear he wants to speak to the lad behind it, I can only presume about the murder last week.

Now he's only five steps from me. I look towards the two guys who've obviously been instructed to dispose of this idiot copper who clearly doesn't realize where he is. Both hooded teenagers flick open matt-black butterfly knives. I need to get this copper out of here. But to do so will blow my cover and we'll both be killed.

He looks young enough for this to probably be his first plain-clothes visit to find someone, and I am betting by his lack of knowledge of those people and this pub that his senior officers haven't sent any uniformed police along to help. It isn't his fault he's naïve, and I can't let him die. Fuck me, I hope this is going to work.

Grabbing the neck of my bottle, I slide off my stool. I move towards the policeman and I put my left hand around his tie and shirt collar, my fingernails scratching the skin on his neck, my grip instant. Bringing the bottle over with a massive amount of force, I look into his eyes. Fear: he knows what's coming.

I need this to look real; I have to fuck this guy up in order to save his life. From experience, I know I have to hit the front quarter of his forehead with the middle of the bottle for it to smash and cut him. The danger is that if I get this wrong, the bottle won't smash and the impact will cause him major brain damage. But I need him out of the pub.

As the bottle connects, I keep my momentum going forward. Bits of brown glass scatter all over my controlling hand near his neck. 'Fucking pig, I'll fucking do every one of you!'

Forcing his limp body towards the doorway, I am now running with him, smashing his bloody head into the doors. They swing open and with one last scream I throw him to the ground outside. 'Tell all your fucking mates they better stay away from me!'

He is dazed but conscious. I rifle through his pockets quickly and grab his loose cash and phone. This is my opportunity, but I need to control the pack of wolves behind me; they want in, they want blood too.

Unzipping my overalls, I start pissing on him. I've not been to the toilet in hours so it's coming out in force, first on his legs then his upper body, to the drunken cheers of my new-found friends.

'Get fucked, you twat! You're all gonna die!'

He staggers to his feet and runs off, bleeding heavily, as I turn to the crowd bursting at the doorway to get out of the pub. I raise the cash up: 'Let's get drunk.'

On the way back towards my stool, I get endless nods of acknowledgement, of acceptance and encouragement. I hand the money to the landlord, who has now replaced his son, who's obviously gone into hiding, and people line up to get a free drink courtesy of the copper I'd just turned over.

Living my cover, I start examining the phone I've stolen, banging it on the side. I need to send a text message to Base; they need to find out who this guy with the Shanker is. We all memorize the number in case of emergencies. I pretend I can't get it to work as I type a brief message:

From 06 tgt with tall slim well-dressed UIDM 6'2-6'4 – need housing.

Hopefully the Operations Centre will send out a message to the team outside and they'll be ready to follow him after the meeting.

Pressing 'Send', I play the part as I wait for the status bar to complete. Come on, hurry up and send!

'Message Sent' icon on the screen. I throw the phone into a pint pot half full of stale beer, destroying the evidence. 'Piece of shit doesn't fucking work!'

'You hate those cunts, then? They'll come after you, you know.'

The landlord brings me over another whiskey as a thank you without actually saying so.

I drink the glass's watered-down contents in one go and wipe the beard around my mouth.

'Maybe I'll get my kids back. Fucking bitch ran off with one of those pigs. All they do is arrest innocent people. They want to go after these Paki twats stealing all our jobs.'

I'd just tuned up a copper, so being a drunk racist complemented my cover. It fitted my profile perfectly.

Continuing to ignore the meeting, I notice the zip on my coveralls is still undone. It doesn't shock me, what I've just done; no adrenaline come-down, no remorse. Have I gone a step too far this time? No, I saved his life. This place would have killed him if I hadn't stepped in.

I know I have to get out of here now, though; can't risk getting caught up in a mass arrest when the police riot vans turn up because one of their own has just been attacked. Nodding towards the landlord, I lean over the bar to talk to him, using my stool as elevation.

'Mate, is there another way out of here? If I get lifted again, I'll go down for pure time.'

Using my newly found alliance is a great way to make sure that if I need to I can return to this community again; you always want to keep that door open. I've been over-exposed to the targets here, but that could prove an advantage later down the line. Right now, though, I need to clear the area.

The landlord signals me round the back and lifts the bar hatch for me to go through. I walk past the targets, still deep in conversation; I notice the man with the Shanker passing him a piece of paper with a name and what looks like an IP address.

I don't have a photographic memory, unfortunately, but just like the Emily elephant story back in Thames House I make up a visual extreme story out of it as I walk behind the bar to the rear fire exit by the pub's bins: 'Massive dagger covered in blood stabbing a woman with massive tits who was swinging two golf clubs at a meat hook.' The Shanker's bodyguards don't give me a second look; they are uneasy and know they have to get him and the well-dressed man out of here. It shows how good their operational security is when they're thinking the same way as me, or is it that I am thinking the same way as them?

Running the numbers through my head, I leave the pub and walk straight towards the main road, the land-lord shutting the door behind me. I notice more teenagers at key transport areas, obviously looking out for police, who are no doubt mobilizing to come and find the heart-less thug who attacked one of their own. Me.

Past the bookies, I make it to my van. I've been drink-ing all day, but need to get out of here. Into the driver's seat and lock the doors. I slide my coveralls off. I need to switch my radio on to listen to the chatter through the car comms.

'Base, Zero Six now complete, Charlie Nine.'

Hopefully the team will also acknowledge and they will take control of the well-dressed man with the Shanker. We need to know where he goes so we can identify him. I know Charlie Five had the entrance to the pub so they should get imagery of him walking out, if nothing else.

'Zero Six, withdraw. Debrief tomorrow 0900hrs, Base OUT.'

What? I stared at the radio hoping for an explanation. When the Operations Centre end their transmission with 'OUT' it means nothing further is to be said or discussed.

Bollocks to that, I need to make sure we found out who the Shanker was with. 'Base, Zero Six. Did you get my message regarding the target contact needing housing?'

'Zero Six, WITHDRAW IMMEDIATELY, Base OUT.'

Still looking at the radio, painter's coveralls down round my ankles.

'Prick!' I mutter as I use my feet to drag my coveralls off. I throw them into the passenger footwell. I drive out of the area steadily, keeping an eye on my speed, listening in hope that I will hear some sort of chatter. Twenty minutes go by as I drive south out of Scotland.

Nothing, not even a no-change or security check to make sure everyone on the ground is OK. I have to assume they all pulled off. Why? Why would they pull off from something as massive as this? A brand-new contact potentially supporting one of the most dangerous terrorist organizations in Europe was massive. Was this because of what I did to that young plain-clothes police officer?

No way: our operational priority would supersede any charges of attempted murder and once they knew I was saving his life it would all be recognized as the right thing to do to protect him.

First services on the M6 motorway, I pull in. It's getting dark. I walk into the toilets. Standing at the urinals, I can smell the booze oozing out of me. I need to sober up. I must eat a lot and drink water to try to flush my system for a few hours before I hit the road again. A change of profile would be a good idea too.

The great thing about service stations in the UK is they have everything you need. Clothes, food, phones; you can even buy a camp bed, for fuck's sake! A red check lumberjack shirt, white T-shirt and blue baseball cap will dramatically change my profile if anyone is looking for me. The chances are no-one is, but I've always lived by the same principle: a covert operator operates for life. Throwing some sandwiches, crisps, muffins and pastries on top of my new clothes, I find the basket gets heavy when I top it all off with three bottles of water.

Sitting on the corner of a huge seating area, pulling the price tags off the clothes, I think about the job today. I had to take that copper out: they were going to kill him. Doing it any other way would have got us both killed and the Shanker would have gone underground instantly. We needed to find out who this guy at the meeting was.

I have to pass the IP address and the name WHIT-LOCK on to the Operations Centre at the debrief tomorrow. Stuff like that you usually need to relay immediately, but the fact that they essentially told me to go off grid until tomorrow means I have to keep it to myself for now.

A few hours pass as I trough my way through the synthetic service station food and make my way to the van. I need to get home and get some sleep, ready for the debrief tomorrow.

Chapter Five

In the morning I was sitting in the debrief room waiting for the rest of the team. Usually this place was a hive of activity, people getting spare batteries for their radios, getting target information, but that day it was silent apart from the odd admin support shuffling papers in the adjacent office.

Eventually the frosted glass doors swung open and in walked the branch director. I'd only ever met this guy once, when I officially joined MI5 from the military. This can't be good.

'Boss,' I said.

I went to stand up and shake his hand, try to defuse any arse-kicking I was about to get.

'Don't bother standing, this won't take long.'

Feeling like I was about to have my arse handed to me, I sat very still and waited for the director to talk. To look at him you wouldn't guess he was a senior figure in MI5 with a serious shot at becoming the director general of the service in the next five to ten years; he was short, very thin and quietly spoken. 'Right, the police officer yesterday. Explain,' he said.

'They were going to kill him. Two locals directed by the CIRA counter-surveillance team working for the Shanker saw the plain-clothes police officer enter the pub. I saw them pull out two butterfly knives and believed they were about to kill him. If I hadn't done what I did he would have been dead.'

The director wasn't taking notes, he was listening but he'd already made his mind up what he was about to say.

'OK, I wouldn't have done what you did but I understand why you did it. We do, however, have a problem here.'

I couldn't contain myself any more and stopped him in mid-sentence. I needed to know if we had found any information about the well-dressed man with the IRA commander. 'Did we house the contact with the Shanker? He was—'

'Don't interrupt me again! Forget the contact – you were filmed pissing on a member of Strathclyde Police! That pub was being used to launder money for a Russian gang, YOU were caught and now Special Branch are looking for YOU.'

'Boss . . .'

He wasn't having any of my reasoning here. I was about to get a message and there was no way I could twist this to my advantage.

'You went too far. Your team don't trust you. You've got real potential but you've got to remember where you are and what we do. The service has a proud history, and despite your experience with us in Northern Ireland, we can still sack you if you fuck up.'

Sitting back in my chair, I looked away from the director, who was leaning forward as he gave me this bollocking. I was fucking fuming, but couldn't help wonder if I really had gone too far. I saved this guy's life, that's all that mattered.

'The copper, how is he?' I asked.

The director sat back in his chair with a sigh as if to say he'd been talking about this constantly since last night and had no sleep. 'Fractured eye socket, superficial bruising. Probably going to spend the next few months having some mental therapy or whatever.'

Hearing that didn't make me feel bad for him, actually I was pleased he wasn't more seriously hurt. Trying to look remorseful, I turned back to the director as he continued, his posture now more friendly.

'Listen, when your handler brought you in all those years ago from the military he assured me you would be a great asset. You are unique, but you've done things I struggle to defend.'

I was going to get sacked here, I knew it. What the fuck would I do if I didn't do this? I couldn't handle the nine to five, all that social media soap opera bollocks. I didn't fit into that mould of the masses; the service needed me as much as I needed the service.

'Your team is back on for a job in Wolverhampton tomorrow evening, and before then you've got to reassure the other operators you can be trusted. I've kept you out of the shit so far, but I can't do it any more. This police officer was my last favour to you.'

As he walked out of the debriefing room I felt like I'd been let down by the very team I thought had my back. Didn't trust ME? I couldn't understand why my 'team' was acting like this. I saved that copper's life. That's all I do, protect this country and save lives. I badly needed to get to the gym and work this off before I took it out on someone.

Cold grey block-work surrounded the battered free weights, punch bag and the creased blue mats on the dusty floor. As I swiped my pass against yet another locked door to gain entry, the strip lighting flickered into life; the gym was empty. Thank God, as I could feel my anger starting to spill out of me.

Walking straight over to the heavy canvas punch bag, I didn't bother putting the gloves on. I stretched out my left hand, running my fingers down the bag as if I was hunting for the weaknesses in its filling. Where could I cause maximum amounts of damage quickly? I was humanizing this inanimate object. This bag was going to pay for the dressing-down I'd just had from the director.

I wasn't the best boxer, nor did I hold any martial arts belts. I was no Bruce Lee ninja. I was, however, dirty and relentless. Our unarmed combat training is conducted by United Kingdom Special Forces, usually the SAS in Hereford. The instructor notably called me a 'vicious little cunt', which, coming from a member of the most formidable Special Forces unit in the world, might have been a compliment, or might not.

I was always the 'demo guy'. The person who the instructor used to demonstrate how to take someone out. I got the feeling that was because he wanted to knock me down a peg or two and teach me a lesson in humility. Control is key when you're fighting for your life: you need to be able to go from standing still to kill in a second.

Turning the aggression off to develop the ability to handle the adrenaline is a skill in itself. I suppose over the years I've also maybe lost the sense of knowing when enough is enough. If a target can get up when you've put them down, you run the risk of having to put them down again. Men in particular have a lot of weak points: testicles, throat and eyes being really easy spots to hit hard continuously, to allow you to then concentrate on the vitals like ribs, kidneys and the base of the skull.

What most people struggle with when fighting – real fighting, not your typical drunken pub brawl – is breathing. The last thing you want to happen as an undercover operator is to end up on the floor with someone who is trying to kill you. Ideally you put them down to allow you to escape. But that could take anything from a few seconds to a minute. You need to remember to breathe, to allow yourself to think and feed your muscles. The more controlled your breathing, the better chance you have of thinking about your surroundings.

Speed is key, and Krav Maga is very typical of the fighting style we use. Multiple quick strikes. I'd been destroying the weaknesses in this punching bag for at least five minutes now, not thinking, reacting to the way the bag moved, exploiting the next weakness. Taking a break, I stood over the water fountain, drinking the slightly stale water. I noticed that the metal bowl was filling slowly with my blood as the water fountain washed away.

I'd been using my elbows on the bag so much that they had become raw and I'd split the skin. Turning back to the bag and wiping the water away from my beard, I caught a glimpse of myself in the mirror. I looked angry, frustrated, isolated. I was alone in there. I desperately didn't want my team to disown me. I needed to belong to a family, and this was all I knew. I had to regain their trust.

I remembered the very first time I felt like my team had a problem with me. When you first join the service at the end of your training, all recruits attend situation-awareness training, run by the SAS using Special Branch police officers due to their high security clearance levels. It's all designed to focus an operator's senses to react to any given situation, albeit in a disused army barracks.

On the fourth day I was driving in a scenario that was a vehicle hijack. You, as the driver, get hijacked at gunpoint by one of the 'role players'. The right thing to do as he screams he's going to kill you and demands the car keys is to give them to him, exit the vehicle and let him drive off. Better to risk losing an operational car than losing your life, was the thought process.

I was fresh to the service, having been recruited from Special Operations in Northern Ireland. Even though I was tapped on the shoulder by my handler, I still had to do the training; if nothing else it helped me learn the different operating methods and tactics before joining my team.

Prior to any scenario you're not told what to do or how to react; it's designed to gauge your most natural and honest response to each event. As I drove the battered car round this ageing camp, I could tell it was used for all sorts by the cracked windscreen, ripped seats, smashed back window and the fact that every single panel on the vehicle was heavily dented.

I'd done a lot of stuff like this, in selection for Northern Ireland. It's fairly standard among covert operating agencies. Turning the corner, I noticed a makeshift set of traffic lights. Knowing the central locking was disabled on this car, I was expecting some sort of hijacking situation. And it came.

As I slowed down for the red light, a van pulled across the back of my car from a side street, blocking me in, while simultaneously another van prevented me from driving forward. Into the front passenger seat burst 'Mr Scary', who was in reality a Special Branch officer who'd obviously lost a lot of weight recently, judging by the sagging skin around his neck. He was armed with a Glock 17 9mm pistol, typical of undercover police in the UK.

He was screaming that he was going to kill me if I didn't hand over the keys and get out: all standard stuff, so none of it fazed me. I was calmly reaching for the keys to switch off the engine and hand them to him when he clearly got overexcited and jabbed the side of my head with the barrel of the pistol.

Something switched in me. Instantly leaning back, I pushed his pistol onto the steering wheel with my right hand, allowing me to grab the Glock and his wrist at the same time. Left hand free, I grabbed his neck and smashed his head against the windscreen, which was the last hit the glass would take as it cracked into a full spiderweb. I was holding his weapon hand firm and his right arm was now outstretched. A perfect strike with my left palm straight on to the back of his elbow, giving me that familiar pop that let me know I'd dislocated his joint nicely.

'STOPPPP!'

The course chief instructor stormed over to me, in his stereotypical SAS no-nonsense walk, while the course medics clambered to get to the screaming mess next to me. I took the pistol from his hand and exited the car, removing the magazine and pulling the top slide back, checked it wasn't loaded.

The chief instructor was the same SAS corporal who did all my firearms training in Hereford and knew me from my days on the training team for the Military Special Operations Unit. 'TC, what the fuck have you done?'

'He pulled a gun, I reacted.'

'You broke his arm, you twat!'

Technically I knew I hadn't broken his arm, but arguing that point would have made me look like a right prick. As he walked past me, barging my shoulder hard enough to let me know he was pissed but not enough to knock me over, he starting talking to the medic while phoning for an ambulance.

The rest of the operators and role players started to gather around me, knowing they had to give the medics space to ease the crying fit coming from the car. One candidate on the course, a former professor who looked a dead ringer for Jesus, strolled up to me, glancing over at the car. 'What happened, TC?'

'Mate, fat fucker jumps in, all going well until he jabs

the Glock into my head. Not my fault he's too weak to stop me reacting. These SB guys haven't seen a gym in years!'

Looking at the faces around me, I could see I didn't have their approval. By rights, there was no way I should have been able to do so much damage to an undercover copper. Walking back to the makeshift canteen, which was basically a metal shipping container with a kettle and white patio furniture from the eighties, I wondered if I had gone too far.

No, this was all about testing our natural reactions to real situations. If this happened in real life I would do the same, probably more.

The SAS instructor followed up behind me, quietly growling my name to stop me in my tracks. As I turned he explained what was happening. 'Right, ambulance just coming through the gates now. He's being taken away to hospital – suspected dislocation of his right elbow and severe concussion. What the fuck?!'

'He's clearly out of shape, and he got too excited when he hit me with the Glock, I didn't even move that fast. He should have been strong enough to resist that!'

Moving closer to me, he became more authoritative. A dressing-down was heading my way.

'Firstly, it's role play. We're not killing people. Secondly, and listen to this carefully, there's a reason he is weak. He's lost twelve stone this year. That's why he has so much excess skin. He's had bowel cancer. It very nearly killed him. It's his first week back.'

I didn't even see the chief instructor walk off. I felt

sick. Fuck me, what a prick. As the ambulance drove past me and out of the gates, I knew I had to brush this off. It was shit that I'd done this to someone who'd been through so much already, and coming back to work on what should have been an easy week helping out 'spooks' turned out to be a nightmare for him. But, if I kept dwelling on this it'd blunt my skill set. Fuck him, he got excited and I made sure he paid the price for that. The team will laugh about this in a few months, I'm sure. I hoped.

As I left the gym I felt more at peace but had to clean myself up, I was pouring with sweat, and my elbows looked like I'd just lost a fight with a cheese grater. I'd gone to the basement gym to try to work this aggression out, but if any of my team saw me now I'd look like the thug they thought I was.

Chapter Six

This world was all I knew for the vast majority of my adult life. I call it 'my world' because it's completely different to what everyone else sees. Normal people go about their lives knowing terrorists and mass murderers exist, and now thanks to today's media coverage they are fairly educated in where those threats might come from in the future. Does it stop them living their lives in the modern world? No, does it fuck. The day after the London bombings on July 7th 2005, most people were using public transport again. Yes, everyone spreads the videos the extremists make on Facebook, but the general public never really know how dangerous the situation is. They work on the unconscious assumption that there are people and large agencies out there protecting them.

Over the past decade the focus on spies and the intelligence services has shifted from the James Bond/MI6 sole operators in a distant land to the ones fighting on our streets. No longer is the emphasis on finding the terrorists in foreign countries, because the terrorists are here. They are your neighbours, your colleagues, people you pass on the street. Mohammed Sidique Khan was a teaching assistant. He blew himself up on the 7/7 Tube and bus bombings in London. The fight is already on our streets.

That's why people like me exist. To hunt these fuckers down and destroy them. We notice everything. All it takes is a brief handshake or a subtle nod passing one of our existing targets in the street to put that unknown on our 'grid'. Every individual we are interested in ends up on the grid with a code name. It's at that point that the intelligence officers rip the target's life apart. It's like splitting an atom, I imagine; I'm no fucking scientist.

One thread leads to ten more. So you start with the basics. Who was the person our Tier 1 high-profile target shook hands with on that street, or who did our target drop call, or send a Facebook request to? Anything that leaves a digital footprint linking our target to an unknown is flagged for analysis, but usually the best new targets come from ground operations. Physically seeing our target in some way associate with an unknown male or female can lead to an intelligence goldmine. What usually happens in this situation is we notice something out of the ordinary or a new face and we 'take them on', which essentially means the team splits and we keep surveillance on our existing target and also follow the new unknown individual, and crucially try to 'house' them.

By finding out an address for an unknown person we can do two things. The Operations Centre carries out all their background checks on that address: names associated officially, mobile and internet IP addresses linked to it, whether work or domestic. From that we can associate emails, calls, text messages, social media accounts, known associates, vehicle documents, travel visits through ports. Absolutely everything that is done electronically and that leaves a digital fingerprint. The second thing, and slightly more important for operators like me, is it gives us a starting point to wait for this unknown if they don't carry mobile phones with them or they are a relatively 'clean skin'. Even if they don't leave much electronic sign, we have a physical place we know they have been before. Housing targets is vital to our operations.

In Bradford, Yorkshire, before the London Olympics, my team was deployed on a four-man-strong terrorist cell. Their intent was to blow up multiple targets around the country; you couldn't call them London-centric. We had the working assumption that it was going to be the Olympic venues but had no intelligence to suggest that. The group was only highlighted to us because the main ringleader, a black Muslim convert who worked in a post office, made an unusual mistake after we'd watched him for nearly a year. This young male converted to Islam while he was in prison briefly, for theft. Prior to that we had absolutely no interest in him, and he didn't even make it on to our grid when he converted to his religion – why would it?

The day he got his target name was when a British IP address showed up on an extremist website promoting jihad. That was the day we tore his life apart.

Once we have a location we use our telecommunications liaison to go to all the mobile phone providers and request the relevant comms data. It's an important relationship between the British intelligence agencies and the telecoms providers; they have to give us the information by law, but it's always asked for politely in true British style.

Most people around the modern world are traceable. Your mobile phone is one massive data logger, but perhaps not in the way the general public thinks. The perception that you just have to turn off your phone's ability to use its built-in location applications to stay 'off the radar' is wrong. Every time you move from one area to another with your mobile phone, it gets its signal from the cell towers for that particular area, whether you are walking from your home to the shops and back, or travelling the length of the country. Cell phone towers are everywhere and easily recognizable. The higher-populated areas have more cell phone towers or mobile phone masts to cope with greater usage demand. Each time your phone latches on to a tower, it registers a unique identification number, which is time-stamped. This means nearly everyone in the UK can be tracked if they have their phone on them. Most of the time the phone will ping off more than one tower at one time, thus enabling us to more precisely locate where the target has been.

This particular male was given the code name GLASS WINDOW, and he was, by current extremist standards, very good at keeping his operational security tight. Truth is, you can't hide from us for long, but he never used the internet in his own house to send messages or view martyrdom videos; his home was clean, he thought. For months we watched him, monitored his calls, emails, text messages – absolutely everything about his life we knew, apart from the other three members of his terrorist cell.

We finally caught a break when he slipped up, and it

gifted us the entire terrorist group, their methodology and attack planning. GLASS WINDOW was usually exceptionally careful, but even the best can drop the ball. And GLASS WINDOW handed out his team's prison sentence when he threw his old SIM card into a high street bin, which our team saw.

His mistake allowed us to find another thirty-two targets just from that four-man group. It's then down to the Operations Centre and the intelligence officers who work in Thames House to try to prioritize who we take on and find on the ground, which isn't an easy task when you have thousands of people to watch.

I couldn't do all that office shit, I knew my place was on the streets. Operators are completely different from the staff working in Thames House. You won't catch one of the office people starting their car the way we do, leaving the driver's door open as you start it in case your vehicle is rigged with an improvised explosive device (IED) designed to blow you up. The idea being that you marginally increase your odds of staying alive if the explosion has a route of escape out of the open door and will likely throw you out of the car rather than trapping you in a metal exploding coffin when you turn the ignition key.

I'd like to say that when I walked into the briefing room or the garages at the Operations Centre I would switch into full MI5 mode, leave all my personal shit at the door and become the ultimate professional; equally it would be fantastic to say when I left an operation to go home I'd switch back into loving family man. Truth is, I was like this all the time, always switched on, assessing absolutely everything around me.

I hated the phrase 'sleeping with one eye open' – it's bollocks. I've never met anyone who can physically sleep with one eye open and manage to take in their surroundings while asleep, but thanks to Hollywood the general public assume we have some sort of magic powers. I have always been a light sleeper though, probably born out of my childhood, always being ready to run at a moment's notice from someone coming to evict us out of our beds. Luckily I don't need a lot of sleep and manage on four to five hours a night or day, depending on when I'm working.

Using a really simple system, and with experience, you can instantly get a feel for the situation in front of you. It's not black magic or some secret fucking ninja skill taught to spies, it comes from surviving on the streets. In fact a lot of career criminals do it without knowing, particularly those from Eastern European countries. We have a saying in the surveillance teams: it's not the target that will kill you, it's the third party. Because we work almost entirely in the most deprived areas in the UK, the level of crime and assaults is obviously a lot higher.

Everything I see is assessed, whether I'm walking into a backstreet internet café or passing through arrivals at an airport; everything is questioned. What's missing from this picture? What's not here that should be? What's here that shouldn't be? Is everyone moving naturally? Why is that vehicle parked facing the opposite way from everything else? Why has that male got his hand in his

97

pocket? Should that old couple be sitting there? Is it the right weather for someone to be wearing a large heavy coat? Is this person communicating with anyone else here? Why is that car wing mirror pointing at the wrong angle for a driver's natural position? Why has someone got two mobile phones? Why would someone be dressing down like that yet have a £150 Military G Shock watch on and a wedding ring? Why is that person sitting bolt upright in a parked car on a residential street?

The list of questions you ask yourself is endless and constant, and it isn't focused around terrorism, it's figuring out if everything you see and feel in the area is right or not. The problem with being like this is that it spills into your personal life. I remember being in the local supermarket with my family when I noticed a man and a woman walking up the escalator approximately twenty metres in front, talking to each other, nice and relaxed. As they got off at the top of the escalator, they split purposely without talking, the male breaking left and doubling back on himself so I could see his face. He was of Somali descent, in his early twenties, with a short patchy wispy beard and wearing a heavy large coat. The female walked away and diagonally right, straight into the supermarket towards the clothes area. Having only glanced at her side profile, I couldn't get many facial features but she too was in her early twenties, European white, wearing a black hijab covering her hair. My wife recognized the look in my eye that indicates when I've spotted something, and gave me a knowing but disappointed glance as she took my son by the hand and continued towards the fruit and veg isle.

I hated the effect I had on my family sometimes. I wish I could be the husband and father my wife and children deserve, who would happily wander around the shops stopping at every single item that remotely looked like a toy, spending the next twenty minutes explaining to the children why they don't need yet another action figure or toy gun. I wish I could be the type of guy who doesn't have to know where all the exits are when I walk into an unfamiliar building, or weave in and out of traffic when taking my son to the park as if to avoid a situation that pins my car in without escape – otherwise known as normal commuter traffic. I wasn't that person, I was the person who hunted the scum of the earth and was ready to eat their fucking faces off if they dared think about hurting my country.

I never feel duty bound to phone the police when I see people up to no good, if I spot someone shoplifting or dealing drugs; it's a way of life for some people. I know that life because it's how I survived as a kid, but when I see odd behaviour it draws me in. I had to know if these two were about to kill people or simply out on the rob. If they were stealing I couldn't give a fuck, but getting close to the male would determine that either way. He was walking to a large group of people by all the TVs, laptops and general electricals.

His demeanour was focused, taking the odd glance to see where the uniformed security guards were stationed.

He knew exactly where to go and was walking faster than normal. As he took his phone out of his pocket and started to make a call I was roughly fifteen metres behind him, knowing I needed to get close enough to understand the content of this call to make a judgement. His clothing was large and bulky, and that on an unusually hot day.

Using the unwitting shoppers, I got close enough to hear the call. 'Yeah, I'm doing it now, get ready.'

OK, here we go. I had no other choice; this guy was about to do something illegal, whether terrorist-related or not, but this supermarket was busy and he was nearly in the centre of a massive crowd. There were nearly fifty people looking at the latest iPads and flatscreen TVs on the display stands. The problem I faced was that if this guy was about to try to blow himself up, I needed to kill him quickly enough so he couldn't trigger anything, and I hadn't seen any improvised switches or wires on him yet. Fuck me, my wife had my keys; they could have been useful right now. Looking to my immediate right, I grabbed a thin but long stylus pen off the display cabinet, the type used on touch-screen tablets, and with a quick yank I ripped it away from the thin wire attaching it to the stand. It was made of a very soft blue plastic, but hopefully I wouldn't be stabbing this fucker repeatedly with it, one quick puncture wound through the base of skull into his brain with this should do the job.

By the time I turned round with the stylus pen in my right hand, the male was kneeling down behind a large TV box. It looked like he was trying to remove something from either his socks or his trainers. I scanned the area for a second, looking for his partner, the female. No sign. I couldn't see my family either. I needed to get them out of there before anything happened, but if I didn't step in something bad was definitely going down. OK, we're dead here no matter what. If I take him on and it goes wrong, he blows himself up, we die. If I go for my family and he blows himself up, we die. So we're dead anyway, and whatever I manage to do now is a bonus.

My plan was to come over to him from behind and wait until the last possible moment to disable him. I still couldn't be sure what this unknown male was up to, but worst case scenario was a lot of people were about to die, so if it came to it I'd have to shove the stylus into the base of his skull if I saw a weapon or anything resembling a detonator. I was five feet away from him now, still walking forward, stylus in my right hand with my thumb near the tip of the pen, trying to give it a bit of strength, ready to kill this guy, four feet, three feet, two feet. I started to lean over with my left hand outstretched to lift his chin up so I could control his body. Where the head went, the body would be forced to go, and it'd also give me the chance to make the puncture into the base of his brain, hopefully killing him instantly. I still didn't know what this guy was going to do, but once I had control of his head I'd know for sure.

He stood up quickly, holding the TV box, which made me stop in my tracks; this wasn't typical behaviour of someone who was about to martyr themselves into paradise. The TV box was stretching this guy's arms to full capacity as he struggled with the weight. I could see it now had a small hole in the bottom. As he walked away from me I knew he was not about to kill everyone. Watching him stagger, I stepped on what was clearly a security anti-theft device he'd ripped out of the TV box to allow him to walk through the scanners at the exit of the supermarket without setting any alarms off; fucking hell, this was bold to say the least. He continued walking back towards the escalator where he had originally split from his partner in crime. Trying to continue my walking pace naturally as if I wasn't, a few seconds ago, about to kill someone for stealing a TV, mistaking them for a potential mass murderer, I caught a glimpse of the female, who was obviously running counter-security surveillance for him. She joined the male on the escalator going back down towards the exit with a receipt in her hand, clearly for deception purposes as if the couple had actually just bought this TV.

Dropping the stylus at the feet of the crowd, I worked my way through the supermarket, looking for my family. I was highly aware that my movements were caught on camera, but the good thing was that I knew in a store this size the cameras wouldn't all be live-monitored, though they would be recording everything. Thankfully I didn't actually kill this guy or make contact with him at all.

As I saw Lucy and my son playing near the bread and eggs, my wife noticed me approaching, and asked, 'OK?'

'Yeah, all good.'

I didn't need to elaborate. My wife always knew if I

wanted to talk about anything I would, but how on earth do you explain being twelve inches away from killing someone for stealing a TV? Especially to the woman who loves me enough to start a family with me, how am I supposed to explain that how I react to situations is normal and absolutely necessary to keep the public alive? Lucy is everything to me and is an incredible mother to our son, and I knew that with our background in Northern Ireland she would understand my hyper-vigilance to things like this, but as much as I wanted to explain, I didn't want that side of me to impact our family life together. Most people would see the way I reacted to someone stealing a TV as extreme; some might even say I was out of control. I would, and always will, argue it's people like me that keep you safe in your beds at night, that allow you to have the freedom to choose who you fuck, where you drink, or, in this case, the freedom to steal a 42-inch TV in broad daylight!

Ask yourself: those people in your office, even your family, what would they do if faced with the split-second decisions we have to make every day? Then ask how they'd switch from family mode into MI5 operator mode every single day without being able to fully explain how their day has been to those who'll never fully understand. You can't do it.

I openly admit I see things differently from the masses, but it's not an over-reaction to things, it's pre-empting mass murder. That's one of the main differences between the intelligence officers who work on the desks in Thames House and operators like me on the ground. They react to intelligence they receive either from the surveillance teams, agent handlers or from electronic eavesdropping, whereas we provide the intelligence and have to react instantly to certain situations if we think something like a 'hard stop' is needed. Which is basically when we call in armed police or Special Forces to arrest a target with force, deadly if there is an immediate threat to life. By law, MI5 doesn't have any powers of arrest, which to some people may sound daft, but it allows us to focus on our covert intelligence-gathering work and let the police and justice system arrest and prosecute our targets for us. The last thing the world needs is for spooks to be caught up in red tape and bullshit paperwork when we have terrorists and hostile foreign agents running around the country.

After our family big shop was done we travelled home by car, returning by a different route from the one we had taken here, as usual. We got held up at traffic lights waiting to take our next turning, and I noticed the couple who had stolen the TV only half an hour ago walking in the distance. A true sliding-doors moment. They will never know how close he had been to me ending him. I had a nice warm feeling that they had got away with stealing something as big as a TV in broad daylight. It took balls, and was probably caused by desperation in whatever personal situation they were facing, but I admired them for that. I knew what they must be going through to try to survive, and in my head I hoped they would continue to survive. It's that understanding of survival, what people are prepared to do in order to make ends meet, that lets me live in the most deprived areas in the UK. Whether someone is a terrorist, mass murderer, career criminal or out-and-out fucking psycho, they recognize their own. Those willing to do extreme things to get them to their endgame, the same as me.

Chapter Seven

Ian Grey was my handler in Northern Ireland. He was responsible for running my covert counter-terrorism operations for nearly five years. He was the type of person you imagine when you think of someone from MI5. He could speak four languages fluently, was able to foresee the Islamic threat on the UK mainland before it really started to happen, and to top it all off he had a photographic memory.

Ian openly admitted he couldn't operate on the ground like I did. He was always going on operations to oversee an arrest or an armed incursion but he had the wrong profile to work on the streets: very typical, elegant clean-shaven English gent. Distinguished-looking. Instead we needed people who'd blend in. People whose appearance didn't draw a crowd.

Along with all the other MI5 handlers and desk officers in charge of our covert military unit, Ian was under an assumed identity, which is pretty standard practice. Even though every military operator had Top Secret clearance, officially called 'Developed Vetting', we all had 'known-as names' or aliases. This provided another, albeit thin, layer of protection to our personal lives. We were after all going after the hardest terrorists and killers in the world, who were actively looking for people like us.

If one of us was caught we couldn't compromise anyone else on the teams or from MI5 because we didn't know anyone's real name.

Ian recruited me to MI5. He was the closest thing I ever had to a dad. He gave me just enough feedback on debriefs so I knew I was doing a good job without over-fuelling my ego. He guided me through the intelligence world and always encouraged me to question everything I saw on the streets and 'think of the picture'. It's to officers like Ian that this country owes a huge debt; because of his actions and people like him, tens of thousands of people are walking around blissfully unaware that they could have been murdered years ago.

Most days he would ask for a debrief from me either in person or on the secure encrypted telephones. Some days even the most hardline terrorists don't do anything of interest. Sometimes all they will do is jump in the car, go to the local takeaway and return home to watch a night of shit TV. But you try telling Ian that a target hasn't done anything of interest. He would always ask me to think: *What have I missed? What have I noticed but discounted?*

He entrusted to me jobs no one else could do or wanted to do. He was, in short, a fucking legend, a true hero, and he played a crucial part in how I went on to operate with MI5 officially.

That particular day I was sitting in the operations briefing room in Thames House, which had a typical lay-out: a big screen at the front showing the Sky News reporting of David Cameron taking his place at Number 10 after Gordon Brown lost the election, with a lectern that controlled all the imagery shown to the operators about to deploy, a big atomic digital clock so everyone could sync their watches with the operations room officers, then approximately five rows of seating on an incline. Obviously I always wanted to sit at the back of the room. It was probably a combination of wanting to see everything without anyone being behind me, which is typical of surveillance operators of our background, and just being the naughty one in the team, always doing whatever I wanted to.

Briefings usually start exactly the same way. 'Good morning, team, please take a moment to sync your watches and I will begin the briefing on Operation GRANITE at 0901 hours.'

As the briefing officer started giving us the background history on the operation and what the job was, the frosted glass door half opened and the director in charge of our branch, known to us only as Director A leaned in just enough to catch my eye and signalled to me with a backwards head nod that he wanted to talk to me outside the briefing room, clearly in private. This was unusual to say the least; we'd have virtually little to no contact with the senior levels of MI5. The flow of intelligence was restricted on purpose; we were told to hunt the bad guys and either report back or stop them in their tracks, and only they know the true reasons why we were on the streets. The purpose was to keep surveillance operators like me objective and not allow us to be led by working theories. We had all the information we needed, like their potential endgame and attack planning targets, weapons, intentions, associates, etc. But we were never told, for example if agent runners were on our operation or if our target had a lot of CIA or MI6 interest.

As I made my way down towards the door of the briefing room, I could see the odd team member looking round at me; we're all spooks, after all, we want to know what's happening, nosy bastards, all of us. I was nervous: was a previous operation coming back to haunt me, had my wife called and something was wrong with my son? The director looked at me, then put his hand on my shoulder. He never showed compassion.

'Ian was found dead yesterday,' he said.

'Get fucked, fuck off . . . FUCK YOU!'

I didn't feel upset, nor did I cry. I wanted to beat the shit out of the director for telling me. He just looked at me as I knocked his hand off my shoulder and adjusted my footing, ready to floor him.

'I've brought this personally to you before the whole service is told. I know . . .'

'YOU DON'T KNOW SHIT!'

I was angry. If I wasn't careful, I'd have my team pulling me off the director as I beat the living shit out of him.

His face went cold, like a portrait, instantly hardening up as he stepped away from me to lean against the corridor wall. He continued to look me in the eyes, probably expecting me to well up and break down into a sobbing mess on the floor.

I quizzed him intently without waiting for a full response: was it hostile action, was he suffering with a long-term illness, where and who found him? His face was ice-cold in response to my quick-fire questions; he knew I was furious. I wasn't sure if I was angry at finding out that Ian had died or at the fact that I didn't find out until a day afterwards.

'Let's walk, I want to show you something. You won't deploy today.'

The director knew I wasn't in the right frame of mind to deploy operationally. Walking through the corridor maze that is Thames House, we went towards the stairs leading down to the canteen. The canteen was a fantastic facility and the food was actually very good and cheap. The service wanted to make sure the non-operational staff didn't have to leave the building to eat, as a constant stream of MI5 employees going to and from the local coffee shop would make them easy targets for terrorists, foreign intelligence agencies or well-organized crime syndicates. The support staff, as we quite often referred to them, were great at their jobs behind the bomb-proof walls of Thames House, but they lacked the operational awareness on the ground that we relied on to stay alive.

'Good morning. Two large lattes, please.'

Although the canteen was a nice place to be and a safe haven for employees to relax in, it wasn't for me. I felt awkward there, not inferior but just out of place. Virtually every office-bound employee around had a degree, they were all highly intelligent and everyone was in typical smart office wear: shirts, ties, suits. Even though we all worked for the best intelligence agency in the world, I never felt these were my people. I felt like a caged animal in this building.

After we got our coffees the director led me to the furthest corner of the canteen, and when we finally arrived at the table, he muttered to me to sit down. I could feel myself stop and stare at him, expecting more respect: fucking telling me to sit like a dog. I never had a problem with authority but this guy was really starting to piss me off.

'So, we have coffee, no one can hear us. Tell me what happened. No bullshit.' I bowed my head slightly lower to make sure I had his eye contact before I continued.

'Boss, what happened to Ian?'

Taking a slow drink of his coffee, he adjusted his seating position and held his cup with both hands as if he was seeking some comfort from the warmth of it.

'OK. This is what we know to be fact. Yesterday morning Ian was found dead by his cleaner. Single shot to the side of his head, and a gun in his hand.'

Sensing I was about to interrupt with another barrage of questions he continued. 'LISTEN! And do NOT push me on this, TC. You will not do any digging on this. This is not being investigated. It was suicide, his family will be told of the official cause of death, and that is the end of it.'

The fact that the director was using my Northern Ireland known-as name from the days when Ian recruited me showed me a degree of respect. I knew that, especially as he'd told me personally. He didn't have to do any of this, which immediately raised my suspicions. Why tell me personally? The director didn't owe me anything, and if this was a tragic event then the service would honour him properly, not shut someone down. This felt very much like I was being ring-fenced from enquiring into his death.

One thing I know about Ian: he wasn't the type to kill himself. He and I shared the same opinion on suicide. I'd come across it a few times in my life: you kill the problem, not yourself. I sat back in my chair like some sort of despondent kid who'd just been told he can't have the trainers everyone else at school had got. The director changed his tone, much softer, and he removed his focus away from my eyes. He shifted in his chair so he could see most of the people eating their mid-morning sausage sandwiches and drinking their very reasonably priced coffees.

'I've seen the service change a lot over the years, TC. I miss the Cold War, fun and games with the Russians. They respected us. I've been stuck behind a desk too long now, I hate it. Fucking hate it. What do you love about being on the ground?'

Feeling as if I was in some sort of mad counselling session, I decided to play whatever angle the director was running. 'I don't do this for Queen and country, I don't do it for you or even my team. It's all I know, I couldn't do anything else. I'm not one of these mega-brainy educated types from Oxford or Cambridge, I blend in on the streets, it's my home.'

The director, still casually looking around at all the other service employees sharing light conversation with their colleagues, smiled thinly before he continued. 'So you're the saviour of our country, are you? The one person who can solve all our problems, simply because you're the runt of the litter?'

'I'm not the last resort, I'm the only option. I can't do half the shit the people in here can do, but YOU need people like me to get alongside the scum of the earth. I don't do it on my own, but what I do, I do extremely well. Could you do what I do? Could I do what you do? We're all individual cogs and if I'm the dirtiest and cheapest cog in this machine then so be it.'

In truth, if someone else had been called a runt in such a disrespectful way they would have flipped out or broken down crying. It didn't bother me though, at all. I know I've come from nothing. A filthy unwashed street kid who lived off cheap tins of beans for the majority of his childhood. But it's that background that allowed me to filter into the hardest areas and terrorist groups in the world.

MI5 has a lot of different names, depending on whom you talk to. Its official name is the Security Service. However, worldwide it's commonly known as MI5. You find the intelligence officers who generally sit behind the desks disseminating and prioritizing the targets on the grid refer to the service as 'the office'.

People like me, and there's probably only a handful still operational on the ground who have been recruited specifically, refer to the service as 'Box'. This goes back to the days before it was officially recognized by the British government and simply refers to its Post Office Box 500 address. Most people who work under the direction of the service, for example when I was with the undercover military unit in Northern Ireland, would always refer to the officers we knew to be MI5 as 'Box'.

I think it's that mentality that has kept me alive on the streets all these years. After all, following an Islamic extremist down an otherwise deserted street in the dark hours of the night after he'd just purchased a crossbow from a local gang isn't that safe, but because I didn't think of myself as an MI5 officer, more someone who belonged on these streets, they were mine and I'd walk anywhere I wanted. That attitude and mindset kept me safer than most.

I was proud to be an MI5 officer, even more so a surveillance officer. The director knew that. He was still holding his coffee like it was a freezing cold day, relaxed and people-watching.

'Why are we dropping it? You must know he wouldn't do this,' I said.

He took a last sip of his coffee, then placed the cup on the table before standing up and adjusting his suit jacket. 'Everyone has their demons. He was in this game a long time. If nothing else, TC, at least we know he's not suffering any more.'

As he turned to walk away, I knew I'd been shut down from asking any more questions about this. The director had one more thing to say before walking back towards the stairs at the entrance of the canteen. 'Take the day off, go get drunk or whatever it is you operators do.'

I looked down at my coffee, which had now reached that stage of no longer being hot but not being quite cold. I started looking around, slowly sitting back in my chair.

I had all my operational kit on. My service ID card and passport were in a Tubigrip around my right ankle. The last thing I was dressed for was a drinking session; ironically, though, if I were able to deploy with my team today I'd likely be drinking from a can of super-strength lager on a street corner watching for our target.

A few minutes had gone by when I found myself looking at an obviously new and very young employee, clearly just out of university and by the look of him either in some admin role or low-level HR position. Thin, tall, around twenty-one, twenty-two years old, stereotypical geek. Breaking my gaze on this boy was one of the canteen staff bringing me another coffee. She knew I was about to say I hadn't ordered a second one.

'This is from the elderly gentleman you were just sitting with.'

Watching her walk away, I poured way too much sugar into my coffee. I thought about the different levels of knowledge within this building.

It's all need to know and everyone in this building respects that. The woman who just brought my coffee, despite working in Thames House for years, wouldn't even have known Director A's name, his role or the devastating news he just told me.

The one person I trusted completely in this agency was now dead. It wasn't the fact that someone else close to me had died; that happens in my world, it's part and parcel of doing dangerous work. What really grated on me was the fact that I wasn't given any answers at all; this was being swept under the carpet and, as far as I could see, the longer I stayed in this line of work, the bigger the carpet we were going to need would be.

I couldn't believe Ian, the man I knew, would kill himself. It felt like it was being shut down quietly, either to protect his integrity or his family. Maybe the director was right that I shouldn't go asking questions. Whatever Ian's demons were, he was free of them now. All I knew for sure was that this iconic and powerful agency had just become that much lonelier for me.

My handler, mentor and one of the best intelligence officers I'd ever met was dead and his body was now cold. I never knew his real name.

Chapter Eight

In the run-up to the London Olympics we started to notice a shift in Islamic extremists' tactics and the way they operated. Usually, home-grown terrorists who affiliate themselves with al-Qaeda or Daesh lack the operational experience to evade us. Some will have returned from training camps in Africa, Syria or Pakistan, and the odd one will have had combat experience in Afghanistan, Iraq, Palestine or Africa. But the majority up till then had very few anti-surveillance skills and certainly no counter-surveillance expertise.

Anti- and counter-surveillance are very different pieces of tradecraft. We use them every single day on the ground as operators. Broadly speaking, anti-surveillance is the art of evading anyone who may be trying to follow you. For example, a career criminal who thinks there is a chance he's being followed while driving his car at night, which just happens to be full of drugs, will use simple and very crude aspects of anti-surveillance. For instance, slowing down coming up to a set of traffic lights and, just as they turn red, speeding up and driving through them, knowing that any vehicle following wants to stick with his car. Changing direction suddenly down a side street without indicating, driving a full loop around to then go back on the way he's just driven down – we call that doing a 'reciprocal' or 'recip' on the net and most of the time it happens when a target is driving around a roundabout to try to catch out any surveillance teams.

Anti-surveillance is quite often done on foot too; you don't have to be driving a car to do it. It all revolves around being able to move freely without being followed, whether you identify any surveillance or not. MI5 surveillance teams employ rigorous and sometimes complicated tradecraft every day to avoid being seen, it becomes second nature to us, but the tactics we use are sometimes used by our targets and they catch out normal police surveillance teams all the time.

Counter-surveillance requires a lot more planning and involves more people. We run counter-surveillance operations all the time for our agent handlers, or for our own operations in which we are deploying against the Russians or Chinese. Whereas anti-surveillance is designed to avoid being followed, counter-surveillance is designed to identify operators working within a surveillance team, their vehicles, equipment, how they communicate and ultimately how big the team actually is. Obviously there are different degrees of counter-surveillance; if a crime syndicate was running 'counter' to detect a police team then they would only likely be able to identify people, vehicles and potentially how they communicate, although it would be unlikely that they would be able to hear the encrypted transmissions.

MI5 'counter' is, as you would imagine, incredibly in-depth. If we were providing cover for an agent handler we'd agree the route of travel he'd take to meet his agent.

We'd design the route so it would take a natural path to the meeting while providing opportunities for identifying any hostile surveillance along the way.

It's a huge effort and takes a large team positioned along the predetermined route. In high-profile operations we'd be tracking the human intelligence source our agent handler was about to meet. The thing that gives the game away is always their behaviour. Being natural and living your cover are the keys to being a good operator. Never be seen to talk to yourself; only nutters and undercover police talk to themselves. If we have to speak on the radio we do it covertly, so we either pretend we are talking on our phone, or do it at natural points that allow your body to move away from anyone who may be watching your face. If we feel we can't talk at all, we can use our radios to signal a limited amount of information nonverbally. This would be started by our team members in their cars asking us questions and we'd reply with signals for yes or no. We also have a signal to tell the team we are in danger and need extracting immediately.

I'd seen terrorist groups deploy various forms of anti-surveillance and counter-surveillance including counter-electronic surveillance, which is designed to identify and disrupt our eavesdropping capability. Usually this came from the Irish groups hell-bent on destroying the Good Friday Agreement. I'd never experienced any 'counter' from Islamic extremist terror cells, until now.

Our target was extremely high profile, number three on our grid. He was responsible for facilitating groups of young men he'd had radicalized to fight British and

American troops in Afghanistan and Iraq. He funded his operation with stolen credit cards and various other criminal activities. He knew he was on our radar because we had tried to recruit him a few years earlier; however, his arrogance and belief in his position within the UK as the voice of sharia law was too strong and we couldn't turn him. He was, however, an incredible source of intelligence because his associates and those he was radicalizing weren't that bright and would easily reveal either to other people or via social media what their intentions were. This target first came on to our grid in 2008 and was given the code name SHARP PENCIL.

Camden Market in London is a brilliant place for operators to work in, and my team had spent countless hours there over the years watching targets. It does, however, present its own challenges for a surveillance team, even one as good as ours. Usually there is at least one undercover police operation in place looking to identify stolen or counterfeit goods being sold on the stalls, and it's also a breeding ground for pickpockets looking to take advantage of the tourists that flock there. This makes the area 'red hot'. Anyone who's up to no good, whether they be a terrorist or a low-level criminal, is watching out for undercover operators, and thanks to the teams of police trying to be covert when they are all over six foot tall, clean-shaven, wearing outdoor walking clothes and not buying anything, our targets such as SHARP PENCIL carry on with their normal day, refraining from doing anything operational.

We'd never liaise with the normal police on our

operations; they weren't cleared and to be honest we didn't trust them. Police counter-terrorist teams and Special Branch were cleared to Secret and in rare cases the odd one held Top Secret clearance, particularly if they had served with us in Northern Ireland, so we would sometimes share real-time information with them about an operation, but nine times out of ten we would operate on our own. We didn't trust anyone, but that's how we got things done.

It was a Friday, and as we left the garage to deploy surveillance on SHARP PENCIL the team leader asked the Operations Centre for an update on the location of the target.

'SHARP PENCIL left his HA [Home Address] at 0923hrs wearing a dark brown shalwar kameez, carrying a white bag. He's currently in the area of Camden Market just south of Camden Lock bridge.'

'Roger that, all call signs acknowledge down the list.'

As the rest of the team popped up on the net with their vehicle call signs, confirming they had heard the message about SHARP PENCIL leaving his home address. I waited my turn and started to accelerate through London traffic.

'Charlie Two Two, roger,' I acknowledged.

Weaving my way through the mass of London commuters, treating all the red traffic lights as a 'give way' rather than a 'stop', I started to make good ground. The team was working well together already, using bus lanes and overtaking the heavy traffic on the opposite side of the road when there was a gap in the oncoming traffic. It's like a choreographed piece of ballet, all very smooth: we can see what our team mates' cars are doing without talking on the net, one car blocks the traffic naturally and we all pass through. London is great for this as the bus lanes, cycle zones at traffic lights and junctions' hatched boxes all give us space to slice through the city wherever we want.

The big thing to remember is we have to choose our places to do this; you can't do it in front or behind targets or even in the immediate vicinity because it raises the tension in the area and, although a target may not see it, they will sense something isn't right. Our vehicles aren't fitted with sirens or blue lights either, because if you know where to look for the blue lights even in the unmarked 'covert' cars the police use, they're still really obvious to see. If we can see them, everyone else can as well, including our targets and their associates.

As the team approaches the markets, we all start taking different routes and breaking off from each other in a way that probably resembles a group of fighter jets suddenly splitting and breaking formation during a display. If this operation goes to plan, the team won't come together again until the debrief. The team leader is now on the net telling each team car where to go. The aim is to have Camden Market well covered, with people further out as a precaution. We were all over him.

This is all done without the public, the target or even the police knowing we are there – everything natural and blending in to the area.

'Charlie Two Two, can you go close in to find SHARP PENCIL?'

'Charlie Two Two, roger, figures three.'

'For information, SHARP PENCIL's just south of the bridge.'

'Charlie Two Two, roger.'

Now my team knew I was only three minutes away from the market and starting to search for him, and I knew he hadn't moved; to be stationary this long he was more than likely to be with friends within the market or having something to eat. This was out of character, though, because he wasn't usually up before midday.

Switching my radio on as I turned into a side street, I saw the bridge and the market in front of me, already rammed full of people. Leaving the car, I sent a quick transmission to my team letting them know I was searching in the area. I loved this part.

'Zero Six out on foot searching.'

I could hear the whole team now on the net, plotting up in the area, saying what they could and couldn't do or go with. Stacey was close in too with the camera; I could see her approaching from the north on the other side of the bridge. As an operator, once your radio is constantly receiving transmissions from your team, it gives you a huge sense of confidence that everyone is working together well and you become unstoppable.

There was an urgent signal over the radio.

'Signal heard, STAND BY, STAND BY. Zero Six, do you have control of SHARP PENCIL?'

Still unable to talk I signalled back to the team on the radio to confirm I had control of the target.

As I walked amongst the hundred or so pedestrians in

the area I noticed SHARP PENCIL leaving the market and striding away from me towards the bridge, northbound.

'Roger that, Zero Six, you have control.'

'Zero Six, Stacey can?'

It's always best if you're on a foot follow to have an officer with a camera provide a commentary when you're in a busy area like this; it lets you move naturally with the target without having to keep a constant eye on them and gives you the freedom not to talk, plus vehicle crews have maps they can refer to and give accurate locations of where the target is at all times.

Signalling back to Stacey on the radio, I hand over control to her. This was perfect as I could blend in to the environment even better now I didn't have to give a full commentary on the net.

'Roger that, Zero Six, I have control of SHARP PENCIL walking northbound on the east side of Camden High Street towards the bridge and the junction with Chalk Farm Road.'

The whole time Stacey was giving the commentary I could hear the camera snapping away, capturing images of our target as he walked further north.

'From Seven One Zero, SHARP PENCIL is NOT carrying a white bag, he's empty-handed, wearing a dark brown shalwar kameez, continuing north on Chalk Farm Road on the east side towards the junction of Hawley Street. Zero Six, if he continues past me can you?'

It's important the team knows what each member can and can't do. I was in a good position here.

'Yes, yes. Once he's past you I can take control.'

No one else was talking now on the net apart from me and Stacey, but I knew the team was manoeuvring around our positions like satellites moving around a planet. We give our targets enough room to go about their business without ever seeing us.

As SHARP PENCIL continued walking I could see the top half of his body through the crowd approximately thirty metres in front of me. When he walked past the camera I took control of the follow.

'Zero Six, all yours.'

I knew we had good photographic imagery of SHARP PENCIL due to the constant camera clicks every time Stacey sent a transmission.

'Roger, Zero Six has control; he's walking northbound on the east side of Chalk Farm Road past Costa Coffee towards Stables Market, very relaxed, no look-backs.'

When following any target you have to give your team as much information as possible in quick concise transmissions: where he is, what direction he is heading and towards something easily recognizable. Whether or not he is operationally aware is important too, because if he starts looking back on his route and deploying some sort of anti-surveillance we'd change how we followed him. SHARP PENCIL seemed very relaxed. I was wondering, however, where his white bag went.

'Zero Six, permission?'

The team leader always asks for permission to talk when a target is under control to make sure he doesn't speak when an operator is about to send a critical message.

'Yes, no change, go ahead.'

'Base, do we have any other intelligence to suggest what SHARP PENCIL is planning today?'

'Negative. Nothing.'

'Roger, thanks, Base. Zero Six back to you.'

'Roger that, from Zero Six. SHARP PENCIL IN, IN Stables Market, I can't go with but have direct on the exit.'

'One Eight can.'

'Roger, thanks, Sarah. Stations stay sharp here, please.'

The team leader was right to make sure everyone was on top of their game here. I couldn't follow him into Stables Market as he might recognize me, and despite a lot of people funnelling into a small entrance into an open-air marketplace I'd just followed him up this street. I'd go and get a coffee in Costa Coffee, sit inside, watching through the shop window at the exit, and wait for him to leave. Sarah would go into the market to watch what he did and feed him back to me, waiting outside. Once she heard SHARP PENCIL was clear of the area, she'd leave and rejoin the team.

As I stood in line waiting to order my coffee I could hear the team talking over the radio. I could spare a minute or two here to live my cover in this shop. I knew Sarah was walking towards the exit, and everyone in the team knew she would have sight of SHARP PENCIL if he quickly left the second marketplace he'd been in this morning, and the advantage of this one was that this was the only exit he'd use.

Trying to cope with a radio that is filled with a ton of

voices all constantly talking might put a lot of people off from ordering something as simple as a cup of coffee, but our brains learn to file certain information coming in constantly and you develop the ability to recall that information whenever you need it.

I sat down with my coffee in a takeaway cup, on a seat that gave me a full view of the exit, in case the target came out without Sarah spotting him. Still no word from her and the minutes were ticking by; he hadn't come out while I'd been watching and Sarah would have seen him exit if he'd left as she approached.

A radio signal came over the net suggesting someone needed to say something but couldn't talk openly.

'One Eight, is that you?'

Sarah signalled yes.

OK, she was trying to communicate but clearly couldn't talk; she hadn't signalled that she was in trouble, so I knew what the team leader was going to ask next.

'One Eight, do you need help searching for SHARP PENCIL?'

Confirming she did, it didn't take long for one of the team to volunteer.

'Six Seven can?'

'Thanks, Six Seven.'

The whole team is always desperate to get in on the follow; it's part of our make-up, we want to be part of the hunt constantly. The one place you really feel like you're at the sharp end of an operation is when you're in control of the target. I could see Amrik moving towards the market now too from the north end. He'd infiltrated himself into a large group of tourists also heading into the marketplace, which was smart and exactly what I would have done. Amrik broke up the profile of our close-in team as he was Muslim and dressed in his shalwar kameez. That was the difference between us and police teams: the range of profiles we had was incredible.

As Amrik entered the market he had a head-on with our target, who was leaving at exactly the same time. Amrik did the right thing and continued to walk into the marketplace naturally with the crowd, but his profile was now blown as SHARP PENCIL would have seen him.

It's moments like this we desperately try to avoid; having a head-on with the target meant Amrik was now out of play to get close to SHARP PENCIL. He was one of the few Muslims on the team so to have him potentially seen and remembered was a big blow, especially if we needed to get close to the target when he went to last prayers at the mosque.

Drinking my coffee, I heard a standby signal cut across the net seconds before I saw the target leaving the market.

'From Zero Six, STAND BY, STAND BY! SHARP PENCIL OUT, out and north on Chalk Farm road on the west side.'

The standby signal came from Amrik. As soon as I saw the target leave I picked my coffee cup up naturally and walked out of the coffee shop without looking at the target. I gave the team my update.

'Roger that, Zero Six, three more out on foot, please.'

The team leader knew this was the second time I'd had

control already this morning and with SHARP PEN-CIL going in and out of places we needed more people on foot to control him properly without being noticed. Within seconds my radio filled with that familiar safe feeling of your team springing into action to back you up.

'Zero Nine backing.'

'Two Nine, roger.'

'Zero Eight, roger.'

The principles of mobile surveillance hadn't changed a great deal for the last thirty or forty years; our ability and technical support had, though, and it's a combination of that and our day-in, day-out experience on the ground that makes MI5's A4 surveillance teams the very best in the world. I didn't need to look behind me to see my team mates, I knew where they would be. The target was still walking north on the west side of the road. I was about twenty metres behind him on the east side of the road. Simon, who was 'backing' me, would take over control if the target took a turning down a side street or if I felt over-exposed, He would be in the vicinity and ready to take over. Sue, who was known as 'Two Nine', would be on the same side of the road as me but even further behind Simon. As a team we were so used to operating together that we could virtually do a foot follow without radios.

SHARP PENCIL continued walking north without looking back at all, and was walking back towards the general direction of his home address. So far, very little intelligence had been gained here, but as always you have to question absolutely everything you see. The biggest questions I had were: where did the plastic bag go, and what was the purpose of this trip? He carried on walking north to the junction near his home address, which we had well covered.

'Base, do you read, Zero Six?'

'Yes, go ahead.'

'If SHARP PENCIL takes his next right towards his HA, can I let him run to you?'

'Yes, we have good picture of his front door.'

'Zero Six, roger.'

Passing the parcel around the team had worked so far and only Amrik had got caught out when the music stopped as the target had left the second marketplace. So far, so good.

'SHARP PENCIL looking to cross the road west to east, HOLD BACK, HOLD BACK!' Issuing the other guys on foot the order to 'Hold Back' gives them time to get into cover like a shop or to move behind a crowd so the target can't see them.

'Yeah, he's moved west to east towards the end of his road. Base, if he goes down his street I will let him run to you. Zero Nine, can you confirm him down the street?'

'Zero Nine, yes.'

'Base, roger.'

So the plan was very simple and working nicely. Once SHARP PENCIL was out of my sight down his home street, I'd take myself off the street by going into a greasy-spoon café, and let Simon continue walking north on the west side of the road to catch a glimpse of the target heading towards his home address. The danger of just letting him run on the assumption that he was going to go home was that he might jump into a car and we would lose him completely.

I ordered my bacon butty with brown sauce from the world's filthiest café, and got confirmation from Simon that the target was almost at his home address.

'Zero Nine, SHARP PENCIL ten metres away from his HA. Base, all yours.'

'Base, roger, SHARP PENCIL IN, IN home address.'

My team leader popped up on the net, asking people to reposition now for a quick foot or vehicle move if the target decided that he was going to leave his home within the next few minutes. Because the team would have been moving their positions constantly around during our foot follow, we'd have most of the vehicles in position already, but those of us out on foot now needed to get back to our respective vehicles. It was going to take me around ten minutes to walk back to my car, and I needed to maintain my cover. I might well still deploy in this area again today so I had to remain invisible to the locals.

I could hear the net starting to go quiet as the transmissions became less frequent, but I knew the intelligence picture was still unfolding because SHARP PENCIL had electronic intercept on his house. This meant that the boffins back at Thames House in A2A were listening to everything he did via the eavesdropping devices planted throughout his building and his car. He was pretty much tied up, as were his associates.

Approaching my car, I was the last one out on foot, as

I'd heard the others tell the team leader on the net that they had returned to their vehicles.

'Charlie Two Two, complete.'

'Roger that. North, please, ready for a vehicle move.'

Reversing the car, I flicked the door locks to secure the vehicle, switched my personal radio off to save its battery and turned on the radio in the car. I concentrated on driving out of the area southbound and worked my way round to the northern position. It was smart to now keep me away from the target, even though he wouldn't have seen me.

Once your target is at their home address and you start your repositioning ready for another move if they come out again, you still drive faster than most other road users but usually you wouldn't go through red lights or use pavements to get round traffic – there isn't any need – but if the target is getting away or not under control then you do everything humanly possible to get control of them quickly. As I wove in and out of the lighter than normal London traffic, I had to change the look of my profile, I slipped my jacket off one arm at a time with one hand on the steering wheel. I paused from undressing briefly to change gear; I'd now transformed the colour of my top half from light green to dark blue.

Changing your profile can be as simple as a making a subtle colour change. Unless you've been spotted up close and your face has been remembered, then at a distance you could be a completely different person. It has to be done subtly and at the right point – you can't just do a fucking Superman walk into a phone box wearing a suit and leave two minutes later dressed as a tramp.

Glancing down at the map I'd pulled on to my lap from the door pocket, I flicked through to get the right page for the target's address, constantly glancing to see where I was on the road and making sure I wasn't about to smash into anyone. I finally got the right page and could settle into a fairly simple drive to my new position.

'Stations, security checks down the list, please, starting with Charlie One.'

The team leader needed to make sure everyone in the team was safe; the areas we operate in are dangerous and the speeds we drive at mean we are more likely to have a serious crash if something goes drastically wrong, so every fifteen minutes he'd make sure everyone shouts up on the net to say they are OK. The team started replying, but when it got to my turn to say I was fine, I was interrupted: 'WAIT OUT, WAIT OUT! STAND BY, STAND BY, SHARP PENCIL in his green Toyota Avensis heading northbound running free!'

Fuck me, this was now going to be a scramble to get hold of him because not everyone was in position yet. Why the fuck didn't the Operations Centre give him out leaving his home address? I could hear the anger in the team leader's voice.

'Roger. Base, did you SEE him leave the HA?'

'Negative.'

Bollocks, we'd lost him.

'Roger that, any stations north to assist?'

'Charlie Two Two, negative, still coming into the area.'

I knew I was being counted on here to get hold of SHARP PENCIL as he drove away from his house, but

I wasn't in position yet. If I was going to break a lot of road traffic laws, I needed extra assurances here that I would be backed up from Thames House. Usually we are allowed to break the speed limits, drive through red traffic lights, mount pavements – all the usual stuff you'd expect us to deal with when hunting the world's most dangerous terrorists. We have something in place for extreme cases, though, called STEEL BADGE, in which we are given permission to bump cars out of our way, though never to hurt other road users. If a gap is slightly too narrow for our car we can use minimal necessary force to squeeze through, which can cause damage to other cars and invariably involves the police chasing us. Such permission isn't given very often, usually only when we know a target is about to blow something up and there is a direct and immediate threat to life.

'From Charlie Two Two, do we have STEEL BADGE in play?'

'NEGATIVE, NEGATIVE.'

Base was extremely quick to react to my request for STEEL BADGE permission to get to the north position and find SHARP PENCIL without worrying about creating a bit of mess. They obviously thought he was on a normal day out without any attack planning, but I still needed to get through this traffic quickly; coming the long way round to save me driving through the area I had just crossed on foot was hurting me.

Another set of red traffic lights. I could see a smoky old Mercedes at the head of the queue and I guessed it would be driven by someone elderly, which meant I could cut them up and pick my way through the oncoming crossing traffic while everyone else was held at red. Dropping down a gear into first, I bumped the car wheels up on to the pavement to give me just enough room to slide on the outside of the traffic. As I pulled up alongside the dark blue Mercedes, I could see it was a woman probably in her early seventies at the wheel. Lights were starting to change from red to amber, oncoming traffic had stopped and I was now in front and accelerating away, 35mph, into third gear, up to 50mph, into fourth gear and resting the engine, still accelerating up to 80mph.

I was about two minutes away from the rough area where SHARP PENCIL was last seen and about to transmit to let my team know just as Stacy shouted up on the net: 'STAND BY, STAND BY! From Charlie Seven One Zero, I have control of SHARP PENCIL's vehicle northbound Highgate Road, Kentish Town. Doing this at a distance, can anyone help out?'

Stacey was right to be asking for help. She was close to him back at Camden Market and we needed someone to take control so she could move away out of the area.

'All stations, that's a STOP, STOP, STOP!'

So far that day, SHARP PENCIL's movements hadn't been overly out of character. Yes, we constantly question everything we see and don't see, but sandwiched around that is the experience of knowing people. Humans are creatures of habit, predictable. As operators it's one of the first things we learn. Think about when you go about your normal day: you probably wake up virtually the same time and go through the same routine, whether that be eating, making a coffee or using the toilet. When you take the kids to school or travel to your place of work, it'll be nearly always similar to the previous time. When you go into your local supermarket you'll collect your trolley or basket and probably start at the same place each time and buy mostly the same things. You'll wear similar clothes most of the time, make your favourite drink the same way.

Once you get round the fact that the people we hunt are the scum of the earth, they become predictable; people stop at seemingly random places and do strange things. There was absolutely nothing to suggest that what SHARP PENCIL was doing was out of the ordinary, but we still needed to get a grip of him. We'd been on him for years. He was a fucker, and smart, so we had to be on top of our game when he was out in the open.

'From Charlie Seven One Zero, SHARP PENCIL is out of his vehicle now, walking to an address on the east side, no house number, doing this at a distance.'

'Charlie Two Two, roger, is the house north or south of the school?'

I didn't know this area at all, but driving towards Kentish Town I could see a school marked on the map, so I replied, 'South of the school entrance, approximately fifty metres, vehicle parked outside the house on the east side facing north.'

This was perfect; I was coming in from the north end and would wait further up the road to get control if he moved away in a vehicle.

Driving down the side streets, I box round to be facing north on a different road.

'Charlie Two Two in position for a north move on a standby.'

'Charlie Seven One Zero, roger that – thanks, mate.'

I could sense Stacey's anxiety. This was starting to get risky having the same operators and vehicles close to the target.

Parking up a few doors down so I could see where SHARP PENCIL's car would have to pass if he drove north I turned down the volume on the car's radio. The team leader was asking permission from Stacey to ask Base to give us information on house addresses in this area; there was absolutely nothing showing on the grid. The Operations Centre had done a great job in identifying that there was a drugs arrest a few years ago at a house that was roughly in the same area our target had gone into, but nothing terrorist-related.

'Charlie Two Two, can you check a possible driving north, please? I've been blocked by a bus.'

'Yes, checking now ... STAND BY, STAND BY, that's SHARP PENCIL driving north on Highgate Road towards the school.'

'Roger that, Charlie Two Two, all stations, we'll go with this.'

The team leader was happy that we'd got hold of the target again despite the scramble earlier. As I slowly drove up on a side road, I glimpsed the rear of his car. This was perfect timing as he'd have no way of seeing the profile of my car. I needed to get behind him now, and accelerated towards the junction, praying there would be another car or two to use as cover between us.

'Vehicle now approaching the roundabout with High-gate Westhill, no indication.'

I still wasn't behind him at this stage, I'd nosed my car to a junction approximately twenty-five metres behind his car but to his right.

'Target vehicle exit one, exit one, northbound on Highgate Westhill. I have control.'

Thankfully I made it look like I wasn't in a rush to get anywhere and two cars, a red Golf and a blue Mondeo, followed SHARP PENCIL's car and I slipped in behind them. They provided my cover as I took exit one on the roundabout too. While I was in control of the vehicle, maintaining visual the whole time, I was determined to make sure nearly if not all of my car's profile was hidden.

'Vehicle still northbound, speed three zero past the junction of South Grove.'

'Roger, Charlie Three Five backing.'

SHARP PENCIL was driving his car fairly relaxed, sticking to the speed limits, but my immediate concern wasn't him, it was the two cars in front of me. Each had three males inside, all appearing very agitated, their heads constantly back and forth to each other, in their mirrors, looking down side streets. It felt like they were gang members looking for someone or they'd spent most of the day so far taking drugs.

'Stations, be aware of a blue Mondeo, last three Victor Mike Victor, and a red Golf last three Mike Zulu Papa, behind the target's vehicle; occupants seem very agitated.'

This was unlikely to be related to our operation, but

when we've had people die or attacked on operations before they have been spotted by a third party, because local gangs always know when their area is red hot and there are people around who shouldn't be. We always aim to pass over control as much as we can when we are following targets, unless we're on extremely long motorway follows where you can get away with being behind the same car for long periods. I handed over the follow to the backing car, Charlie Three Five and pulled down a side street. Not long after, it came over on the net that the suspicious cars I'd pointed out earlier had pulled away too.

The car journey went on for the next few hours as SHARP PENCIL drove around seemingly aimlessly, making the odd stop at a takeaway to get some fried chicken. The team leader had asked the officers in the Operations Centre if any intelligence was coming out of the eavesdropping devices we had fitted in the target's Toyota Avensis. Nothing had come back yet but there was another large job running at the same time in Bournemouth and nearly everyone was working on that operation.

As it started to get dark, SHARP PENCIL was driving back towards the area of the mosque he usually attended. With it being Friday, we expected him to go for food once he had prayed with his associates, but despite him being a 'true Muslim' we hadn't seen him pray yet.

The team had been handing over control all day, constantly swapping around to keep our cover. When I heard Charlie Seven One Zero take control of the vehicle follow

I was surprised, because Stacey should have changed that vehicle at the garage hours ago. SHARP PENCIL finally got out on foot roughly five minutes away from the mosque. Now it was raining and dark I was happy getting out of my car and following him again because I'd changed my profile and most people keep their heads down in weather like this. The operator in front of me who had control of SHARP PENCIL would tell me on the radio where he'd gone and carry on past, then guide me in or clear the corner for me so I wouldn't be walking into a trap.

I loved this weather, but fucking hated it at the same time. Freezing-cold rain was hitting my face, with only the yellow glare of the streetlights offering any sort of warmth in this shit side street. We were back in the target's traditional ground where he'd spend most of his time; the only thing littering the streets more than the full bin bags of rubbish were the local gangs dealing drugs. This had been an incredibly long surveillance follow, I hadn't eaten or been for a piss for hours and thanks to the strong coffee I'd had that morning in Camden my bladder was about to burst.

'SHARP PENCIL walking east towards the rough area of the mosque, can anyone help me out with a street name?'

Fatima was in control of him, I was about twenty metres behind her, but knew why she was struggling with street names down here. We hadn't deployed down this street before and most of the graffiti suggested we'd struggle to find a street sign anywhere. We weren't getting an answer from any of the vehicle call signs. This didn't happen that often, but we were obviously in a communications black spot.

'You are going out, mate, and I'm still backing.'

This was a rough area, so I relaxed the voice procedure to give her a bit more confidence that I was in her ear and backing her up. I was comfortable in places like this but equally Fatima could go into areas I couldn't; we all had our strengths and right now she needed to feel mine – that I was calm and there was nothing to worry about.

'Thanks, TC. He's still walking down, but if he turns off I will clear you round?'

'No worries, mate.'

I was hoping that even though we couldn't hear the team on the radio they would be able to hear us. Fucking typical. First we lose him leaving his house, now the radios go silent when we're out on foot.

'TC, he's turned left down that alleyway. If I clear you round, can you go with and I'll try to get round to the mosque?'

Alleyways are always shit and never a good idea. He was probably using this one as a cut-through. We'd had such a long day, we couldn't lose sight of him now. If we got sight of him going into the mosque then at least we had a new starting point but if we lost him now we'd have no way of knowing for sure where he was.

'Yeah, mate, let me know if you can see the end of the alley, please.'

If Fatima could see straight through it would be slightly safer knowing it was clear; last thing I wanted to do was go walking into an alleyway with the target holding a knife waiting for me, especially as I was dying for a piss!

'OK, SHARP PENCIL down the alleyway and no sign, I can't see the other side. I'm going to continue to the mosque, see if I can pick him up there.'

Fuck's sake, this wasn't good at all. The target had been out all day without doing anything glaringly out of character, but we needed to keep hold of him to make sure the whole day wasn't a waste. We couldn't talk to any of the cars or the Operations Centre and we were in one of the hardest areas in London on foot with no back-up, and I was about to turn down an alleyway.

'Roger that, mate, checking the alleyway now.'

Forcing my legs to keep moving, I could feel something deep inside my gut willing me to stop walking down this alleyway. I was being stupid here. The target wasn't in attack-planning phase, he was a facilitator. I shouldn't be going down this alley when I couldn't see the end of the narrow dark tunnel. Was it my ego forcing me to continue walking or the will to keep hold of the target? Walking into the mouth of the alleyway, I was now committed, because turning around would look unnatural to anyone who might be watching. The target turned down here roughly forty-five seconds ago and it did look like a common through route for locals; that didn't make me feel any better though.

'MIKE ZULU PAPA.' Shit, it was the red Golf with the gang members from earlier, parked on the street just up from the alleyway, now empty. It made sense that the occupants either lived near here or did business in this area but as I walked further down the narrow alley all I could think about was why this car was back. My train of thought was broken by the overpowering smell of cat shit as I worked my way through bin bags and puddles.

I could feel my heart racing. I wanted to speed up and get to the other end. Choosing my steps, I tried to remain as quiet as possible and resisted the urge to look behind me. If I was about to walk into a drugs deal I could probably talk my way out of it but if I was walking into a trap I'd be screwed. Navigating the slight curve of the alleyway, I could now see I was about fifteen metres away from the exit, which was lit by the rear lights of a vehicle I could hear driving away. As the light slowly disappeared I emerged from the alley. No sign of SHARP PENCIL on a small street lined with terraced houses in need of repair.

Stay calm, don't speed up. Stay focused. I whispered into my radio, needing to hear from Fatima to make sure she was OK. Crossing on to the other side of the street to put some distance between me and the alley, I walked to the end of the street, hoping I'd come into an area in which my radio would work with the cars.

'Alley clear.'

'Roger, no sign near the mosque, I have direct of the entrance.'

'ALL FOOT CREWS, SECURITY CHECKS.'

The team leader had clearly been trying to reach us for a while and was getting worried. I didn't know whether this was a good sign or not. On one hand we could now talk to the car teams, but on the other we'd have to tell the team we'd lost control of the target. Fatima and I had both got on the net to let the team know we were OK, when we all got a very abrupt message to stop the operation.

'TC, Fatima, shout your positions immediately; we're coming to pick you up.'

'I'm direct on the mosque, ten metres north of the Tube entrance on the east side.'

'TC, can you get to Fatima's position in thirty seconds?'

'Yes, yes.'

Something had gone wrong here; surely us losing control of the target hadn't been such a massive fuck-up that it warranted two operators coming together and being picked up? Everyone on the net was dead quiet apart from the team leader who was talking a lot faster and louder than normal. Turning out of the street, I could see Fatima's position. As I walked over, I saw one of our team cars already pulling up to her, and she got into the front passenger seat as I walked towards the rear of the vehicle. I could see the odd local teenager walking past taking notice of the car and us getting in; it didn't look right. We'd never be so obvious as to do things like this. We looked like an undercover unit here; it looked shit.

The car accelerated away before I'd even put my seat belt on in the back. I adjusted it to give me enough slack so that I could sit forward to speak to the team leader, who was driving through every single red light we came across. I asked what was going on.

The team leader ignored me for a brief second, then he pressed the car's radio push-to-talk button and shouted, 'All stations, all stations, STEEL BADGE, STEEL BADGE!'

He was still accelerating as we hit 90mph.

I could hear the engines screaming as everyone in the teams acknowledged in turn. I'd never seen my team leader like this before. He was scared, as though he'd spent the last half-hour panicking. I glanced at Fatima; her eyes were wider than normal. This was frightening her. Still no reply from the team leader as he interrogated the operations officers on the net. 'Base, anything further on SHARP PENCIL?'

'Negative. Local police CTU informed.'

Just as the team leader was about to press the talk button again to reply I could see he was going to try to make the car six inches slimmer than it actually was between two buses. The wing mirror smashed off on Fatima's side of the car, making her jump; she was really starting to lose her composure now. Trying to comfort her, I put my hand on her shoulder and squeezed it.

'Roger, figures three out now, security checks, stations.'

This was the second security check in as many minutes, so I knew we were in trouble. Releasing my grip on Fatima's shoulder I sat back, tightening my seat belt again, knowing it was fairly likely we'd lose the other wing mirror at this speed. The whole team acknowledged the security checks with their vehicle numbers in double-quick time, engines still working at full capacity in the background of each of the radio transmissions.

Eventually we pulled into our covert garages away from Thames House, and even this was odd because we hadn't deployed from here that morning. Was the building under threat? As we went through the huge security gates, armed police manned the gates on the street and behind them, uniformed soldiers holding their rifles, clearly on edge. Whatever was going on, people clearly thought it was about to happen any moment now. It wasn't until we made it into the secure garage compound that my team leader relaxed and slowed down. I was never one to flap and panic in situations like this, and as far as I was aware nothing had actually happened yet; hopefully not, anyway. No point in panicking, it only made the situation worse.

Half of the team were already in the garage in a Docklands warehouse, leaning on their cars, deep in conversation about what had just happened. These old buildings are getting harder to come by, but until the developers got their hands on it, it was still ours. I still had no fucking idea what was going on. The three of us got out as the rest of the team arrived. It looked like we were about to have our debrief here. Behind the last team cars I noticed the operations officer who'd been running our support that day walking in too.

'OK, roll call, let's make sure everyone is here.' The operations officer was taking the lead on this, and as the team leader ran down the list of operators, we all shouted back with varying degrees of sharpness, 'Here!', which I'd never, ever done before. It was clear now that the threat wasn't against our buildings, it was against our team.

'We now know that the white bag SHARP PENCIL had when he left his house was passed to one of his associates. It contained walkie-talkies and video cameras. His vehicle recorded what was being said on those walkie-talkies from SHARP PENCIL's in his car. He had recruited a team of approximately twenty males to run counter-surveillance for him. To save me explaining the hours of audio footage recovered by A2A I've brought this brief clip.'

As surveillance operators we'd hardly ever be given access to eavesdropping audio like this. While the clip was playing I watched the faces of my team, and I knew from how pale they were turning that a few of them felt sick as the realization started to kick in. First all we heard was static and general driving noises, but then came the very real voices of the team that was hunting us: 'Yeah, yeah, bruv, that fucking white van is back, same reg.'

'Sweet, so how many we have now? Six, seven?'

'Let's take one of them. We'll wait on the cut through and take them straight to Imran's.'

'Everything is ready, bruv. We'll do 'em quick, though, they might have trackers on an' shit.'

Some of the team were now looking over in my direction with the realization that it was me they were planning to take hostage as I entered that alleyway.

Pressing stop on the Dictaphone, the operations officer continued. 'The plan was to take one member of your team in the back of a rented van as SHARP PENCIL left the alleyway near the mosque. We believe they would have been moved to the house on Highgate Road in Kentish Town. That house was just raided by Police CTU Green team and they found a video camera, a black flag and three butcher's knives. The floor was covered in plastic sheeting.'

The operations officer told our team leader quietly that she'd update him the next day if she got any more intelligence, then walked out of the garages. Our team leader waited until she had left to start talking to us. 'How did we miss this?'

We all looked at each other, waiting for someone to speak. This hadn't happened before: never before in the UK had so many of us been identified and set up for execution on British soil. For whatever reason, the target's team backed out at the last minute, which meant I kept my head on my neck. No one wanted to offer any opinions. Some of the team were clearly shocked and frightened that one of us had come so close to being beheaded.

The team started slowly and quietly discussing as a group and some individually with each other how we could possibly have missed this. SHARP PENCIL's friends had managed to follow us all day, employing some of the same surveillance tactics we use until they were sure they had our entire team. I could sense the air of defeat among us.

'Let's get back out there!'

The team leader looked at me as I said this, and his face said it all really. He wanted us to calmly discuss our tactics and methods and how our entire team was compromised, not make suggestions for getting everyone back out on the ground.

'These are our fucking streets, they are NOT in control, we are!'

'TC, we're not going back out. Let's see what intelligence comes through and let the intelligence officers do their job. They'll decide when and who we go out against next.'

I was furious, not at the target for daring even to think about trying to take me hostage as I left that alleyway, but for the lack of aggression in the team. It was like we were in hiding, but we were meant to be the hunters, not the fucking prey. I understood the need for a level head and to look at the big picture, but every fibre of my being wanted to destroy those pricks. Who the hell did they think they were to try to threaten us? We stop fuckers like this from killing the general public every single day, but now that we were the ones being targeted my team didn't know what to do.

I knew what I wanted to do, but recognized it was the dark side of my personality taking over. My team leader was right, I acknowledged that deep down, but I was struggling to keep hold of my professional edge. I wanted to tear those guys apart, SHARP PENCIL and all his fucking team, I wanted them dead. I was well aware that the Security Service's policy does not allow us to commit random acts of revenge or murder and that I couldn't legally do what my ever-darkening soul wanted to. If I'm really honest, I understood that the amount of intelligence gained from that day's operation would be massive.

The blood was burning through my veins, and my team could see I was angry. They left me alone as we organized transport from this compound to our houses. We were confident we weren't followed to the garages but we had to be careful. We'd leave in blacked-out minibuses one at a time and be dropped off at our homes. It took hours to get the whole team out and back to their loved ones.

Finally I arrived at home, gone midnight. I knew my family would be asleep as my wife knew never to wait up for me. Walking through the door, I noticed another letter from the credit card company: final demand. How the fuck does someone from MI5 who's saved countless people over the years and was nearly beheaded just a few hours earlier end up in debt? I fucking hated this, I was a good operator, in certain situations I was one of the best, yet because I wasn't earning enough I was struggling to do my real job of husband and father. My family never asked for anything, but I wanted to give them everything I could. I grew up with no money, but now with a good job and career I still had no money.

I checked the figure of how much I owed the credit card company, realizing it was another three weeks till payday. I wondered why I was risking my life to save everyone else's when I was drowning in debt. This was all I knew, and all I was good at, but I had to bring more money in, otherwise the people I should be protecting first would start to suffer: my family. Then an awful thought drifted in – if SHARP PENCIL and his crew had managed to kill me, my family would be financially better off, because the service would pay them high six figures as compensation for my sacrifice. I hated thinking like this. I had to put more hours in and get some overtime money.

Chapter Nine

Working up north was always my favourite place to operate, because I grew up there. I felt like I knew these places.
Even Moss Side, an area of Manchester that over the
years has had a troubled history with gang violence. As a
kid I used to float around squats in places like this, sleeping illegally in various types of buildings before ending
back at home guessing how much my dad had to drink
that morning. It's actually a lot easier to go unnoticed
doing things like this when you're of primary school age,
not old enough for your friends to notice at school and
tell someone but not young enough for people to worry if
they see you on the streets alone. All the boys at second-
ary school wanted to be Liam Gallagher from Oasis and
wore all the latest Gore-Tex jackets from Sprayway and
Berghaus or a Ralph Lauren sports jacket with Rockport
shoes. That sort of clothing would be more than our
monthly food budget so I would live in old tracksuits
from charity shops and ripped trainers. I never thought
then that I'd be back here wearing the same type of
clothes, trying to blend into the community as an officer
for MI5.

Whenever we deploy in potentially dangerous areas
like this we have a briefing not just on the target and the
wider operation but also on any criminal activity we need

to be aware of. For example, if we are going to be working on a Saturday night on the streets in an area where rival gangs are actively trying to kill each other, we need to know. Not because it would stop our operation, but so we can look out for it and, if needed, use that information to help us live our individual cover stories.

I knew these sorts of areas so I wasn't fazed at all when we were deployed there. As a kid I'd kicked cans around in front of shops and terraces in places like this. I knew the dealers round here would be really sharp, but the runners were the ones who knew absolutely everything that went on in this tight little patch, the ones riding around on their mountain bikes, taking drugs from the dealers to the buyers. Constantly weaving around the street corners and roads, they had absolutely no respect for the police, because the majority of the time the police wouldn't come into this area, unless mob-handed, as it was far too dangerous at night.

It was in rough areas like this that we'd constantly look out for everyone in the team: you always want to make sure everyone is OK, and particularly in Moss Side. We'd look to have everyone in their team cars for that added level of protection. Operating at night meant it was also a lot easier to hide in a vehicle in the dark. There aren't that many people on these streets past midnight unless they are dealing or buying drugs or looking for prostitutes; either way, if you're on foot at night here, it's likely you're up to no good, which means you're fair game for being targeted by the locals that run these streets.

On our way, the team leader came up on the radio and

asked if we could see the back door of our target's house. The target was suspected to be Chinese foreign intelligence, and we had no other information at all other than that we needed to see what he was doing in the midnight hours. This was a brand-new lead so it was understandable that the intelligence was thin at best.

As I settled to the north of the target's address I heard on my car radio that two of our team vehicles had driven through to try to get a direct view on the back way from the north as the property faced south. The layout of houses here is very much stereotypical northern city: rows of terraced and semi-detached houses in neat little blocks, all overlooking each other. I had a feeling that we might be able to get direct on the back door of the house but it would have to be someone on foot. I knew no one else in the team either had the right profile or the desire to be on their own out here at night.

'From Zero Six, I could have a look at getting this on foot from the park to the north.'

'Roger, Zero Six, do you feel safe here?'

I knew he was going to ask that. As a team leader he was responsible for the team's safety and wellbeing, but I knew he wanted results. So did I. My profile was perfect for this area tonight. I had my tracksuit on, tucked into my socks, Rockport shoes and my JD Sports drawstring bag in the car, containing a couple of cans of super-strength lager.

'Yes, fine. I'll get out now and move into the park.'

'Roger that, Zero Six. Stations, radio silence while we have him out on foot, please.'

The idea of keeping the net quiet and free from transmissions was because it was highly likely that I might need to ask to be extracted quickly, and I couldn't do that if the team were constantly talking to each other. Before I left my vehicle I switched off the car radio and switched my personal radio on, while reaching behind the passenger seat and grabbing my chav crash-out kitbag. Before you leave your vehicle, you always check your covert radio is working, especially in dangerous areas like this.

'Anyone read, Zero Six?' I asked.

'Yes, loud and clear.'

'Roger, likewise. On foot now.'

The park was roughly 150 metres ahead of me as I walked south. I couldn't see the target's house yet; it was just too dark. Holding my drawstring sports bag with my lager in, I could hear the distant sirens of emergency vehicles and some shouting from the street adjacent. Nothing to worry about. At this stage I was slowly morphing into the area. I felt at home again, and thankfully for once it wasn't raining, although this meant there was a high likelihood of the streets being busy because it was dry.

Once I got into the park, I moved towards a see-saw covered in graffiti. Taking a seat, I got a clear and direct view of the back door of the target's house. This was a fantastic position and if I was lucky I could stay here for a few hours without any issues. With my super-strength lager for company I looked like I belonged here. I needed to maintain my cover, even though I was alone in the park, and I wanted to avoid talking if I didn't need to. I opened the first can of Kestrel Super-Strength.

I signalled over the radio for the team leader to ask me a question.

'I hear you, Zero Six. Do you have direct on the back door of the address?'

Staying nice and quiet, settling in to the area, I signalled back that I could see the back door.

'Roger that, Zero Six, you have direct – thank you.'

Returning the drawstring sports bag back to my back, I settled in, soaking up the environment. It was cold and fairly quiet apart from the odd drugs-runner on his bike in the distance. I had been on the see-saw for around fifteen minutes before the team leader started interrogating me using the tone system to get a clear picture of what the target's house looked like.

'Zero Six, signal if you're OK and ready for questions?'

Taking another swig of this beer that tasted like paint-stripper, I let them know I was ready for questions.

'Roger, that's "yes", thank you. Are there any lights on at the back of the target's house?'

Negative

'Roger, negative on the lights. Do you need a break?'

Another no.

'Roger, we heard negative. Will check with you in fifteen minutes.'

With no lights on at the house it was looking like our target had already left, or wasn't about to leave for a while. The only movement I could see was the odd mountain bike cutting down the side streets, but thankfully no one had come near me yet. I didn't know where the team cars were; I knew they'd be close, but the main thing was that everyone knew I was in this park.

Nearly an hour went by and, other than the four security checks from my team leader on the radio to make sure I was OK, nothing had happened. The park was a fairly large open space at my back and I caught a glimpse of what looked like a local runner on his mountain bike riding across behind me. I was fairly sure he must have seen me. One of two things was going to happen: either I'd be left alone or I'd be approached to see what I was doing or if I wanted to buy any drugs.

Lights on downstairs at the house around the back door; this was likely our target coming out. I couldn't move away in case I walked head-on towards the target; if he was Chinese intelligence it was likely he'd be very aware of his surroundings. Probably one of the reasons he was choosing to live around here was that no one apart from me would be crazy enough to operate in gangland Manchester in the middle of the night.

Back door open. I could see a Chinese male leaving the house, illuminated briefly by a hallway light, which he switched off as he closed the door.

Giving the team my stand-by signal, the radio filled with transmissions as the team immediately switched on.

'We hear you. STAND BY, STAND BY! Zero Six, vehicle crews will take control now; return to your vehicle.'

I couldn't. The target was walking away from me about 100 metres in the distance, but my car was to the north behind me and I had a gang of lads closing in fast, blocking my path. I could hear the team moving with the target and slowly edging out of the area.

The last thing I wanted to get into now was a fight with some kids trying to prove a point to each other. If it came down to it, I could probably fight my way out of a small group if I took the initiative of surprise and speed, but the local gangs round here always carry knives and in some cases small guns. The shouts the confident teenagers were directing at me were growing more aggressive as they closed in behind me. I had to confront this.

The see-saw bounced slowly as I stood up and turned around to face this hostile gang of seven males, all of them, I saw, in their early twenties. Too big to fight off. I signalled to the team I was in trouble, transmitting the emergency signal over my radio.

'Roger, Zero Six, you need help. Coming in now, stay on this channel, everyone else switch to channel 6 and stay with the target.'

My team leader was leaving the follow to come and help me. I just hoped he would make it in time.

'What the fuck you doing round 'ere?' the leader of the gang asked, aggressively sure of himself. He was around 5ft 10 tall, dressed very similarly to me in a tracksuit with Timberland boots, smoking. He had a look in his eyes I recognized: he wasn't scared, nor was he angry. He was secure in his surroundings and what he was saying to me; he knew he could back up anything he was about to threaten me with. I tried to play down the aggression and keep hold of my composure and cover. Taking a drink of my now nearly empty can of lager, I acted as if I didn't know they were meant to be threatening,

'Nowt, been kicked out again.'

The gang started to surround me and close in, two of them on mountain bikes circling all of us, laughing and swearing. This was everyday life for them. One of the gang behind me shouted out, 'Tax 'im!'

The leader lurched forward, grabbing hold of my track-suit top on my chest. The impact made me stumble back slightly, which I emphasized to allow me to adjust my footing. It looked like this guy had the advantage, but in reality I was picturing ramming my beer can into his eye socket. Now his face was an inch away from mine I could smell on his breath that he'd been drinking heavily.

'This is my park, you twat, fucking hear me? Eh?'

OK, enough was enough. I'd have to take this guy out. I couldn't hear my team leader on my radio but I knew he would be closing in to help me, so I'd probably have to fend these guys off for no more than a minute. A minute is a fucking long time, though, if you are losing a fight against a gang of seven who clearly are used to this life. It reminded me of growing up, being around this crew. One thing was certain, though: if I managed to take out the leader, the rest of his crew wouldn't back down, they'd pile in. Loyalty to each other is all these lads had. I needed to act fast and hard.

As the gang leader swung me around to throw me towards his mates, he noticed my radio.

'He's five-o, he's got a radio, look, look!'

There was an instant shift in the gang's demeanour:

strangely, the leader softened his approach, while a few of the other quieter ones became more aggressive. I had to play on the gang's belief that I was undercover police, but I also needed to make my team aware that I might have a way of walking out of this cleanly if I could win over the leader of the gang, who just a moment earlier had wanted to kick the fuck out of me. He became the focus of my attention. I wanted my team leader to know exactly what was happening. I kept my radio transmitting so that the team could hear absolutely everything that was being said.

Staying relaxed, I side-stepped into a better position where no one was directly behind me and gave a nod that said, 'OK, you guys have sussed me out.'

'Lads, I'm looking for a paedophile who tried to snatch an eight-year-old boy from this park earlier today.'

Everyone universally hates paedophiles, and it showed on the faces of these lads as most of them bought the story straight away — apart from the one or two that clearly still wanted to bounce my head across the park.

'I'm with an undercover police unit working with Interpol. This paedophile was last seen in this area, wearing a green waistcoat. He's white, nearly six foot tall, about forty years old, with bright ginger hair. Have you guys seen him?'

I'm not sure why I mentioned Interpol, I guess it was the adrenaline-fuelled reaction to a sudden fight or flight situation, but I went with it anyway.

As soon as I stopped transmitting, I got a reply from my team leader: 'Zero Six, do you want us to come and get you?'

I was now fairly sure I could get out of this, so I signalled back that I didn't want them to come in. If my team piled in now we'd lose the target and end up in a brawl with these guys.

'Roger, negative heard. Get out of there as soon as possible. I have eyes on you.'

This was good; my team leader was within running distance of me somewhere now. As the gang swapped ideas about who my fictitious paedophile might be, I still needed to get out of there. I got on the radio again and started to lay the groundwork for my extraction.

'Lads, are you here all night?'

They nodded unanimously to confirm they'd be there all night because it was their patch. For the first time I could see my team leader's car at the corner of the field and the main road with its lights off.

'Great. Listen, I need your help . . . Wait.'

Still transmitting, I pretended to receive a message, aimed at letting my team leader know what I needed next and giving the gang just enough to go on to allow me to leave unharmed.

'Roger that, Zulu Six Seven, sighting confirmed in Oldham on the High Street. Moving there now. Foxtrot Oscar Mike, pick me up on the main road now.'

A lot of what I was saying was bullshit and my team leader would have known that, but I was trying to make it sound consistent with what they would expect an undercover policeman to sound like. It gave the gang just enough information about the paedophile being spotted somewhere else and that I was rushing there to arrest him.

'Lads, I have to go and get this scumbag, but if he comes back here before I get to him ring me on this number.'

Taking a phone out of one the gang members' hands, I quickly typed in my service-issue mobile phone number with the last two digits changed. Returning his phone, I turned and started running towards the main road, my bag and can of lager bouncing on my back. Glancing back towards the gang, I shouted, 'Remember, if you see him, ring me!'

Five metres away from the edge of the park I could see my team leader, accelerating fast towards the main road with his lights on. Hitting the brakes hard, he stopped just as I got to the junction. I jumped into the car and swung around for my seat belt as the team leader drove out of the area fast.

'You OK?'

'Yeah, no problem.'

After changing the settings of the car radio to channel 6, I picked the map up from the footwell. The team was still with the Chinese guy, who was in a taxi by the sound of it. The team leader gave a quick update to let everyone else know I was OK and that we were back with the follow.

'Charlie One One, complete and back with.'

No time to process what had just happened and – perhaps more worryingly – what could have happened; I had to focus on this task and make sure we controlled the target. The team leader didn't go into any detail with me either; we were too busy now concentrating on the follow. He just sent a quick message back to the Operations Centre to make sure no other teams went into the park I had just been in. 'Base, acknowledge – no crews to go into area around the park.'

'Yes, roger.'

And as easily as that I rolled back into our operation, not thinking about my previous cover or the fact that all I could taste was stale lager. It wasn't until we got back to the garages at the regional Operations Centre that it started to sink in what real danger I had been in at the park. In the changing rooms, I was on my own; everyone else was in the canteen, getting coffees and bacon sandwiches as it was just coming up to breakfast time. I grabbed my wash-bag out of my locker to go and brush my teeth. It felt like that super-strength lager had been dissolving them all night.

I flushed the toilet, walked over to the sinks and started to brush my teeth. In the mirror, I looked tired. Trying to freshen up, I somehow managed to put most of the water all over my top instead of my face. It gave me an excuse to get changed before I went home. From my locker I collected my spare set of normal clothes, returned to the sinks and started getting undressed out of this chav-tastic tracksuit so I could travel home in comfort and leave 'work' here.

I caught the reflection of myself in the mirrors, but didn't quite acknowledge what I was seeing: scratches on my arms and two large fist-shaped bruises on my chest. That fucker from the park must have hit me with more force than I had realized. I couldn't even remember him or anyone grabbing my arms, yet I had three very distinct scratch marks around the insides of both biceps. Why couldn't I remember that? Surely it wasn't that traumatic? But my brain had somehow blocked that memory.

The bruises didn't hurt but were already starting to turn a deep purple. This was going to be difficult to explain to my wife. I knew I would be opening a can of worms if I tried to explain what I was doing in Moss Side on my own, drinking in a park, ending up having to talk my way out of getting my head kicked in by a local gang. How the fuck was I meant to have a loving and open relationship with my wife when everything I did at work involved me putting my neck on the line to make sure we kept hold of the worst kind of scum to walk this earth?

I knew that if I was to protect my family from worrying every time I left the house, I had to bury this and not mention it. I'd been through a lot worse. Thankfully, I was having issues remembering the details anyway so it made it that much easier to keep it to myself. If I couldn't remember everything then there wasn't any point saying anything. I just hoped this bruising faded quickly or I got an operation that would mean I'd be away from home for a few nights to give these two massive bruises time to blend in to my pale skin.

With my 'going home' clothes on, I put my washkit back in my locker and saw that the tracksuit top I'd had on in the park was actually ripped on one of the arms, so I quickly threw it in the bin. I had to get rid of any evidence, anything that reminded me of the incident in the park.

Staying on task is what being an operator is all about, living your cover to allow the best intelligence capture possible. If you need to sit in your own piss as a tramp for six hours in the freezing cold in order to make sure you let your team know a high-profile target is coming out, then that's what you do, and if I had to hide the fact that I'd had a lucky escape in Moss Side, then that's what I'd do. Operators don't have mood swings, we stay constant so our team knows exactly what we can and can't do. Someone's memory putting padlocks on certain things to prevent them from becoming traumatic is a really bad thing, and would instantly lose the confidence of the team.

Chapter Ten

We'd been on this Russian job for weeks now. I loved working against these guys; they truly understood how to operate on foreign soil, and, despite posing as diplomats based out of the Russian Embassy in Kensington Palace Gardens, they were anything but diplomatic. Most of the time foreign intelligence operators from the Russian SVR were here to advance their own technical or military progress. They would hardly ever try to recruit members of the British Parliament because they knew the risks of being caught were incredibly high.

Britain is a world leader in military tech, especially equipment that requires lasers, so its defence companies and civilian tech firms that become the targets of hostile intelligence agencies. They operate high levels of security and counter-intelligence to prevent corporate espionage, so they were still a difficult nut to crack, but with the right squirrel it was not impossible. I loved the Russians, though, because despite them trying to steal secrets they would do it in a way that was subtle – no sledgehammers involved unless it was a reprisal on one of their own defecting agents.

I always thought of the intelligence officers from the SVR, who are basically MI6's counterparts, as the stealthy bank robbers. Not the sort that would stick 10kg of military-grade explosives on the safe door, blow it, and walk out with the loot, but the type that has everyone looking in one direction while they flirt with the security guards. Once the vault door is open, they leave virtually everything apart from one seemingly insignificant piece of jewellery. Then they close the door behind them and it is weeks before anyone realizes anything is missing, by which point they are either out of the country or have planted enough 'evidence' somewhere else to mean that everyone chases their tails for years before they truly understand what's happened.

Stealing secrets with a feather, that's how the Russians did it. This particular job started out following a Russian SVR officer as he left the Russian Embassy in his Mercedes S Class with the 248 diplomatic plates, but over the weeks we'd stopped our surveillance of him and changed instead to watching the woman he'd recruited to steal some information about a piece of equipment used in satellite imagery. The Russian had recruited a tall blonde in her early twenties and encouraged her to start a relationship with one of the assistant engineers on the satellite projects. She had massive debts, which he used as the hook to get her to do what he asked. It was starting to work too; we'd watched this blonde woman and the slightly overweight engineer go on a few dates, sharing some late-night drinks as they grew closer.

The Russians' hope was that once the blonde had completely embedded herself in the engineer's life, they could gradually start hacking his emails and phone messages. This data would be pieced together with further information the blonde would glean from him during some pillow talk about his job. This was clever, as it distanced the Russians from the situation. It was the sort of tactic that large defence contractors always tried to make their employees aware of, but many never believe that the young, attractive blonde is only interested in them for the Top Secret equipment they have access to.

We'd heard rumours of corporate espionage between two leading defence contractors who were bidding for the same piece of military work; a project worth hundreds of millions of pounds. During a budget meeting, the rival company had managed to hack into the CEO's mobile phone, which was on the boardroom table, switched off. Using very illegal, but extremely clever techniques, they managed to switch on the CEO's phone without activating the screen, and turned on the microphone, enabling them to listen to the whole meeting.

It had been another long shift and the whole team checked into a hotel, because we were at least three hours away from our regional Operations Centre, plus we were back on this job first thing in the morning. At reception we all signed for our room keys using our normal alias names; we all did our fake signatures and postcodes for home addresses we never visited. Walking into my hotel room, I threw my kitbag down next to the bed and headed straight for the toilet. One thing you rarely get the chance to do when you're an operator is take a piss, so you need a bladder the size of a basketball.

Collapsing on the bed and switching the TV on in this small room, I started to take all my kit off, ready to get in the shower and get some sleep. I felt heavy; everything was an effort. This operation had us racing all over the place and I hadn't eaten for at least eight hours, which meant I was running on empty. Leaving my trail of clothes behind me, I dragged myself to the shower, battling with the mixer tap on the wall to get the balance between freezing cold or scorching hot just right. I closed my eyes and allowed the water to warm me up.

I'm not sure how long I'd been in the shower, but I was starting to fall asleep standing up. 'STAND BY!' Holy shit, my radio must still be on, had I missed the call to get back on the ground? Fuck.

Diving out of the shower, I lost my footing on the tiled floor and slipped into the door frame. I had to get all my kit on quick and rush down to our vehicle in the hotel car park. Shit. I had no idea what was going on. I could hear gunfire . . . Gunfire? I stopped, half-naked with only one sock on, grabbing my radio. Taking a moment to listen to the transmissions, I realized it wasn't my team. A few more seconds and it dawned on me that it wasn't even my radio giving the commentary on all hell breaking loose. It was the TV – some action scene in a film. Sitting on the edge of the bed again, dripping wet, I felt stupid. How had I mistaken the sounds from the film as coming from my team? Maybe I was more tired and hungry than I had thought.

I began to shiver in the cold hotel room as my body desperately tried to warm itself. My one sock now soaking wet, I wrapped a towel around me and tried to find my phone to call Lucy. I needed to hear her voice and make sure my son went to sleep OK. As I pulled it out of the pocket of my crumpled jeans, I saw a text message from her saying that she was going to sleep and to text her when I'd finished to let her know I was safe. I knew I couldn't phone her now; it wouldn't be fair to wake her up, potentially waking up the whole house at this late hour, and she'd know I was lying if I said I was OK. How the fuck would I explain I'd just thought the TV was my team radio? I felt dizzy and disorientated and my arm was starting to sting like fuck from when I'd fallen into the door frame stumbling out of the shower.

Right, I needed to get a grip here. I was hungry, dehydrated and tired. At this time of night the only place to get food was the vending machine in the foyer. Ducking my mouth under the tap in the bathroom, I glugged down as much water as I could, threw on my jeans and trainers and headed downstairs, the key card for my room in hand. Life as an operator isn't glamorous; it's probably the polar opposite to what people think working for MI5 is like.

Standing at the vending machine, my clothes were sticking to my still-wet skin. I spotted one of my teammates outside the entrance smoking and using his phone, probably talking to his girlfriend. Finding myself making quick choices between chocolate bars and crisps, anything with a high calorie count, I fired all the change I had into the machine, grabbed my snacks and walked back up the stairs to my room as quickly as possible. I didn't know why I wanted to get back up there so quickly, but all I felt was the desperate hope that I wouldn't see anyone else from my team tonight.

Making it back to the safety of my room, I threw all the snacks on to the bed; I wasn't even hungry any more, I was tired. Before anything else I'd need to prep my kit ready for the morning, and then I could go to sleep knowing I wouldn't be flapping around first thing: radio batteries on charge, phone plugged in, passport and ID next to some clean socks and pants. Ready to go.

Stripping off again, I rearranged the room, pushing the bed right up against the wall that housed the small bathroom, and moving the bedside table against the door. I put my car keys on top of it so if the room door did open while I was asleep, I'd get a noisy prior warning. Grabbing a towel from the bathroom, I dried my hair and the rest of my body, which was still slightly too damp. Switching all the lights off, I climbed into bed, rearranging the pillows so that I could get as close to the wall as possible. I started to drift off, seeking comfort from resting my forehead against the ice-cold wall. This wasn't how most people slept, I knew that, but it reminded me of being in harsh conditions as a kid, allowing myself just enough comfort to fall asleep, but not so much that I wasn't alert. That kept me sharp back then, and I hoped the method would continue to serve me as it always had done.

Out of the darkness I could see a hand coming down towards my face. Swinging my arm out to bat it away, I sprang out of bed with an almost unnatural burst of energy and speed. Standing in the middle of the room, I tried to see who'd just tried to attack me, but couldn't make out anything in the blackness. Backing towards the window, I ripped at the curtains to let some light in. Flashes shone in with every tug at the curtains, and eventually I managed to open them fully. I could see the whole room. Empty. The fucker must be in the bathroom.

I moved forward quietly, able to hear the low whine of the battery chargers on the table to my right. The keys were still on the bedside table, which hadn't moved. The security chain was still in place on the back of the door. As I checked the bathroom I already knew it would be empty. I'd had another nightmare. Realizing I was safe and that it was nothing more than a bad dream that had woken me up, I tried to catch my breath. My heart was racing. How the fuck had I managed to spring out of bed as quickly as that? I couldn't do it like that when I was awake! The adrenaline that had flooded my body was now ebbing away, and I felt the harsh cold of the room again. I needed to get back to sleep, but I was frightened of having another nightmare.

I was meant to be this super-hard spook recruited from Military Special Ops, but here I was curled up in a foetal position in the corner of the room, too scared to fall sleep. Fuck's sake. Trying something different, I grabbed the pillows and quilt off the bed and took them to the other corner of the room. Making a makeshift bed from the pillows, I wrapped myself in the quilt to keep warm. Listening to all the sounds that surrounded the hotel, I felt my eyes getting heavy again. I had to be up in three hours and the only thing ready for the job was my watch, which was emitting its luminous glow and providing the only bit of light in the pitch-black room. I knew I would be fucked if I didn't at least get an hour's sleep to take the edge off.

It felt like only five minutes had passed before my alarm went off. I always made sure it was incredibly loud and annoying, in order to force me to get up and switch it off. I must have set it wrong – there was no way it was 0530hrs already. Fuck's sake, it was. My eyes felt like they were on fire. Right, I only had thirty minutes before I had to be in my car, travelling to the target's address. I walked to the bathroom and switched on the tiny kettle, desperately needing some coffee to give me a caffeine kick. Once I was clean and my hair didn't look like I'd been sleeping on the floor, fighting with invisible demons all night, I finished getting ready and grabbed my kitbag.

Thankfully, no one else from the team was in the car park as I left the hotel and headed towards the target's house. I was probably the first one on the ground, but I switched my car radio on and waited for the rest of the team to start shouting up that they were coming into the area. Opening the bag of crisps I'd bought last night, I heard the team leader check if anyone else was on the net yet. I quickly swallowed a mouthful of the unhealthiest breakfast I could choose and responded quickly, 'Yes. Yes, Charlie Six One Two is in the area.'

'Roger and good morning, we'll wait for everyone else to get on the net then I will brief the team on air.'

I started to feel more awake; this job was a welcome break from the Islamic extremists and Irish targets. It actually meant for the first time in ages we were allowed to drive the nicer cars and wear more normal clothes, because we were generally in more civilized areas. The blonde woman that the Russian had recruited had left university with huge debts and had been trying to support herself as an escort. She held a receptionist's job at an executive suite within Farnborough Airport, just minutes away from the satellite engineer's place of work.

When the Russian intelligence officer recruited her, it gave her the opportunity to live a better life without having to sell herself. He also promised her a new identity, a paid-for home and a job with the ministry in Moscow if she helped him. She had no family, so this offer was perfectly pitched to lure her, and she got to work almost immediately. We knew from the eavesdropping equipment we'd planted in her flat and at the engineer's house that he was unwittingly revealing enough so that, once they'd pieced it together with the emails, text messages and voicemail, the Russians would be able to replicate this technology in Moscow.

As I ate the rest of my snacks in Farnborough Airport car park waiting for the team to arrive so we could start the job, I rang my wife; they'd probably be mid-breakfast now so hopefully calm enough for her to talk. As I unlocked my phone . . . BANG BANG BANG!

Fuck me! I moved the gear stick into reverse, piled on the revs, was about to release the handbrake to get the car out of there when I looked out of the window to see what had just battered the car. Parking attendant, cunt. I put the car back into neutral, let the engine revs die back down to idle and dropped my window about an inch.

'What's up, pal?'

'Ticket, you have ticket, parking, yes?'

This guy was probably from Ghana judging by his accent. I took the parking ticket out of the cup holder in the centre console and flashed it to him. He walked off, having no clue that I wasn't in the right mental state for him to be banging on the car windows right now. As I wound the window back up with the electric switch I could hear a faint, 'Hello . . . Heeelllllloooooo?'

I'd pressed 'call' just at the point the parking attendant nearly gave me a heart attack. Picking the phone up out of the footwell down by my feet, I heard the voice I'd needed. Ten minutes of talking about my little boy, and how he'd kept her awake at night singing 'We Wish You a Merry Christmas' at the top of his voice, and my wife's plans for that day after the school run. Normality. Some people call their lives boring, mundane, but right then I would have killed for normality. I desperately wanted to be home with my family, but knew how important this job was. If the Russian managed to steal all the secrets he needed from the engineer, he'd be advancing his country's technology research and development by at least thirty years.

'Do you think we'll be able to have a holiday this year? Nothing expensive, can be camping in the Peak District, just anything to get away.'

My wife was doing an amazing job raising our son and creating a home for us. She was a remarkable woman and I felt like I was failing them in some way. I was so wrapped up with my team I wasn't focused on being a father and because I wasn't prioritizing properly I'd let the finances slip too. This had to change, but I had absolutely no idea how to do it. How was I meant to split my time between national security and my little family? All the while I could feel myself being pulled apart, cracks starting to appear that I couldn't plaster over and carry on. The little fractures in my armour were becoming larger.

'Thanks, stations, everyone is now in the area. We have Charlie Six One Two close in direct on the entrance waiting for HUNGRY WORM.'

'Just to clarify, I can see the entrance to the executive suite and the vehicle access at the barriers of the car park but can NOT go with.'

'Roger that, Charlie Six One Two, we have stations close in to react on your stand-by.'

It was fairly unlikely that this blonde woman had any sort of anti- or counter-surveillance training by the Russian, but I still needed to be clever about this. I couldn't follow her out of the car park if she left the building; despite her lack of operational training, people are still intuitive and she would suspect something wasn't quite right even if she couldn't identify exactly what was wrong.

'Base, permission?'

'Go ahead, no change.'

'Stations, DIRTY BOOT has arranged to meet HUNGRY WORM. The details of the meet have been sent with a florist. We don't have any further intelligence, just a heads-up.'

'Charlie Six One Two, roger.'

I was now looking for two things, the blonde woman

and a florist. This was a smart play by the Russian, arranging to meet HUNGRY WORM by some sort of coded message. It gave him distance and it could be argued either that he didn't send the message or if he did it was merely a gesture of affection rather than espionage. The intelligence about DIRTY BOOT's use of a florist was unknown; it was probably pieced together from previous surveillance and electronic intercept. We wouldn't send anyone into the florist to see what the message was just in case the florist the Russian used was recruited too and tipped him off. We needed both HUNGRY WORM and DIRTY BOOT to be as confident as possible that we weren't watching their every move.

The problem was we had absolutely no idea where this meeting was. We needed to cover it to gather enough actionable intelligence to present to the Russian Embassy and kick this guy out of the country for trying to steal our tech.

Nearly twenty minutes went by before I caught my first glimpse of the blonde.

'From Charlie Six One Two, that's HUNGRY WORM walking towards the entrance of the executive suite, white waist-length jacket, black knee-length skirt, white shoes, hair down, carrying a black handbag.'

'That's HUNGRY WORM IN, IN the executive suite. For information, she walked in from the area of the barriers, she didn't drive a vehicle into the car park.'

'Roger, thanks, any close-in stations see how HUNGRY WORM arrived?'

'Negative, but there's been regular buses over the past

few minutes on the main, I don't have sight of the bus stop, though.'

'OK, roger that.'

The close-in cars had fucked up here. The team leader's response said it all; we had me inside the car park watching the entrance to the building, and the cars close-in outside should have been able to see the barriers from the main road and any bus stops or likely drop-off points. It was highly likely that she arrived here by vehicle – bus, taxi or car driven by someone else. It was too far for her to walk from her home address in those heels.

'Close-in stations, can you get direct on the bus stop, the barriers and the main road north and south, please?'

Today wasn't the day for fuck-ups.

I was getting hungry again and could start to feel my eyes getting itchy and hot. I was tired and focusing on my mirrors for this long was starting to take its toll on my sleepless body. Luckily I didn't need to wait long until I got something else to focus on. I saw an unmarked white courier van pull up to the barriers of the car park. As it entered it made its way slowly to the entrance of the building.

'Stations from Charlie Six One Two, be aware a white courier van has pulled up to the entrance of the executive suite, one female has exited the vehicle wearing a green fleece and walked to the rear of the van.'

'Roger, thank you.'

'Further, the last three of the VRN of the van are TANGO, FOXTROT, DELTA. It's unmarked and at distance looks like a Volkswagen Caddy. Female removing flowers from the back of the van and is now towards the entrance.'

'Roger, close-in cars get the full VRN imagery as it leaves then let it run, please.'

There was no need to follow the florist's van away from here; even if the woman in the van was onside with the Russian, taking her on would split our team and we'd need every single asset available to make sure we got DIRTY BOOT bang to rights.

'That's the woman in the green fleece back out into the van, van reversing, and towards the barriers.'

'And out of sight to Charlie Six One Two.'

'Charlie Eight Five Zero, imagery obtained, full VRN WHISKY ALPHA ZERO SEVEN TANGO FOXTROT DELTA. Vehicle now running free to the north.'

'Thanks, stations, good work.'

'Charlie Six One Two, permission?'

'Go ahead.'

'Base, do we have anything on HUNGRY WORM's phone?'

'No string.'

'Roger, thanks. TC, back to you.'

'Roger, no change.'

The blonde had obviously been told not to use her mobile phone to send messages to the Russian, hence no valuable electronic intercepts. It always made me smile when people referred to eavesdropping intelligence as 'string'. It's only the older officers who've been around a bit who call it that. It comes from the days when eavesdropping audio was recorded on cassette tapes and before that reels of tape. I remember Ian Grey briefing me on operations starting with, 'Latest string intelligence suggests . . .'

'STAND BY, STAND BY! That's HUNGRY WORM OUT, OUT and walking towards the barriers, dressed as previous.'

As the close-in cars acknowledged, I resisted the urge to change my body position. I couldn't go with her, but I knew this was potentially the start of a very busy day and the pick-up of your target determines how well the day is going to go. Get control of them straight away and you're golden, fuck it up and you're playing catch-up all day.

'From Charlie Six One Two, for information she is not carrying anything other than her handbag, now five metres from the barriers.'

'That's HUNGRY WORM through the barriers towards the main and out of sight to me.'

'Roger, Charlie Eight Five Zero has control, HUNGRY WORM walking towards the bus stop; she's just looked at her watch and is now static on the west side of the main at the bus stop.'

'Roger that, is she alone or can we send someone on with her?'

'From Charlie Eight Five Zero, she's alone and most of the buses have been fairly empty.'

We couldn't risk sending anyone on the bus with her with it being so quiet. We'd have to watch her on to the bus and pursue it like a normal vehicle follow.

'From Charlie Eight Five Zero, a number 82 single-decker bus is approaching from the south and pulling up to the stop. That's HUNGRY WORM ON, ON to the bus, VRN to follow.'

'Roger, stations, we'll go with this.'

'VRN KILO NINE EIGHT SEVEN KILO MIKE PAPA. Bus now heading north, can anyone take control?'

'Charlie Seven Five can.'

'Roger, all yours.'

As the bus travelled away from the area, we had no idea where she was going, and could only assume she was on her way to meet the Russian. We were blind here; we had to gain the advantage to avoid alerting the blonde or, even worse, the Russian. As the team leader asked the Operations Centre if they knew the destination of this bus, the team was constantly handing over as it made its third stop already. I was still in the car park and useless to the follow. I had a few minutes before my team leader would start checking up on my security. Fuck it, we needed to know what message was sent by the Russian.

Just before I left the car, I flicked my radio on so I could hear what the team was doing in case HUNGRY WORM decided to come back to the executive suite. I had to be careful here because DIRTY BOOT wasn't being monitored today and could well be in the area. I walked across the car park towards the entrance of the executive suite. The team were still following the bus but were concerned about being spotted. The Russians knew what to look for and could be providing counter-surveillance for her.

As I approached the large frosted glass doors of the

executive suite, the automatic sensors responded to me and opened swiftly. Moving into the large open-plan building, I could see the reception area where HUNGRY WORM would work; the place looked empty, so either the blonde didn't get any cover and just left work or another receptionist was on their way. I had no cover story at all here, so I'd just have to improvise. I was proper risking it here. No one knew I was in HUNGRY WORM's place of work and I doubt I would have been given permission to do so through fear of compromising the operation, but I needed to see if I could see the message that'd been sent with the florist.

The receptionist station was impressive and clearly designed to appeal to the corporate market. A fresh bunch of flowers sat next to a computer screen that had gone into screen-saver mode. There was a CCTV dome camera directly behind the desk. I was now officially here. Grabbing the leaflets next to me, I start reading about the building's facilities and upcoming events. Folding the leaflet out, I raised it slightly higher as I leaned against the high counter surrounding the receptionist desk behind it. I had to look natural here and I was banking on the fact that if anyone was watching the CCTV live feed of me they wouldn't be looking at my eyes, so I moved my head now and again as if reading the leaflet and peered over the top just enough to see the desk.

No greeting card on the flowers on the side I could see. I couldn't check the other side of the flowers because it would look too obvious. Scanning the rest of the desk, I finally saw it. Fuck, upside down! I needed to adjust my position to allow me to focus on the hand-written message. Looking at my watch, I shifted half a pace to my right and picked up a different events flyer. Employing the same tactic as earlier, I looked ever so slightly over the flyer and focused hard on the small greeting card.

My beautiful lady, meet you same time at the Crescent.

I needed to get this to the team leader. I had to be ready to be severely bollocked for doing this without permission, but I could hear the team getting stretched as the bus now headed south on the dual carriageway. Checking my watch again and having a look around, I lived my cover as if I'd given up waiting for someone, and walked towards the exit. As the glass doors once again recognized my presence, they slid open.

'Sir, can I help you?!'

Fuck. Turning around, I saw a security guard, about my height but twice as wide, his shoulders nearly bursting out of his clean pressed white shirt. Short, neat hair. His purposeful swagger, he was ex-military. I knew how to get this guy on side straight away; I needed to make him feel important.

'Yes, brilliant. I need your help. I'm trying to organize a skydive for Sport Relief. I'm not sure I've come to the right place, though. You guys seem a bit upmarket?'

His posture changed straight away as he clearly enjoyed feeling important and part of an executive company.

'We don't really cater for things like that. We manage private flights for CEOs, and A-list celebrities. Things like that.'

'Ah, that sounds exciting – bet you see all sorts, eh! All

right then, I thought I had the wrong place, it must be one of the offices in the airport building.'

Turning back towards the exit, I took my opportunity to leave. As the security guard turned back towards his door hidden into the building's wall, presumably leading to his office where he was monitoring the camera, I half turned towards him.

'Thanks again, mate, have a good one.'

The trick to living your cover is to be natural with the environment, to blend in without creating a sign. Now, if anyone asked the security guard about me then he would remember me, but unless he was pushed he wouldn't think I was a threat or out of place. It's a balancing act. I just hoped the message I found was worth it and I wasn't about to fall head first off this tightrope.

Walking back towards my car, I pulled my service-issue phone out of my pocket. I needed to get this information to the team leader but with the confidence of the team in me at an all-time low I couldn't put this out on the net.

> Don't ask how, no compromise. Greeting card on blonde's desk said: 'My beautiful lady, meet you same time at the Crescent.' I'm back in my car now.

It took the team leader about thirty seconds to reply to my text message.

'Roger, we'll discuss this later.'

Yep, that was me in for a kicking later, then. Fuck it! I tried to help this operation. I was already the naughty boy of the team. Can't be in any more shit than I already am,

I thought. I had to get with the follow, and judging by the team's comms I had about five miles of ground to make up. Driving slowly out of the car park, I waited until I was well out of sight of the executive suite and potentially the security guard, then started accelerating hard to catch my team up.

'Base, permission.'

'Go ahead, bus continuing south on the Alpha Three Three One.'

'Meeting place between DIRTY BOOT and HUNGRY WORM is believed to be at the RHS garden in Wisley, specifically the glasshouse. No time, unfortunately.'

'Roger, thank you, Base. Charlie Eight Five Zero, Nine Seven, Three Five and Two Three, get ahead at Wisley, please, page fifty-eight on your map books.'

Obviously the team leader forwarded my text on to the operations officers and they cross-referenced that with the grid and known meeting places or dead-drop sites. Sometimes the Russians would leave packages or encrypted memory sticks at prearranged sites called dead drops. Later on, the intended recipient would see the sign that a drop had been made and collection of the item was permitted. All the sites are covert and quite often hidden in plain sight. Most intelligence agencies use this method when stealing secrets on foreign soil and the British government is no different. We all do it.

'From Charlie One Eight. That's HUNGRY WORM OFF, OFF the bus on the east side of the Alpha Two Eight Seven just before the junction of Trafalgar Court, HOLD BACK, HOLD BACK.'

Turning the car into the nearest side street, I waited around the corner, approximately five hundred metres away. We were still a way off from the RHS garden and the village of Wisley yet. I was starting to wonder whether the intelligence I got from the greeting card was right: had I read it wrong? The team could be on the wrong track because of me.

'STAND BY, STAND BY. That's DIRTY BOOT in a black cab taxi driving south and pulling alongside HUNGRY WORM now, VRN to follow.'

Shit! The Russian was employing anti-surveillance techniques with the blonde. This was designed to make it harder, much harder, for any surveillance team following to keep hold of these two. We expected the Russian to be slippery but the team presumed the blonde would be an easier follow and lead us straight to DIRTY BOOT without alerting him. We now had the risk that the Russian had actually followed us the whole way from the executive suite to this point.

'VRN of the taxi, YANKEE SEVEN ONE ONE ECHO ALPHA ECHO. DIRTY BOOT is facing with a view to the rear of the taxi, HUNGRY WORM is now IN, IN the taxi and continuing southbound on the Alpha Two Eight Seven. Charlie One Eight is NOT with.'

'Roger. All stations, get ahead to Wisley gardens, STEEL BADGE, STEEL BADGE.'

The team leader didn't have to tell us not to drive past the taxi on our way to Wisley; we were all experienced enough to know that would be operational suicide. You want to remain in the shadows around your target as much as possible, especially Russian targets.

I knew from my position I could box round, but the taxi would soon be on a national speed limit dual carriageway towards Wisley, so I'd have to do some serious driving to get ahead of him. Into first gear, handbrake off, map book on my lap, I saw a rough group of streets that would allow me to box round back onto the main dual carriageway and if I got there quick enough I could be in front of the taxi without being seen by either target.

Wheel-spinning away when trying to drive at speed looks dramatic but does fuck all for your progression. The car is another tool for us to use, and it has to be used correctly. Applying just enough acceleration to get away quick enough without spinning my tyres, I approached the first side street I needed to box round to gain the advantage over the taxi. The team was taking a massive risk here; we had dropped both targets now and were all flying towards the Royal Horticultural Society's showpiece gardens. If that was false information designed to throw us off track we'd lose coverage of this meeting entirely.

'Stations for information, HUNGRY WORM's phone now appears to be OFF.'

Typical. All we could do now was fly up to Wisley as fast as we could and hope the surveillance dice rolled in our favour this time. Making the first turn, the back end of the car stepped out slightly as the tyres struggled to hold on to the tarmac as I kept applying the power. I saw two other cars following me down the same side street, both my team cars. Obviously we all held back at a similar time when the bus stopped and taxi arrived. Into third gear as I hit 75mph down this side street. You always have to be mindful driving at these speeds about what you can and can't see. This street was fairly quiet with one or two cars parked along the road so we could see if there were any small children on the pavements or car doors about to open.

Hard on the brakes to make the next turning, the nose of the car dove into the black tarmac as the team car directly behind me grew massive in my mirrors. As we made the next turning we were met with speed-restriction bumps. Thankfully they were the island bumps rather than the speed strips that go the full width of the road and we could straddle them easily. Back on the power and accelerating hard down this long straight, I remembered from the brief map study I did that this road loosely paralleled the dual carriageway the taxi would be on. We needed to keep pushing.

No oncoming traffic as we fast approached a learner driver in a small Ford Fiesta having a driving lesson. Fuck knows what the driving instructor and learner would have been thinking as we blasted past doing 110mph and still accelerating in perfect formation, no indication or lights. Very smooth and slick, but extremely fast, nearly four times the speed limit for this road.

Seeing the T-junction ahead, I stayed on the power. I knew the brakes of our team cars were as good as they could be. All three of us would wait for my cue to hit the brakes to give us all the best chance of getting in front of the taxi. As we continued past the road-warning signs telling us to slow down ahead of the junction, I could see the view opening up, giving a great view of the dual carriageway in both directions. We wouldn't be stopping here, we'd slow down just enough to allow us to take the corner and try to carry as much speed as possible through it.

Leaving it as late as I dared, I hit the brakes and block changed down the gears from sixth to fourth; once the engine revs had dropped enough I changed down again to help slow the car down as quickly as possible. All three of us were now only metres apart, we were making a hell of a noise and there was no way anyone could operate in this area now because our driving had made the area red hot, but we were praying the Russian hadn't noticed.

Double-checking there was still no traffic on the dual carriageway, I kept the power steady as I made the turn at nearly 40mph in second gear. As my turn straightened out I piled on the power again, up into third gear, engine revs climbing. Checking my wing mirror, I saw that the other two members of my team had made the turn too. There was no way I could see, given our distance down the dual carriageway, that the taxi could have made it in front of us. We'd done it, but the hard work wasn't over. Now we needed to make it into Wisley even quicker than we'd made it to the dual carriageway.

Overtaking anything in our path, the three of us set off a speed camera; the blinding flashes filled my car first, then the other two. Things like parking tickets and London congestion charges just got paid by the service.

However, all three of us getting flashed together at 140mph would take some explaining. Not my problem.

'Team leader, from lead vehicles. We are now in position at the gardens.'

'Roger, thank you, can we get imagery as they enter?'

'Yes, and Nine Seven is on foot with her camera taking pictures of the plantlife with a long lens.'

'Great, thank you.'

It's a good advantage for us that the meeting is in Wisley as it does give us the excuse of getting people in with cameras taking pictures of the plants, but you can kick the arse out of it. If you deploy too many people and this Russian knew a normal day here, then it would soon become obvious to him if there were more long-lens cameras than normal. One woman in her late forties with a camera taking pictures of flowers would be enough to get a crystal-clear image of both targets.

Seeing the tourist road signs for the RHS gardens ahead, I took the last turning off the main and parked up in between two cars, facing away from the road junction.

'Charlie Six One Two in position north. I can give possibles for the taxi towards the Wisley entrance.'

'Charlie Eight Five Zero, roger that, I can confirm anything you give towards the entrance.'

Using my wing mirror again to see the main road behind me, I switched the engine off and waited for any black taxis driving past. The net had gone quiet while we waited, no transmissions; the only noise I could hear now was the car ticking from being worked so hard to get here.

'Black cab taxi heading southbound towards the Wisley entrance, out of sight to Charlie Six One Two.'

'Yeah, STAND BY, STAND BY, that's DIRTY BOOT and HUNGRY WORM arriving at the gardens in the same taxi.'

'DIRTY BOOT and HUNGRY WORM now OUT, OUT and walking arm in arm towards the entrance of the main building.'

Hearing the constant clicks of the camera in the background of the transmissions, the whole team now knew we had good imagery of these two. We just needed good intelligence of them inside and we would have enough to stop the Russian from stealing this tech.

'Roger, thank you. Nine Seven, signal to acknowledge the last?'

'Yeah, roger the last, I'm in a good position at the moment.'

'Roger, thank you. Can we have anyone else out on foot, do you think?'

'Negative, place is dead.'

'Roger, thanks, Kate.'

'Stations, we've got the exit covered, Kate inside. We've done all we can do to monitor this meet. Be aware of any counter on the outside positions, please. Other than that we'll wait for them to come out.'

It was wise not to send anyone else in. Our team leader was good at listening. Surveillance teams from other intelligence agencies or police teams would probably have sent more people in, likely to be male, in walking kit, having just had a fresh shave that morning. These things stand out. The place was empty, apart from the staff. The headquarters of the Royal Horticultural Society were now the site of a major international intelligence operation, but it couldn't look like one. We hid ourselves around the area, used other cars and buildings to disguise our profiles and positioning. We could just do with more team members – it felt a bit stretched getting here.

I needed to stay alert; if there was a Russian counter-surveillance team in the area we would need to identify them quickly. My eyes were starting to lose focus now the adrenaline of driving here was wearing off. Rolling my lip in between my teeth, I bit just hard enough to send a pain signal to my brain, switching to digging my nails into my fingertips, doing anything to keep me sharp. I was fucking starving and needed a piss badly.

'From Nine Seven, imagery taken, HUNGRY WORM has shown DIRTY BOOT a brown paper folder. DIRTY BOOT looked at the contents of the folder but did NOT take anything out. The folder is still with HUNGRY WORM and she put it into her handbag.'

'Roger, thanks, Nine Seven.'

'SPLIT, SPLIT, DIRTY BOOT is towards the exit, HUNGRY WORM static in same position.'

'Is the folder still with HUNGRY WORM??'

'Yes, still in her handbag.'

'Roger, let DIRTY BOOT run. We'll stay on HUNGRY WORM and the folder.'

'From Charlie Eight Five Zero, the same black cab taxi

from earlier, same driver has just arrived at the car park again.'

'And that's DIRTY BOOT IN, IN to the back of the taxi, facing out the rear window, vehicle moving towards exit now.'

'Roger that, we stay with HUNGRY WORM and the folder, Base acknowledge.'

'Base roger, we are on it.'

Fuck. The Russian had done us over here and covered his arse properly. By leaving the folder with the blonde he had deniability. He technically hadn't stolen state secrets, and by leaving them with her he made sure he and Russia kept their distance. There would be two reasons he'd do this: firstly he might have seen one or all of our team and decided to go about his day usually to prevent being arrested. Secondly and more likely, he was providing an extra layer of protection in his operational security, planned to receive the documents at a later date and was merely checking them. Fucking hell, these Russians are good.

We could hear the camera clicking away over the net as we got more updates.

'That's DIRTY BOOT and the taxi from earlier out of sight to me towards the exit of the car park now.'

Catching a glimpse of a black cab in my mirrors driving away, I let the team know.

'Good possible for the taxi now northbound on the main, time and distance matches Eight One Zero's last.'

'Roger that, let it run. Stations, we stay with HUN-GRY WORM and the folder. We can't risk a loss here.'

Losing whatever intelligence about lasers the folder contained would be catastrophic. When the general public thinks about threats to national security, most of the time it's terrorist mass-murder events: killing innocent civilians, women and children lying in pools of blood on the streets of our great country. For us as operators in the greatest intelligence agency in the world, hunting murderers masquerading under the guise of religion is preventing us from stopping the really big threats. The threats that would allow a country with a military force much larger than ours to walk straight through our front doors and take whatever they wanted.

The security service's remit is to protect the United Kingdom and its interests. The key to that is 'interests'. An island such as ours relies heavily on being on the front foot and, in some cases, controlling where the next step is. We provide some of the most advanced technical capabilities in weapons technology worth billions. If a country acquired our research and development it would advance their own status and earning potential. Losing the ability to earn billions of pounds would cripple a small but significant country like ours.

The other side of the coin in stealing military tech is losing the defence capability. If certain codes and equipment were handed over to foreign intelligence it could render our submarines and quick-reaction fast jets completely useless. By a million miles, the biggest threat to our country and its survival isn't the few thousand would-be mass murderers living among us, it's the smooth-talking suit like the one we've just allowed to drive away in a taxi.

*

We got another signal from Nine Seven, who still had control of HUNGRY WORM.

'Roger, signal heard. STAND BY, STAND BY.'

'From Charlie Eight One Zero, HUNGRY WORM OUT, OUT of the gardens into the car park, stood waiting looking towards the exit of the car park now.'

'Roger that, stations ready for a vehicle move, please.'

I was already turning the car around before the team leader asked us to be ready for the move. It was obvious she was waiting to be picked up. You couldn't walk far from here, and the way Nine Seven described her demeanour, this pick-up would have been prearranged and was going to be soon. Driving further down this side street, I'd parked up facing the main road, using a parked car and garden wall as cover. I had a gap of around two feet that allowed me to see the main road.

'From Charlie Eight One Zero, a black taxi, different from earlier has pulled into the car park now, VRN to follow.'

'Roger. Stations, we'll go with this if she gets in.'

The team leader was anxious; we needed to keep hold of this file.

'STAND BY, STAND BY, HUNGRY WORM IN, IN to a black cab taxi VRN MIKE ECHO FIVE ONE CHARLIE ECHO CHARLIE, taxi licence number FIVE ONE FIVE SIX.'

'Base, roger.'

'Out of sight to Charlie Eight One Zero.'

'From Charlie Six One Two, good possible for the taxi now northbound on the main, will confirm.'

Seeing the side profile of the taxi drive past the end of this side street, I couldn't see the blonde inside due to the roof pillars of the taxi. This was going to be a balancing act confirming the VRN, especially if these two taxi drivers were in the Russian's pocket and had been told to watch for any suspicious vehicles.

Accelerating fast towards the main road, I hit the brakes hard as I approached and pulled out naturally. Last thing we needed to do now was get blown. Seeing the back end of the taxi move round a bend ahead on the road, I pulled out and started making ground.

'Anything further, Six One Two?'

Fuck's sake, give me a chance!

'Checking the VRN now, give me ten seconds, time and distance would make this our taxi, though.'

Hard on the power, I moved round the bend in the road as I'd seen the taxi do just a few seconds ago. Charlie Echo Charlie, this is the one. I'd give it some distance now and try to clip the back end through the corners, hiding the profile of my car as much as possible.

'VRN confirmed, CHARLIE ECHO CHARLIE, northbound on the main. I'm giving it some room here. I'm non for cover.'

'Bravo Nine can?'

We had only deployed with one biker. Bravo Nine would have been redeployed to help us out at the request of Base, realizing we were going to struggle when we had the split. This would allow the team to follow the taxi at a distance to prevent the cars being seen. The bikes had an incredible ability to hide their profiles behind other cars. Coupled with the speed and braking power of their motorbikes, they could catch glimpses of the taxi through the corners, so being non for cover didn't really affect bikes as much as it did our cars.

'Thank you, Bravo Nine, all yours!'

He must have been following us as he popped out from a side street just in front of me. To any normal road user it would just look like a rider taking his bike out, enjoying the sweeping roads, but his transmissions told the entire team he was here to help us. The whole team knew these guys would be taking over the majority of the follow.

'Bravo Nine to Three, mate, I will hold this.'

'Bravo Three, roger that. Great to have you here, mate.'

'Anytime. From Bravo Nine, vehicle is northbound on the Alpha Three Two Five towards the junction with the Alpha Three One.'

'Roger, Bravo Three is backing on your parallel to the west.'

'Roger, thanks.'

Our bikers are an incredible asset to the team, but when we have two working together like this it's almost a work of art to watch and listen to. Their training and experience and the fact Red team had finished their operation early, allowing the operations officers to redirect Bravo Nine to come and help us, had just saved us getting too close and potentially compromising the whole job. Each time they transmitted, you could feel the effect accelerating and braking was having on them physically.

'Bravo Nine, permission?'

'Yeah from Charlie Eight One Zero, leaving the car park now and have just seen DIRTY BOOT in his taxi travelling northbound, facing forward in the taxi now.'

Bollocks. The Russian must have doubled back once HUNGRY WORM got picked up and started looking out towards the front of the taxi. That suggests he was going to try to see if anyone was following behind the blonde's taxi.

'Roger that, Charlie Eight One Zero, go back and change your vehicle, please. Is Nine Seven back with you or in her car?'

'Yeah, in her vehicle'

'Roger, Bravo Nine, permission?'

The team leader was now desperate to prevent DIRTY BOOT identifying the whole team. It was clearly the Russian's plan to follow up behind the blonde to try to identify a surveillance train following on the road behind.

'Go ahead, HUNGRY WORM's taxi is still north-bound going past the junction of School Hill.'

'Roger. All stations, with the last in mind, get off the main roads and stay parallel behind DIRTY BOOT's taxi.'

'From Bravo Three, I will take the follow on DIRTY BOOT if Bravo Nine stays on HUNGRY WORM.'

'Bravo Nine, roger that.'

'Charlie Nine is close in to support lead biker Bravo Nine on a parallel with HUNGRY WORM.'

We had to stay out of sight from DIRTY BOOT now

his taxi was trying to identify if the blonde was being followed. Having Charlie Nine close in to support with HUNGRY WORM's taxi and our biker, Bravo Three, behind DIRTY BOOT's taxi, we would be able to react if these taxis stopped for whatever reason.

The great thing about our team is profile. Bravo Three was a leather-clad biker. The bikes looked the part, and they needed to be quick and agile to skip through traffic. In contrast the car close in, Charlie Nine, was a dark blue Nissan Note driven by Ken, who by his own admission was at least 900 years old and looked like a perfect OAP on a Sunday drive.

'Bravo Three to Bravo Nine, for information you have DIRTY BOOT's taxi now 500 metres behind HUNGRY WORM's.'

'Bravo Nine, roger that. I'm balancing in between the two taxis now. Can you if I have to use one of these side streets?'

'Bravo Three, yeah, no problem.'

With DIRTY BOOT's taxi closing in on HUNGRY WORM in front, Bravo Nine was about to end up in a Russian-spy sandwich.

Running this follow was a fucking nightmare. Using side roads as small as this, working our way around using the main dual carriageway, which our entire team was trying to use, wasn't ideal.

'From Bravo Nine, that's a STOP, STOP, STOP at a garage on the west side of the main, it's a Texaco. HUNGRY WORM is out of sight to me. Bravo Three, all yours, I'm pulling off.'

'Stations be advised from Bravo Nine, in my mirrors, DIRTY BOOT's taxi is now towards the garage.'

'Bravo Three, roger.'

As the biker transmitted you could hear his engine screaming while he desperately tried to make enough ground up to see both taxis in the garage.

Without saying anything, I could sense the team tightening its grip on these two. They were displaying a really high degree of operational security. We needed to be on top of our game here; squeeze too tight and we risked compromise, but if we gave them too much room we'd be handing Russia our country's pay cheque for the next thirty years.

'Both taxis at the fuel pumps. DIRTY BOOT's is at pump number one, HUNGRY WORM's is at pump number three, drivers still at the wheel of both. DIRTY BOOT and HUNGRY WORM have just walked into the shop at the garage, from Bravo Three.'

This was going to be the handover of the folder, I knew it. Whether the Russian chose this spot deliberately or not was irrelevant. We only had our biker close in.

'Zero Five on foot.'

'Roger. Charlie Nine now close in to support if needed.'

The bikers went in because this was likely to be a quick stop and if these two were handing over the folder we needed to know because after this we knew the two taxis would split again.

'From Charlie Nine, STAND BY, STAND BY, that's DIRTY BOOT and HUNGRY WORM OUT, OUT and towards their respective vehicles.'

'Roger, where is the folder??'

'Unseen from Charlie Nine ... HUNGRY WORM into her taxi now and vehicle out and away northbound, DIRTY BOOT getting into his taxi now.'

Fuck, we had no idea where the folder was or who to follow. This was fast becoming a cluster.

'Bravo Nine has control of HUNGRY WORM.'

'Roger. Stations close-in, any idea who has the folder??'

'Bravo Three negative, they came out as I walked in.'

'WAIT OUT, WAIT OUT! From Charlie Nine, as DIRTY BOOT got into his taxi, his shirt was untucked at the back. Bravo Three, was it untucked when he went into the garage shop?'

'NEGATIVE!'

'All stations go with DIRTY BOOT. Bravo Nine, can you stay with HUNGRY WORM, please?'

'Bravo Nine, roger.'

It was a long shot, but Ken had likely saved this operation. He'd been an operator for well over thirty years now and cut his teeth following the Russians. DIRTY BOOT, by not tucking his shirt in, might have given us enough of a clue that he'd been passed the folder and hadn't smartened himself up properly afterwards. The problem we had now was that clearly these taxis were Russian assets in some way. But we didn't know if DIRTY BOOT was photographing the paperwork in the back or sending it directly to a secure server and destroying the evidence. As dangerous as this situation was, we were also in the middle of a political arm-wrestle between London and Moscow. Get this wrong and it would be extremely embarrassing for Downing Street to explain.

'From Charlie Nine, DIRTY BOOT's taxi moving towards the main from the garage. He's facing to the rear of the taxi again, and it's southbound, southbound, Charlie Nine not with.'

'Roger that, Charlie Nine. Stations, let's leapfrog ahead and ping him through. Base, can you go to channel thirteen, please?'

The team leader was trying to make a plan here. At the moment we were just keeping control of DIRTY BOOT, but he potentially had vital intelligence with him. We needed to stop him and check him and the contents of the taxi but do it in a way that gave us a sliver of deniability.

As the team followed the Russian's taxi southbound, watching the taxi through key junctions and using alternative roads to get ahead, constantly handing control over to the next vehicle ahead in this massive game of leapfrog, the team leader popped up asking permission to tell us the next move.

'Stations, local police are going to stop DIRTY BOOT and conduct a licence check on the taxi driver under the cover of illegal taxi drivers.

'Further, the police team will have a dog with them and fake a drugs find to allow a search of both occupants.'

'Charlie Six One Four, roger, taxi still southbound on the Alpha Three Two Five.'

It took all of five minutes for the police team to stop the taxi.

'From Charlie Six One Four. A police dog car has pulled the taxi over on blue lights. HOLD BACK,

HOLD BACK, taxi is STOP, STOP, STOP on the west side of the Alpha Three Two Five, just south of the junction with Holt Pound Lane, page 56 on your maps.'

'Roger, have you still got control, Charlie Six One Four?'

'Yeah, and can give commentary if needed.'

'Thanks, we have Special Branch with the dog team, but if you can let us know – if they take DIRTY BOOT into custody we'll get out of the area.'

'Roger that. Just one uniform talking to the driver of the taxi now. DIRTY BOOT remains inside.'

The police team wouldn't have been told what to look for; that would have been handled by our Special Branch contact. He was in uniform too so would have looked like a normal police officer, like the other two in the car, but he would have been told one of the two occupants in the taxi was hiding sensitive material. It had to look like a normal licence check on the driver until the dog indicated the presence of drugs, which would allow them to be taken in and searched and the taxi to be impounded.

'Charlie Six One Four, permission?'

'Go ahead, no change. Uniform checking the taxi driver's details now.'

'Roger, Bravo Nine, same deal with HUNGRY WORM. Base are going to coordinate with you on channel one and put in a police stop on her.'

'Roger, Base, switching channels now.'

'Base, roger.'

The police stops now gave the service and the prime minister deniability. The Russians aren't stupid though;

they would know we'd been watching them trying to steal this information, but now we had enough of a story we could spin it if it became a press war when we kicked the Russian 'diplomat' out of the country.

'From Charlie Six One Four, police have taken the driver of the taxi into the back of their police car. Dog handler is now letting dog sniff the taxi.'

'Third police officer now out of the vehicle and walking towards the taxi, DIRTY BOOT being asked to get out.'

This was the Special Branch officer we used as our police liaison. The other two uniformed officers wouldn't know the real reason behind this stop and would be gently led to have enough reason to take DIRTY BOOT and the driver into custody to do a proper search.

'From Charlie Six One Four. Both officers now handcuffing DIRTY BOOT and performing search.'

'Yeah, from Charlie Six One Four. One of the officers is now pulling sheets of paper from the back of DIRTY BOOT's trousers and walking him towards the back of the police car.'

'Roger that, Charlie Six One Four, all stations cease and withdraw back to Base for debrief. Acknowledge down the list.'

'From Base, just for information, HUNGRY WORM and driver of her taxi have just been arrested too.'

'Roger that, Base. Pass our thanks to Bravo Nine. Fucking great job!'

I was hungry, and dying for a piss. But it looked like we got them. It would be unlikely any of this would hit the press. Right now I didn't give a fuck if we paraded them both on the *News at Ten* for all to see; I needed food and sleep. I'd been running on adrenaline for so long and now that the operation had finished, I almost instantly crashed.

It was a long drive back to the Operations Centre from here, which is why we were staying in hotels, but now the team leader popped up on the net with the good news.

'Stations, go home. We'll debrief tomorrow first thing at the ops centre, bright and early. Well done and thank you for all your hard work.'

Thank fuck for that. Last thing any of us wanted to do was a mega-long drive back to Base then another hour or so's drive home. Just as I settled into the drive and switched my car communications off, my service-issue mobile started to ring. It was my team leader.

'TC, me and the ops room staff have decided to keep quiet what you did in the executive suite this morning. I will trust you not to say anything to anyone either.'

'Roger that, boss, I won't say anything. Good result, wasn't it?'

I wasn't expecting a pat on the back, rather an acknowledgement that getting that information off the greeting card wasn't going to be held against me if I did something similar in the future.

'It was, but listen. You could have fucked the entire job if you got that wrong this morning. We have procedures and a chain of command. You're not in the army any more and we expect people to think on their feet, but your actions this morning could have had massive implications beyond your career. Just slow down a bit sometimes, mate.'

'Roger.'

Sensing I was angry, he lightened the tone and wished me a good evening with my family when I eventually got home. Yes, it was risky getting the information from the flowers, but if I hadn't the Russians would have been clear away with the information in the folder. I should be on a high with the rest of the team, knowing Russia's best weren't good enough for us. Yet all I could think about was my team leader telling me to slow down. I had so much respect for him and he was a fantastic operator, but being blamed for something that didn't actually happen was really pissing me off.

Admittedly, if I had got the information wrong or had been caught then it would have been bad, but we take risks every day, the reward was worth the effort.

The following morning at the debrief, the operations officer told us that DIRTY BOOT had been escorted to the airport and told to leave the country. HUNGRY WORM was still in custody and more than likely wouldn't go to jail as she was providing information on the Russian and how he contacted her. She was treated as an asset and moved to a new area, had her identity changed and given a new job in Scotland. The fat engineer who was head over heels in love with the blonde was never told how he lost a file from the mountain of Top Secret paperwork that he brought home with him to carry on working late.

The engineer's boss was made aware of his lack of

personal security, and his subordinate was warned not to be so fucking stupid again. He was a bright guy, though, and probably knew that being bollocked and the sudden disappearance of his new-found love were connected. Embarrassment was his only punishment.

Chapter Eleven

'Fuck you, pig!'

The young policewoman I directed my abuse to looked shocked, but she'd get over it. We needed to survive here.

I had to take control; the crowd was growing. The police were moving in with their riot shields and starting to replace the normal uniformed police who'd been trying to keep control of the situation as the cleric continued to tell everyone how Blair and Bush should be arrested for their 'war crimes'. Danny was new to the team and this was one of his first operations. I had to get him to live his cover, because we were the only ones in this crowd who weren't covering our faces and shouting 'Death to America'.

Showing aggression towards the police was hopefully going to achieve two things: it'd show the young male crowd that we hated the police too and allow us to move freely within them, but secondly and more importantly it would show Danny we were OK and hopefully give him the confidence that we weren't going to be pulled off the streets and beheaded, with a bit of luck.

As the riot shields grew closer I started to sense some of the more vocal males taking a strong interest in us. We stood out a mile. We weren't in shalwar kameez like the other hundred or so males here, and our faces were the only two, apart from the cleric on the loudspeaker, that weren't being hidden by military-style shemaghs or bala-clavas. I had a responsibility for Danny here, and I could see the fear in his eyes as it got louder from all directions; the cleric on his platform and loudspeaker behind us call-ing for sharia law and how all non-Muslims are infidels, his every word filling the crowd with cocaine-like energy. And to our front the police had us completely ring-fenced to try to control the crowd and stop an all-out riot, which ironically incensed the crowd and gave them even more will to become more threatening.

'You, you, what you doing here? You ain't Muslim.'

Four of the crowd had started to bear down on me and Danny. I could smell this guy's breath through the black and white shemagh covering his face, his eyes were black, aggressive and focused on me. Out of my periphery I could see two of them holding Danny's arms just above his elbows as if they were about to take him away. As I was constantly getting battered by a riot shield to my left shoulder, I could see the cleric behind this fucker with the awful breath; he'd stopped talking on the loud-speaker and was watching what was going on with us two. Bollocks, if this crowd wanted to take us these police wouldn't be able to save us; I'd just told one of them to fuck off.

'It ain't right, the way these cunts treat you. I shared a table with some Muslims in lockup, and they were proper good to me. All these fuckers do is arrest innocent people, I've fucking had it!'

Turning away from my would-be captives, I shoved

the police riot shield back, hitting the very top to knock it out of balance for the massive copper holding it. I knew from my time in Northern Ireland where to hit the weak points in these shields. As the shield pivoted around the hands of the copper, I grabbed the bottom of his shield, pushing him further back. This was my opportunity to get me and Danny out of here.

'Pigs! We ain't doin' nuffin' wrong!'

The young lads released their grip on Danny as he started hurling abuse at the riot police too. It didn't take much to win the trust of these guys, but on the flip side I'd properly pissed off one of the biggest coppers here and thanks to the way me and Danny looked it was going to be easy to spot us if they decided to charge the crowd and start arresting us.

The cleric started shouting on his loudspeaker again as the one with the bad breath guided me and Danny through the crowd towards the entrance of the mosque.

'You need guidance, brother. Can you read?'

Resisting the urge to tell him, 'Actually I'm dyslexic but I only found that out when I gained Top Secret clearance to work for MI5,' I continued to live my cover, making sure I had Danny right next to me now.

'Did a bit when I was locked up, why?'

Living your cover is a combination of playing to your audience but remaining true to who you are. If you want to ask a question then nine times out of ten you'd ask the same question. No one rolls over for everything, and people, especially ones with shady history behind them, know when they are being played. My cover, although I'd just manufactured it in the previous few minutes, was an angry guy with no direction straight out of prison.

'Brother, read this. It will save you and fill that void you have.'

Fucking hell. Despite being in a near full-on riot and only moments earlier having been about to get kidnapped by this guy and his mates or be arrested by the police, these words actually stopped me in my tracks for a second. Did I have a void that needed filling? Was something missing that I was overcompensating for? Was I missing my family so much I'd forgotten who I was? I couldn't think about that now, I had to get us two out of here.

He handed me and Danny a Quran each, and we were told to come back tomorrow morning and meet them at the mosque gates and they'd show us 'what to do'. It was moments like this that made my world a funny place to be; here I was pretending to be someone else in order to find one of our targets who'd gone missing, and we'd ended up getting pinned into an extremist protest, but yet once I bared some of my soul by attacking the shields of the riot police one of the crowd had noticed something in me that he was trying to help with. I was under no illusion he would have tried recruiting me to join their jihad at some point in the future, but that wasn't the point.

This young extremist, despite his views against women, the West and our way of life, had recognized something in me he could exploit to his advantage. I just hoped it wasn't anything my team could see too.

Overemphasizing our gratitude for our new saviours, I hugged the guy with the horrendous breath, thanking him and gesturing with the Quran that we would be back tomorrow. At that point the police started a surge forward, trying to push the crowd back, and this was our chance to run for it. Grabbing Danny, I shouted in his face, 'We have to go, fucking move now!'

Running against the crowd but with the flow of the advancing police, we made our way towards the back, past the cleric, continuing to the very rear of the crowd. I could see more riot police advancing towards the rear to try to pin us all in. They were out to arrest people here, and the last thing my team leader would want was for us to be arrested. I'd given up looking for our target, this was about getting out of here now. Danny was still panicking and starting to shut down; he'd clearly never been exposed to anything like this before. His eyes were looking straight ahead, he wasn't taking in his periphery at all and more worryingly he'd stopped talking.

As we fought our way towards the very back of the crowd, the riot police at the back were now about twenty-five metres away and charging towards us. Holding on to Danny's arm with my fingers in his left armpit I was directing him like a toddler: side street, that's our exit. Pushing him down in between two houses, I hoped this was a gap the police hadn't plugged yet. We didn't have our radios because of our closeness to everyone in the crowd. I needed to get us back to my team car and let the team leader know we were OK but we couldn't see the target. I had to sort Danny out first, because if the team saw him like this it's likely he'd be pulled off the team straight away.

As we got to the end of the little street I could see police vans everywhere with their riot covers down over the windscreens, but no cordons in place. We had a straight run through to the other side of the street. Relaxing my grip on Danny, I spoke to him calmly as we walked at a pace that was almost running speed.

'Mate, get to the other side of these houses down that alley there – my car is on the other side, then we'll drive round and get yours, yeah?'

'OK.'

He'd almost shut down here. I felt bad for him. This wasn't a particularly scary situation, I'd been in a lot worse, and we got out alive, but Danny had never seen anything like this and he was clearly from a well-off background. He had a couple of degrees and his own place in London, which for such a young guy on our salaries obviously meant his parents were helping him out.

Finally at my car, I unlocked it and let Danny get into the passenger seat. Engine on, my door now closed and locked, I switch the car radio on.

'Charlie Two Two, complete with Nine Seven.'

'Roger. Did you locate RUBBER PASSPORT?'

'Negative. Riot police on scene, we've extracted.'

'Roger that, good call. Move to the north, please, and we'll wait out for update from Base, all stations acknowledge.'

As the other vehicle call signs responded, I set off driving. I noticed Danny hadn't put his seatbelt on, and I was just about to prompt him when his eyes started to well up with tears. Fuck me, this had taken its toll on him. I had to help.

'Bro, let's get a Maccy's on the way to your car, yeah?'

I roughly knew where he'd parked but he couldn't be on his own yet anyway, so there was no need to push him. Hopefully a burger and a drink would bring him round before we ended up back in the debrief in front of the team. Moving through the drive-through, I collected the food and passed it over to Danny. I saw tears streaming down his face and his lip quivering like a small child's when they'd fallen over at the park.

I've seen a lot of people cry over the years, it wasn't shocking, nor did it strike any emotion in me, but this kid was part of my team. If I didn't help him the team would suffer, which meant I'd suffer. Shouting at him to man up wouldn't work with Danny; he was in his mid-twenties, but still quite naïve in the world. I had to distract him to allow me to get into his head, but I had to be quick before the team leader started to question why Danny wasn't in his own car yet and why I was still out of position.

'Pass me that bag, brother. We're gonna have a bet. I win, you let me have your fries – you win, and you get my fries AND my burger, deal?'

Looking at me for the first time since we escaped the crowd outside the mosque, he tried to smile in a way that said yes. Taking a paper napkin out of the food bag, I unfolded it to make a square.

'I bet you that you can't fold this paper in half exactly more than eight times. So you fold it in half exactly, that's once! Then fold it in half again exactly that's twice and so on. If you can't do it MORE than eight times, you give me your fries . . .'

Handing him the napkin, I watch his focus slowly switch to the folding task. Making constant jokes, I was trying to eat my fries as fast as I could so that I could 'make room for your chips, fucker!' He sniffed and wiped the tears away as he struggled on the seventh fold, the paper now becoming impossibly small.

'Come on, two more folds and my food is all yours . . . apart from the chips I've just had!'

Failing to fold it past the eighth, he smiled. 'TC, that's impossible.'

'All right then, mate, I'll give you another go while we head to your car.'

Taking another napkin, I separated it from the other sheets, making one ultra-thin sheet of paper.

'Thinnest paper, and I bet you still can't do it.'

As Danny focused, I could see him returning to his normal self while I moved through London traffic towards the area of his car.

'Dude, is your car first left off the main?'

'No, second left by the phone box.'

This was good, he was engaged with me again. On his eighth fold, he couldn't make that final fold.

'Mate, there has to be a way of doing that, what's the trick?'

Letting him keep his food, I continued to joke with him.

'No trick, mate, it's just fucking impossible. I think you need to be some mad ninja or a blind monk on a mountain trained in voodoo-jitsu or some shit to do it.'

He was laughing as he stuffed his face with burger at

my voodoo-jitsu comment, but I had to make sure he was OK before he got into his car on his own.

'Dude, you OK? Scary shit.'

Clearing his voice, Danny tried to regain some composure, slightly ashamed he'd become so vulnerable.

'Er, yeah. Sorry, mate.'

'Listen, Danny, there is no shame in being frightened—'

As he interrupted me, I could sense he was starting to beat himself up over this.

'Yeah, but I don't see you panicking. I'd be dead without you.'

'Shut up, you dick, we're fine. Look, mate, I can't do half the shit you can. You've got education coming out of your arse, you remember things and know more about current affairs than most. You found being in a hostile crowd scary, you found being battered by riot police scary . . . So what, it WAS scary! You're fucking human, you bell end.'

Danny started to laugh. He knew what I was trying to do. Giving him a few minutes to move from my car to his and sort his car out, I started to think about the situation we were in. I didn't find it scary: was something wrong with me? Or did I find it scary but my brain was locking it away like it did with the gang in Moss Side?

Hearing Danny shout up on the net, I watched him drive away to his new position. Following him for a few turns, I eventually pulled off and parked up to the north. I had to ring the team leader to let him know that me and Danny needed to be kept away from this target now on foot if we did find him; we would be noticed again because we got caught up in the crowd out-side the mosque. Pulling my service-issue mobile out of my pocket, I could see the screen flashing. It was on silent.

'TC, everything OK on the ground?'

I knew what the team leader was asking without asking it, he wanted to make sure I hadn't done anything crazy. I got results for the team, but he thought I was a bit of a loose cannon, like throwing a lit firework.

'Yeah, yeah, fine. Police got mega rowdy though, start-ing throwing their shields about. Some of the locals gave me and Danny a Quran and we got out of there before the police pinned us all in. We stumbled into the crowd looking for the target before we knew it, hundreds of extremists around us and same amount of police in front of us.'

'OK, mate, no worries. We'll keep you away from get-ting out on foot again on this one. How did Danny do?'

I was torn here, I was loyal to my team – having the back of the operator next to you is ingrained into us – but if something like this shook him up that badly the team leader should know. The fact Danny showed emotion was a good thing, maybe. Fuck knows, it wasn't my call to make and I wasn't about to dump him in the shit.

'All good, mate, lived his cover and moved quickly, no dramas. We stopped for food on the way to his car, I needed a coffee.'

'Great, thanks, mate. Right, I'll let you get off, we've got Base searching for leads on the target so just sit tight for now.'

An hour went by with no updates at all as the operations officers desperately searched for leads on RUBBER PASSPORT. He was born in Syria and moved over with his parents when he was an infant. A fairly successful architect, he became self-radicalized over the course of a year shortly after his wife died giving birth to his first child. Neither survived, and apparently he blamed the NHS nurses for their deaths. The problem we had was, being involved in the building trade, his brother-in-law was involved in building demolitions, which gave him access to explosives. The working theory was RUBBER PASSPORT was going to try to blow up a significant building in London, potentially a power station. To make matters worse, we had no clue if he had managed to acquire any explosives or detonators prior to going completely off grid. No phone movements, nothing from his associate contacts, no business contacts, nothing.

'From Base, an address maybe worth checking is an internet café next to Edgware Central Mosque.'

'Roger that, thank you. Charlie Six Two, can you?'

'Yes. Yes, on route.'

The ops officers would have had to do some major digging to get a vague address like this as a lead. Usually every single detail, no matter how loosely connected to our operation, is available within seconds on the grid, so the fact that this address took over an hour to find was probably down to the fact the intelligence officers were called and asked for more information that wasn't officially available. Usually this means the intelligence has come directly from agent handlers who have contacted their agents to help locate the target.

'Charlie Six Two, can you deploy, please?'

'Yes.'

'Specifically, if the target isn't in the café, can you sweep, and any local vehicles too?'

'Roger that.'

'Stations, update to follow.'

OK, this was shaping up to indicate the intelligence was coming from covert sources, or CHIS (Covert Human Intelligence Sources).

'Stations, I've asked if we can check if there are any traces of explosives in the internet café or vehicles outside that could indicate that RUBBER PASSPORT has been inside or using one of the vehicles nearby. Charlie Six Two, roger so far?'

'So far.'

'Source reporting indicates a potential attack in East London, likely to be a power station. So locating him is a priority.'

If RUBBER PASSPORT had acquired any demolitions and managed to gain access to a power station, London could be plunged into darkness. Over the years we'd discussed high value 'soft targets': sites that weren't military installations that boasted low-level security but if taken out would cripple the country. This particular power station was one of them; if it was taken off-line the majority of London would be without power for around eight months and rationed for another year after that.

I had my doubts whether or not RUBBER PASS-PORT actually had the right access to the power plant's crucial structures. He obviously had access to industrial levels of explosives and being an architect would know exactly where to place them with maximum effect, but he'd need a lot of logistics help, which would slow him down and more importantly help us find him. People always fuck up, and when they do we are there to exploit it.

'From Charlie Six Two, I'm in the area and have driven past the internet café, no sign of RUBBER PASSPORT.'

'Roger, thank you, stations, radio silence while Anna is checking.'

MI5 has recruited female operators for years. They have a few tools for changing their profile that aren't available to their male colleagues: hair, make-up, even pretending to be heavily pregnant. And add to that a woman's natural ability to prioritize and remember details.

'From Six Three, that's me in towards the internet café now, I'll keep the radio on.'

'Great, thanks. Charlie Seven One Zero direct of the vehicle please, radio silence while Anna is inside.'

Getting a camera direct on this suspicious Avensis would let us get imagery of anyone who had anything to do with the car; hopefully RUBBER PASSPORT would come to it and we'd get control of him. If nothing else, it meant Anna had some close-in support if the shit hit the fan.

When Charlie Seven One Zero got into position so it could see the green Avensis, it had a perfect view of Anna inside. Roughly thirty minutes went by before Anna left the internet café and shouted up on the net again.

'From Six Three, that's me walking out of the area now towards Charlie Six Two. No sign of RUBBER PASSPORT.'

'Great work, Anna, thank you. Base, acknowledge.'

'Roger that, making arrangements now.'

'Charlie Seven One Zero, stay in position, please. Everyone else quiet while we get Six Two back in her vehicle.'

It took Anna about three or four minutes to get back into her car.

'Charlie Six Two, complete.'

'Roger, thank you. Base, go ahead with your message.'

The operations officers had obviously given the team leader the heads-up on what was about to happen.

'RUBBER PASSPORT has gone to ground and hasn't been seen for at least twenty-four hours, source reporting suggests he's connected to this internet café, and the vehicle isn't known to us. With that in mind, we've asked local Special Branch to shut down the café while they conduct a search and remove the Avensis for further examination.'

'Roger, thank you, Base. Charlie Seven One Zero, stay in position until target vehicle is removed. All stations

cease and withdraw back to the debrief room and acknowledge down the list.'

I hated it when targets managed to get away. It hardly
ever happened but when it did we could usually pinpoint
how, but this guy had virtually disappeared off the face of
the earth. We weren't even sure at this stage if the source
reporting that linked the internet café to him had actually seen RUBBER PASSPORT enter or not, never
mind use this Avensis.

As the team waited in the debrief room for Charlie
Seven One Zero to return, we got an unofficial update
from the operations officer.

'OK, we think RUBBER PASSPORT has fled the
country with help. The Avensis has been recovered and
industrial demolition equipment has been found in the
boot, and swab results of the internet café have proved
positive for explosives. The site target for the attack is
still unknown. However, we still think it was a power
station.'

'Did we get all the explosives?'

The team was anxious. We still didn't know where
RUBBER PASSPORT was and if we had let anything
slip through our fingers, we didn't want to be the ones
responsible for leaving London without power.

'The brother-in-law has been arrested. Special Branch
found a trade purchase slip that indicates all the detonators and explosives recovered in the car was everything.'

'How good is the source reporting?'

The ops officer paused when I asked this. The team
knew it was a question we would never ask; they would

always question the reliability of the agent handlers' sources, but we would usually operate on a need to know basis. Given the scale of this attack my inquisitive nature overruled my ability to keep my fucking mouth shut.

'Source reporting is solid.'

And with that he let our team leader run the tactics debrief to see if there was anything we could improve on for next time. I'd obviously hit a nerve with my question; my guess is we had someone alongside RUBBER PASSPORT who had gone to ground, fearing for his life after feeding us the information that stopped this attack. That, or RUBBER PASSPORT was in some way part of a bigger operation and was in fact himself the source.

You can never tell with operations like this. As operators we go out and hunt the people we are given pictures of, we identify everything they do and everyone they speak to. Intelligence officers disseminate the information we give them, combining it with the electronic eavesdropping intelligence they get from A2. But when it comes to agent handlers, they live a fine line between passing on intelligence and protecting their assets.

The bottom line is, we stopped the attack. I didn't really give a fuck how we did it. Driving home that night, weaving my way through the traffic in the dismal British weather, I thought about Danny. He was clever, a member of Mensa and articulate. But I couldn't help thinking he should be in Thames House as an intelligence officer rather than on the ground, in the gutters, with people like me. It wasn't down to me to suggest what path people should take in their own careers, but it felt like the team needed operators from a stronger background. We were already incredibly diverse in terms of racial profiles and heritage, but a posh cunt is still a posh cunt no matter what they look like.

Chapter Twelve

The official line of Her Majesty's Government was that we never deal with terrorists, which was utter bollocks, but unless you saw it happening on a day-to-day basis you'd believe the UK's standpoint; after all, why would we deal with or fund terrorism? Because it stops bigger attacks, that's why.

We'd been funding the Irish paramilitaries for years. The IRA and their splinter cells, the UDA and associated Loyalists, all at some point received money, equipment or intelligence from us.

Most conspiracy theorists would have blamed the intelligence world for Princess Di's death and the Twin Towers on 9/11, which is obviously ridiculous, but in reality we sometimes fund and deal with bad people to prevent the worst atrocities from happening. You can't do good without doing a little bit of bad.

We'd known about this doctor in Birmingham for years. He was, until recently, always low level on the grid. Working as a GP in the local doctors' surgery. He would appear completely normal and mundane to the public, but he was in fact hell-bent on killing a lot of people in the UK, while helping his 'brothers' in Syria.

He was a short little fucker, which actually made following him in busy areas hard because you couldn't see him among the vast majority of normal-height humans. As I walked in the security tubes at the Operations Centre I thought about the doctor, where he was currently, what eavesdropping intelligence we had on him, how far along was he in the attack-planning phase; the thought of him actually made me laugh when I punched my personal numbers into the key pad to open the tubes, as it had just occurred to me that the doctor wouldn't actually be able to reach this keypad, due to its height.

Walking towards the stairs I saw Dave – he was on the same surveillance course as me. A great guy, funny and intelligent, and despite coming from an amateur dramatics background he had a real ability to work in hard areas. Plus he was the only one in our team that smoked, which was really handy sometimes. He was waiting for the lift until I convinced him to take the stairs with me: 'You'll get fat like those cunts on the desk, you know.'

Dave had always relied on me to be honest with him during his probation period; every time he had a follow or deployed a new bit of technical kit, even taking photographs, he'd ask my opinion: could it be done better, was it done quick enough? The truth is he was a natural operator. He lacked a bit of conviction sometimes, but that also played to his strengths of being able to assess the situation and prevent getting blinkered like most new operators. This time, though, he was coming to me for an entirely different reason.

'Dude, you're making me look like a rock star at the minute.'

'What do you mean?'

Dave was trying to soften the blow here, but I knew he was talking about the lack of team confidence in me.

'You go off reservation a bit. Now, mate, I love you and you get fucking brilliant results, but . . .'

He was struggling to be diplomatic and stopped talking while we walked past one of the cleaners. It gave me time to think about my response, because my initial reaction was to tell the team to go and fuck themselves, which I knew deep down I didn't mean. Putting the door code in for the deployment room, we both walked in and checked the intelligence boards for today's job.

'Dave, don't worry, mate, I'm good. Yeah, sometimes I step outside the team, but it's to get things done. Team leader knows that, mate. It's all good, but if I make you look good then surely that's a good thing, right?'

Dave knew I was trying to make light of the situation and started laughing as I patted him on his back, walking towards the trauma bags on the other side of the room.

'After all, you need all the fucking help you can get!'

Being one of the trauma medics on the team, I would carry extra kit in my car on top of the normal first aid bags everyone carried. We were trained to deal with the common injuries operators are likely to treat or be subject to. Gunshot and stab wounds, crush injuries from car crashes and, perhaps most importantly, how to save our biker should he come off. Things like removing his helmet, cutting through his leathers and radio kit. I'd done a lot of medical training with the military, but the Security Service training for operators is intense but highly specific. We didn't worry about how to create a sling out of a bandage, any of that shit. Our medical training was how to stop people dying when they were losing massive amounts of blood, plain and simple.

The job today was actually incredibly straightforward; all we had to do was keep control of the doctor and two other 'key holders' while a technical attack team entered his house to install eavesdropping devices.

Zipping the trauma bag up and slinging it on to my shoulder, I picked the oxygen bottle up and walked towards the door. Dave had gone into the briefing room with the rest of the team. I couldn't shake what he said to me; was I really going about things the wrong way? We are the world's best surveillance operators in the world's best intelligence agency and yet I was having another mental battle over whether it was the team being too soft or me stretching the limits of what's acceptable and legal.

Pushing the handle down on the briefing room door, the group leader stopped me. He was my team leader's boss, two levels below A Branch Director.

'TC, can I have a word?'

'Yeah, sure, boss, what's up?'

'Everything is fine, don't worry. As you know, every five years you have a DV review to assess whether your vetting is still OK and valid. Yours has come in early, but it's nothing to worry about, it really isn't.'

I knew the group leader must have been told the real reason behind my early review, but I had no clue.

'She's in the imagery suite round the corner. Sorry it has to be now. I'll take the kit off you and hand it over to your team. You go and get it sorted out and then get yourself home.'

Fuck's sake, If I was about to lose my vetting I would be fucked. I already needed the money, I couldn't afford to be sacked. Right, time to live my cover and play the game. Vetting knew everything about every single Security Service employee: our phone records, emails, social media accounts of us and our families, everything. If we were about to have an affair or buy a house, Vetting would know about it first.

'Hi, Tom, please sit down.'

Shit, formal names. At least she didn't full-name me; that's a positive. Sitting down, I remained relaxed, keeping my body positioning open and non-combative. I knew Vetting studied body behaviour so I had to get her on side quickly. I had no idea what she was about to say, so anything that could sway some friendly feelings towards me would help, otherwise I was about to try to scramble out of the lion's den.

'OK, your DV review isn't due till next year and I know you've held this level of vetting for a long time now, so this isn't anything to worry about, but a few things have been highlighted and we want to make sure you're OK.'

'Yeah, yeah, fine, what sort of things?'

'Tom, I know you're struggling financially. Being financially vulnerable makes you a target for foreign intelligence agencies unless we know about it. We can and do help a lot of employees. Let's just go through your debts and some of your recent investments.'

This was humiliating. Now I knew my group leader knew I was skint. That was the look on his face when he took the trauma bag off me: it was pity. I could feel my blood boiling and my core temperature increasing fast. I didn't feel angry though. I felt embarrassed.

'So first let's talk about the limited companies you've invested in and then we'll go on to your credit cards and how we can solve those issues.'

I bowed my head like a schoolboy who'd been told he's letting himself down by not washing and doing his home-work, but she lowered her body to catch my gaze.

'Tom, you're not in trouble, I'm here to help you.'

Raising my head and adjusting my body positioning, I knew the time had come to man up to my situation. I had a lifelong battle scraping through on the bare minimum. I've always wanted to provide for my wife and family. I didn't want to be rich, just to have enough money to last the month rather than my bank account being heavily overdrawn by the first weekend after payday.

'Talk me through the companies you're involved in.'

'Yeah, I didn't think it would be an issue as it's not intelligence-related, they are limited companies registered through Companies House but completely unrelated to my work here. Not actually making any more from them, unsurprisingly. First one I started when I was over the water with the Special Ops unit. I don't run any of them day to day.'

'OK, Tom, that's fine. We knew they were unrelated to your work with A4, what we wanted to check was your future plans if or when they become successful. Usually you'd be required to ask permission to gain employment outside the service.'

'Sorry, I didn't realize that. I don't run the companies day to day, it doesn't impact my work and IF they make any money I certainly won't be leaving the office, it would just go to reducing my debts and paying the mortgage off.'

'That's absolutely fine, though obviously we will ask if you do need to increase your workload to inform us and we'll give our consideration.'

I swear people from B Branch don't talk normally. 'Give consideration!' Why didn't she just say, 'Tell us and we'll think about it'? I couldn't let little things like that show on my face now though, this tiny little woman from B Branch was probably one of the most powerful in Thames House, and she could save me or end me.

'So, Tom, credit cards . . . We see that your repayments exceed your income, which is why the debt is growing. We have our own in-house charity as you know, and sometimes we can make a case to pay your debt off and in turn you pay back that over time from your wages. Would that be of interest to you?'

'Absolutely! How easy is it to get the charity to agree?'

'In a word, not very. But, we look to protect our employees and I think with a young family you would certainly be considered. Is there anything else apart from the card statements I have in front of me that you owe money on or is an extra expense?'

Looking through the raft of statements, she had absolutely everything. As I looked at each paper in turn I heard my team leaving the briefing room and heading out down the stairs towards the cars. I was an MI5 surveillance officer, recruited from Military Special Operations, and while my team geared up to travel to Birmingham I was sat here staring at my mobile phone missed payment bill. How the fuck had my life come to this? I was blessed with a rare set of skills that allowed me to keep my country safe, but I couldn't do the basics of providing for my family. It was at that moment that I felt like I was failing.

'Tom, do you want to join your team?'

She could sense how vulnerable I felt. I'd never felt comfortable talking about money; I'd always deflect if the conversation came up. I felt like the little boy in the army careers office. I wanted to belong, I was determined to make something of myself, but a part of me still felt like I wasn't quite good enough.

'Yes, please.'

Putting her hand on mine, she shook it with reassurance.

'Go, I'll sort this out. Check your service email when you get a chance this week and I'll give you an update. I'll speak to your group leader and get you some extra shifts too, he owes me a favour.'

Running out the door, I jumped down the stairs five at a time to catch my team. Through the tubes I could see the first cars leaving the gates. As I jumped into my car the team leader was parked opposite me, and he leaned his head outside his open door.

'Back with us today, then?'

'Yeah, all sorted – apparently I've got to stop shagging animals!'

'Ha. Come on, you prick, let's go. I'll brief on the air separately, channel three.'

In reality I knew my team leader would have been told I was struggling financially, or if not now he would be soon when I started picking up extra shifts. The battle I had now was all the extra shifts would take me away from my wife and son for even longer. I hoped the charity would help out, but the only way I could focus on today's job was to compartmentalize my money problems and slip back into operator mode.

I switched the car radio on to channel 3 and turned the volume up on the loudspeaker. I had a few hours of motorway driving ahead of me towards the doctor's work address.

'TC, you on channel three?'

'Yeah, go ahead.'

'Roger, the main team channel for the job today is channel four, channel four. Operation COINAGE, as you know, is the investigation into the supply of equipment to terrorist organizations in Libya and surrounding areas. The target, PENNY BLACK, is suspected of being in the attack-planning stages, working towards conducting hostile operations, either on the mainland here in the UK or overseas against coalition forces. Roger so far?'

'So far.'

'Today's task is to keep control of PENNY BLACK, also his wife BROKEN BRANCH and his only son FALLEN LEAF, to allow a team to bug his house. No other keyholders are known. PENNY BLACK is at the doctors' surgery, address on your PDA, and his wife and son are together shopping in Wolverhampton, according to the string from A2A. We are going to plot up around the surgery; another team has deployed on the wife and son.'

'Roger that. I'll give you a shout when I'm in the area, switching to channel four now.'

'Stations, give Charlie Two Two a radio check on channel four, please?'

'Loud and clear, bud.'

'Likewise, cheers.'

Hitting the motorway, I relaxed into the drive, no need to bust a gut getting down there. The technical teams wouldn't deploy until we had the doctor and his family identified and under control, and they would be travelling towards Birmingham too.

As the overhead gantry signs passed by, my mind started to drift back to my vetting interview; could this really be the end of my financial worries? I hated being away from my family constantly. The pace of operations was relentless but the increased hours meant more money. The service was going through its 100-year anniversary since Vernon Kell started the organization in 1909. As part of the celebrations, the service had commissioned a book to document the official history, and various other things were available for employees to buy as keepsakes. The director general, Jonathan Evans, gave me a personally signed copy of the book. I also got the service-issue watch. It was a privilege because only around a quarter of

MI5 employees got the chance to buy a watch and I believe even fewer got a signed copy of the book from the DG.

My wife and I couldn't afford the watch; we both knew we didn't have the money but we wanted my son to have something of significance he could pass on to his children, and their children after. It was more money than we had paid for our family car. I'd always liked nice watches, but had never been able to afford one. We took the money from two of our many credit cards to pay for it. I was sure it would increase in value and when my son was old enough to have his own children or get married I would pass it on to him; surely by then I would have paid back all this debt.

I've always been a bit of an entrepreneur at heart, looking for opportunities to make money, which is why I got involved in some companies, anything from imports and exports of games consoles, trying to take advantage of the currency exchange rate, through to selling goods on eBay. It's that side of my personality that applies well to being an operator. Looking for opportunities, how best to take advantage of the situation I was in. I just wasn't quite sure why I was failing to bring in enough money yet.

As the time rolled by I was getting close to the target area, and I could hear the technical team pop up on the net as they started to move into the area, ready to get into the house when we had control of everyone.

'A4, do you read, team leader?'

'Loud and clear. We'll give you a shout when we have PENNY BLACK under control.'

'Roger, thank you, we won't need too long.'

Hollywood spy films would have you believe it's all gloss and shine when 'bugs' are planted in houses or cars. The truth is less dramatic. And doesn't unfold against a tension-building movie soundtrack. It involves careful preparation to make sure that it goes as smoothly as possible. Entry follows rigorous surveillance, so the team knows what to expect. The target didn't leave the house much. That complicated things.

Picking locks is an art and any seasoned locksmith will tell you that you can pick the same lock in the same conditions with the exact same tools ten times and each time it will unlock in a slightly different way. Sometimes you'll get a pin that sticks or doesn't want to lift properly. An examination of the locks is conducted prior to the job to eliminate that problem.

'Base, do we know if PENNY BLACK is inside the GP surgery?'

'Confirmed, entered at 0930hrs, hasn't left. Red team have control of BROKEN BRANCH and FALLEN LEAF.'

'Roger that, thank you.'

There was absolutely no way the doctor could escape us and make it back to his house. Hopefully, once the technical team left the house having installed the eavesdropping devices, we'd be able to pull out of the area. This was a simple babysitting operation.

'Entry team leader, do you read, A4?'

'Go ahead.'

The team leader was talking in hushed tones, meaning he was ready to go.

'We have control of the whole family, you're good to go.'

'Roger, gaining entry now.'

'Roger. Stations, radio silence while the entry team are on target unless we see PENNY BLACK.'

Normally the technical teams wouldn't give us running commentary on what they were doing but in this case everyone was talking. I was starting to think that the doctor wasn't just a horrible short little cunt after all and had some significance beyond being a terrorist facilitator.

'That's us inside, on target now.'

The entry teams are always surprisingly quick getting into buildings or cars. It doesn't matter what lock or alarm system something has, if it has a method of opening then it can be defeated. One of my first introductions to their particular skills was while I was still in the army. Ian, my MI5 handler, was speaking to a guy in his fifties about a parcel they knew was in the Post Office's sorting office. He wanted to get access to the laptop inside, but the parcel was sealed with security tape that was designed to break if tampered with, to show if it had been previously opened.

This guy, who I came to know only as 'Paul', went on to explain that he and his boffins had ways of getting past security tape and resealing the parcel without anyone being any the wiser. Not a problem. Absolutely anything is accessible; if at some point it's designed to be opened, AI know a way of getting in, and closing it back up without leaving a sign. They really are the best in the world, proper sneaky bastards.

'Installing now.'

We would never be told where or what devices would be installed in target addresses or vehicles. A2A, who monitor the eavesdropping audio and video recordings, would know because it would help them distinguish sounds within the property, particularly if they thought the device was compromised and found by the target, which happened quite a lot in Northern Ireland.

No longer than a minute had gone by before we got another transmission.

'Base, entry team is preparing to leave now. Can you confirm exit is clear?'

'Confirmed, you're good to leave.'

It took the entry teams another minute, maybe two, before they sent their last transmission.

'That's us complete and away from the area now. Device installed. A2A, do you read?'

Why the fuck were the monitors from A2A on our comms? This never happened; they would never be listening on our radios, in fact I didn't even know they had access to our communications. Usually if they have anything urgent coming through they would ring the operations officer.

'A2A reading and audio behaving normally.'

'Thanks, guys, A4 and Base, all back to you, entry team OUT.'

'Roger that, thank you. Stations, we are going to sit tight for thirty minutes then pull off back to the Operations Centre. Red team have ceased already.'

I really didn't understand what was going on here. We'd deployed to keep control of the keyholders while the technical team got into the property and installed another bug, but we had running commentary and A2A were on the net too. This doctor was either being run by the agent handlers or the risk for compromise was much bigger than we were being told.

'Stations, Base has kindly allowed us to have a debrief over the air and travel straight to your homes rather than coming back to the ops centre. Cease and withdraw and acknowledge down the list, please.'

Once everyone shouted up and started their drive home, the team leader started the debrief.

'All stations, switch to channel ninety, NINE ZERO now and test call, please.'

Changing the channel on the car radio, I knew I was about to get some answers to today's job, and the team could sense it too as we all scrambled to reply on channel ninety as quickly as we could.

'Roger, thank you, stations. Base is on too. This channel is for A4 only. Entry team and A2A do not have access to this channel.'

'Base, roger, and yes, that's correct.'

'Base, all yours for debrief.'

'Roger, thank you. Stations, obviously you heard A2A on the net and the running commentary from the bugging team. We tried to recruit PENNY BLACK last week. It was felt he wasn't receptive to the thought of working for us, but he didn't discuss this with anyone in his family or close associates. Any station roger so far?'

'So far.'

'Last night we received intelligence that Pakistan ISI

had been told we had tried to recruit PENNY BLACK and he was considering it. We do know that communication came from the doctor but we don't know how he's communicating with the intelligence agency in Pakistan. Hence the extra device installed today. One station roger so far?'

'So far.'

'This is all need to know, but given how unorthodox today's job was and the possibility for PENNY BLACK to be more aware than he might have been previously, I thought it best to let your team know.'

'Roger, thank you, Base. Stations, this is NEED TO KNOW, do NOT discuss this with anyone given the sensitivity of inter-agency relations.'

'Base, no problem. Safe driving, everyone.'

Just when you think this life couldn't get any darker or have any more twists and turns, you find out one of your targets is potentially helping terrorists kill coalition forces while pretending to work for us as an agent, all the while passing intelligence on to Pakistan, who could potentially be passing false intelligence through him to feed to us. Fuck. Me.

In reality what this meant was that the agent handlers would run him as one of their covert human intelligence sources, with a view to gaining intelligence that could prevent further attacks on the UK and its interests. However, we knew this doctor was a tricky little shit who'd passed information on to Pakistani intelligence about the service. Throw into the mix the fact that the agent handlers would be rewarding PENNY BLACK for 'his service' by way of cash, presents and treats, and you are then back in the realms of funding terrorism.

Driving home back to my family, I was running through over and over what just happened. PENNY BLACK was going to be paid by us, he was going to be paid by the NHS as a GP and more than likely he would have a bank account in Pakistan having regular deposits made too. This twat was raking it in while I was having to make arrangements with charities to help pay my debts off. I'd got myself into this situation, and had only myself to blame, but I couldn't help feel bitter when I saw terrorists and career criminals getting away, literally, with murder and having more money than they knew what to do with.

PENNY BLACK would likely go on to become a double agent while continuing to facilitate terrorist groups overseas. Every roadside bomb, every suicide attack in Iraq or Afghanistan, I'd continue to question whether we could have prevented that or did we inadvertently aid it by funding this miserable fuck?

Chapter Thirteen

Early in my career with MI5, I considered going through the surveillance biker training. Our bikers are all operators, with the added specialism of being able to ride one of the team's surveillance motorbikes. I decided against it because I was concerned I'd lose valuable time doing proper foot follows if I was stuck on a bike in full leathers and a helmet.

The bikers in A4 are absolutely the best asset we have. A bike can cover ground much quicker than any of our cars. They are incredibly well trained so like all surveillance operators they are advanced car drivers taught by the police, having the ability to do everything an intercept police car can and would do but without sirens or blue lights, meaning our skill set is much higher.

But bikers go beyond that in MI5. They then attend the police motorbike training and once they have done that they return to the service to learn surveillance riding on bikes, which is intense and extremely difficult to pass, considering the amount of things they learn how to do on a superbike, riding at night with no lights on to follow vehicles in complete darkness being just one of the skill sets.

Today's job in London was a new target we were having a 'first look' at. Very little was known about the target, and the intelligence officers only caught wind of him because he was on the periphery of an extremist cell we had arrested the week previous. I sat in the briefing room with my team as we waited for the operations officer to arrive and give us the key details for that job: address, recent photo, any known vehicles, pattern of life, if we had any at this stage, potential work addresses, endgame objectives. Anything that would give us some help on the ground finding him, figuring out what he was up to and if he had any help.

I was sitting next to Stu, the biker for our team, at the back of the briefing room as the ops officer walked in. As the officer switched on the large screen at the front, Stu passed me a mint.

'Take two, mate, you need them.'

'Prick.'

Despite his huge amount of experience, Stu was still one of the guys, always making jokes and helping anyone who needed it. It always surprised me that he never went for promotion to team leader or even further than that. All he wanted to do was be on the ground with the team on his bike 'getting in the mix', and I loved him for that. He wasn't in this life for a career, he just loved being here.

'Good morning, Green team. I'll start the briefing at 0801hrs. Please take the time to sync your watches . . .'

'Do you want help reading the time on your watch, brother?'

'The hand of Mickey Mouse is stuck . . . now what am I gonna do?!'

The officer briefing knew that Stu was joking around with me, and as the other members of the team started laughing and turning around he raised his voice to keep control of the briefing.

'Operation QUAKE is a result of intelligence gained after the op BEARING arrests last week. The target is MUD SLIDE and this is a first look at him. This is the most recent image we have of him taken from a phone in the arrests.'

Quite often this is the way we get new investigations. A large operation like BEARING will give us stacks of intelligence, not only during the surveillance phase but when we arrest the key players too; it's amazing how quickly some ideologues fall by the wayside when they are faced with thirty years in prison and their family is threatened.

'MUD SLIDE has no history with us, no criminal record and isn't a UK citizen. To date we don't know how he made it into the country. Today's objectives are simple: using the address on your PDAs, we'd like any surveillance possible. Up-to-date photographs, if he uses a mobile phone, GPS it and we'll lift it from the service providers. We have a possible phone number for him but it hasn't been switched on in the last few days. I'm afraid it's a roll of the dice; if you can get hold of him, great.'

As we left the briefing room towards the garage, the team knew today was going to be hard. All we had was an image lifted from a phone and an address on our PDAs. We didn't actually have this address confirmed as the target's home. That was our role today, to try and get as much intelligence as possible to provide a more stable base if and when we came back to this another day. You can't uncover everything in one day, and we might not even see MUD SLIDE at all. We didn't get many operations like this but stuff like this is great for a team's morale if you manage to go on the ground with absolutely nothing and get a key piece of evidence that opens up the investigation.

As we left the garage at varying intervals, I saw Stu already on the other side of the bridge as he popped up on the net for a radio check,

'Anyone read, Bravo Seven?'

'Loud and clear, Bravo Seven.'

'Roger and likewise.'

It took the team about forty minutes to arrive in the area of the address we had been given for MUD SLIDE. The team leader was rightly cautious about saturating the streets immediately around the address. We hadn't been here before and didn't know anything about the target, and this is a dangerous time in surveillance. If we alerted him to the fact that he was being watched now we'd fuck the entire job up before it'd even started,

'Can I have one out on foot to do a walk-past of the address, please? Charlie Seven One Zero, can you see if you can get imagery direct on the front door, please, and any VRNs of vehicles outside? Other stations, cover north and south on the main to react on a STAND BY, and Bravo Seven, wait out the area, please.'

It was a waiting game now. You make your own luck in this game, but we would need a little help too for the target to actually show himself near this address. It didn't take long for us to catch our break.

'STAND BY, STAND BY, from Charlie Seven One Zero, that's MUD SLIDE OUT, OUT of the address, walking northbound, black hooded top, blue jeans, white trainers, carrying a green rucksack on his back, I can't go with.'

'Roger that. Charlie Two Two is in position if he goes to a vehicle to the north.'

I was hoping he'd use a vehicle because it would give us a good bit of intelligence this early on.

'From Charlie Seven One Zero, TC, he's about twenty-five metres north of the address now, continuing on foot, had a brief look back too.'

For targets to be aware usually suggests operational activity, so this was going to be a good day if we could keep hold of him.

'Roger that, and have seen. I have control, MUD SLIDE walking north and has now STOP, STOP, STOP at a bus stop on the east side.'

'Roger that, Charlie Two Two, if he gets on a bus can you go with?'

'Yeah, can't see any bus numbers from this distance but he is alone at the stop.'

'Further, the bus would take him south on the main.'

'Charlie Seven One Zero, roger that, bud. I should get the bus number at least.'

'From Charlie Two Two, large double-decker bus approaching the stop now. MUD SLIDE is ON, ON to the bus and has walked to the top deck, stations be aware.'

'That's the bus now leaving and travelling southbound, southbound on the main. I have control.'

Accelerating gently towards the main road, I was mindful of not creating too much sign locally. We still didn't know anything about this target yet or any other linked addresses. As I got to the junction of the main road I could see the bus now about a hundred metres away with three other commuter cars behind it. I could live with being this far back from the bus at this stage.

'Base, permission.'

'Go ahead, no change, bus continuing southbound past the school and Chinese takeaway to his off side.'

As with all bus moves, it's a big game of hide and seek. Most of the time, buses in London can move through traffic easier than normal passenger cars thanks to bus lanes, but you have to throw into the mix the fact that they are constantly making stops on their routes, so as a team you have to stay back when the bus stops to prevent being forced past, while keeping the ability to stay with it in heavy traffic. London buses in particular are quite aggressive when they pull out so they can quickly get away from the team if you're not totally on the ball.

'Hold back, hold back. That's the bus STOP, STOP, STOP, twenty metres before the garage on the near side. No one has left the bus, and it's now continuing southbound again.'

The bus was now over a hundred metres away from me and I was slowly starting to lose my grip on it,

'Any station help out with this bus, I'm getting held and don't want to show out too much.'

'Charlie Eight Seven can, I'm ahead at the next junction?'

'Great, I'll feed it to you. Once you can it's all yours.'

'Roger that, and Charlie Eight Seven now has control of the bus, for information the VRN is WHISKY MIKE FIVE ONE, TANGO HOTEL YANKEE, it's a number 61.'

'Base, roger.'

'Charlie Two Two, roger and backing from a distance.'

I had no problem staying behind the bus at this distance, it looked like a main commuter road so it was natural to stay on this route.

'Stations, hold back, that's a STOP, STOP, STOP, STAND BY, STAND BY – MUD SLIDE is OFF, OFF the bus and crossed immediately over to the west side of the main.'

'Roger, three, out on foot, please, let's get hold of him.'

This was a busy area and there were a lot of transport links here, so if we weren't careful we would lose control of him quickly. As three members of the team jumped out on foot, I sneaked into the bus lane to undertake fifty metres of traffic and slide back in. The bus was still stationary but at this angle I couldn't see the target at all.

'From Charlie Eight Seven, MUD SLIDE has now crossed back over to the east side of the main, still continuing southbound on foot, he's looking back towards the bus.'

'Base, anything to add?'

The team leader started to feel how the rest of the team

was feeling: this guy was deploying very crude methods of anti-surveillance, and we needed more information.

'Stations, STEEL BADGE, STEEL BADGE, recent text message from his phone three minutes ago: "I'm going to the wedding now with Lucy."'

Fuck, the backpack. Quite often terrorist cells would use coded messages to each other to mask their real intent. In this case, the Operations Centre were thinking that the 'wedding' was a bombing target or location and 'Lucy' was the bomb itself.

'Roger. Foot crews, do you have control and Base, can you let us know if our friends have been informed and on route?'

'Negative, I don't have control.'

'Negative from Eight Seven.'

'Negative.'

Fucking hell, this was going wrong fast. I could see MUD SLIDE at a distance as the traffic started to move.

'From Charlie Two Two. I can see MUD SLIDE, he's now walking southbound again, moving away from the bus stop towards the Tube entrance in the distance about 300 metres away. I'm held in traffic. Bravo Seven, are you able to assist?'

'Bravo Seven, twenty seconds out.'

I could hear the bike's revs on Stu's transmission as Base popped up with another update.

'EXECUTIVE ACTION, EXECUTIVE ACTION, stations, when you have control we will guide in the arrest team.'

That confirmed it then; MUD SLIDE was likely

going to blow something up, the operations centre weren't taking any chances and were going to have the target arrested. The executive action team would be extremely aggressive and would be operating under a kill or capture, given the likelihood that he was going to commit mass murder.

'From Charlie Two Two, MUD SLIDE is out of sight to me and running free. Bravo Seven, can you?'

I didn't want to be a dick on the net to Stu but the team had to know the target was no longer under control and I couldn't see him. Thankfully I heard the engine revs of Stu's bike as he dropped down a gear, making his way through traffic. Spotting a gap, he opened up the throttle and rocketed towards the area I'd last seen MUD SLIDE.

The noise was destructively loud. I only registered the engine revs climbing higher and higher, almost screaming, then I realized that it was a pedestrian that was screaming. An articulated lorry trying to overtake the bus had pulled out too far, too suddenly, and clipped Stu as he tried to speed past, knocking him off and throwing him under the wheels of the trailer.

'STU!! STU IS DOWN, HE'S BEEN HIT BY A TRUCK ... HE'S FUCKING DOWN ... STUUUUUUU!'

'Base, roger, we need control of MUD SLIDE.'

'HE'S DEAD, HE'S FUCKING DEAD.'

The traffic came to a standstill as the truck slowly moved over away from Stu and came to a stop. The team leader replied instantly to my transmission the moment I let go of my push-to-talk button.

'TC, we need MUD SLIDE. Ambulance is on its way.'

The traffic slowly edged forward. Without thinking or removing my gaze from the spinning wheels of Stu's bike, I moved with the flow of cars. It felt like an hour but would have only been a few seconds before I was alongside his bike as normal bystanders started rushing in to help him. He'd come off his bike and hit the trailer first, then been crushed beneath its wheels. The bike's engine was still ticking over as his wheels slowed down and stopped. I think it was that exact moment the wheels stopped turning that Stu passed away on this soaking wet road with bits of rubbish everywhere.

'I have control of MUD SLIDE, towards the Tube entrance, 200 metres away, still walking south on the east side. No change in appearance, still dressed as previous.'

Leaving my car on the side of the road just in front of the truck, I made my way down the pavement as quick as I could. I wanted to look back but I'd become numb. MUD SLIDE was going to pay for this.

'Roger that, TC, EXECUTIVE ACTION team now deploying.'

'MUD SLIDE still southbound, east side 150 metres away from the Tube entrance, walking past the coffee shop with the silver tables outside.'

'Roger, NINE EIGHT is backing.'

'Roger, MUD SLIDE now fifty metres from the Tube entrance, Base, acknowledge.'

'Roger that, TC. If he goes inside can you go with to let me guide the strike team in?'

'MUD SLIDE now in the area of the Tube station, and towards the barriers, going with.'

Just as the target pulled an Oyster card from his pocket and walked to the barriers, I heard the executive action strike team pile into the Tube station entrance, guns out, screaming at him to get on the floor, keeping his hands visible. As the other London commuters fled the area like a family of ants escaping the horror of being caught up in something they shouldn't, the strike team moved in.

I didn't even flinch when the second wave of armed police piled in to make sure MUD SLIDE didn't detonate anything he was carrying. The screams, sirens and shouts all stopped. I felt cold and heavy as I looked back up the street to see the ambulance arriving in the area where Stu was lying. I could see a paramedic first responder car already there. As the crowd gathered near me I could feel the police pushing people back as they looked to see what was happening around MUD SLIDE. I was the only one not looking towards the Tube entrance.

My team leader was with Stu and the paramedics. I could see his car on the other side of the road with his door open. I had no idea how long my radio had been receiving transmissions for, I hadn't heard anything for a while, and Base had clearly been trying to get me to respond, 'Zero Six, radio check?'

'Loud. Yeah. Loud. Clear.'

'Roger, all stations cease and withdraw, team leader is with Stu and he's receiving treatment. MUD SLIDE has been arrested, acknowledge the last.'

'Yeah. Got it.'

I knew Stu wouldn't be getting any treatment, I knew he was dead. The paramedics were clearly trying to do their best for him as he was moved into the ambulance and it sped away past me through the traffic. Even the police cars from the strike team had left with MUD SLIDE and this street in London slowly started to go about its normal day again. The team leader didn't see me standing on the pavement as he spun his car around and followed the blue lights of the ambulance to the hospital.

It took less than thirty seconds to get back to my car. It was quiet, no team transmissions, no sirens on the street, even the police putting tape around Stu's bike and interviewing the truck driver were quiet and slow. The clinical nature of the normal uniformed police dealing with a road traffic collision couldn't be further away from the way the executive action strike team moved and dealt with MUD SLIDE.

As I drove down the main road past the Tube station entrance I saw a police recovery truck coming the opposite way to remove Stu's bike and reopen the road behind me.

'Stations, an update for you on MUD SLIDE. Initial report from the police arrest team is he isn't carrying explosives and was doing a dry run. Base, out.'

Fucking. Cunt. That fucker, he was practising his route to his attack site in preparation for the real event. He wasn't carrying anything that could hurt anyone apart from his imagination. Stu died for nothing. Fucking nothing.

'Base, TC. I'm going home. Debrief me tomorrow.'

'Negative, TC, we need everyone to come in for debrief, we have counsellors here already.'

'TC OUT!!'

I threw my radio at the passenger window. It smashed open and I saw the small battery hit the dashboard and disappear towards the windscreen vents. I wasn't in the mood to speak to some posh prick with a degree on how I should be feeling. I'd had to drive past my team mate as he took his last breath on the road in a puddle chasing someone who wasn't a threat to anyone.

My service-issue mobile started ringing almost immediately. 'Call.' The only people in the country this would be is the ops room telling me to come in for debrief. They can fuck off. Squeezing the phone in my hand, I tried to crush it. I knew I wouldn't be able to but I couldn't help the aggression spilling out of me. Throwing it behind me, I hit the wing mirror with my left hand as the phone disappeared on to the back seat, still vibrating, as the ops room continued to call me.

Driving home, all I wanted was to see my family. This fucking job was a curse. I was blessed with a set of skills that allowed me to protect this country but those skills brought infinite darkness to me. I couldn't remember a full week during my time with the service, both officially and unofficially, where my effort to keep people safe was rewarded with happiness. I was surrounded by death and destruction. The people we hunt want to kill our civilians and sometimes people in our team die trying to stop them. Because of who we are we can only talk to professionals who have Top Secret clearance if we are starting to suffer with mental health issues.

The problem with that is you're talking about Top Secret events, to people with Top Secret clearance in a building that plans Top Secret work. No one we are cleared to talk to has the ability to look at things from a different perspective. I called Stu forward to help out on that follow, he came in without a second's notice and when I thought he wasn't moving quick enough and we risked losing MUD SLIDE I chased him up a second time and asked for help. It was his speed that killed him. His speed was a reaction to me. I killed my team mate. Now how the fuck was I going to explain any of this?

I needed to talk to my wife, but I knew what I would end up doing. I'd either brush over this or just clam up completely. I was shit at talking about my feelings. I think that comes from my childhood. Being told not to cry, to be quiet and having no one to actually talk to led me to develop a sort of protective armour. I was afraid that if I did talk about things I'd either let too much out and not be able to operate on the ground properly, or people would lose confidence in my ability, not only as an operator but as a husband and father.

As I walked through the door at home, my wife met me with her usual smile. I never got tired of how beautiful she was, not only to look at but to be with. She was absolutely without question my one true constant, and I almost felt guilty being married to her. My wife brought so much more to the table than I did. She's always believed in me as a person. She was my walking guardian angel.

'I've just seen a biker die . . .'

'You're joking?? What happened?'

'I tried to help, but . . .'

I felt myself starting to wash over this. I needed to bury it, I didn't want to deal with something like this and I refused to let my family know how dangerous my role was, hunting the scum of the earth.

'It was on my way home, police and ambulance already there. His bike was a mess.' I left it at that.

Sensing that I was a bit shocked by it but clearly didn't want to talk about it any more, my wife took me by the hand into the kitchen to make some food together. I was starving but didn't want to eat. That night, falling asleep, I was woken by my wife's hand on my shoulder.

'You're jumping . . .'

I don't think I was having a nightmare. Maybe it was my subconscious trying to process what had happened today. We'd arrested someone for pretending to bomb something and my team mate died because of it. And in the morning I'd have to deal with the ops room officer as to why I didn't go to the debrief as instructed, and I'd have to go to Stores for a new radio. I wasn't sure which would be harder to deal with, the ops officers or store-room Phil. He could be a right grumpy twat when he wanted to be, and his favourite line when we would ask for a replacement or new bit of kit was, 'What if someone else needs it? It's my last one and they are expensive.'

Q from James Bond, he wasn't.

That night was one of the most restless nights' sleep I've had in a while, but all I could think about was how tired my wife was going to be as she nursed me through the whole night, giving me her reassuring hand while I shook and twitched through whatever my brain was trying to process or lock away.

Whether everyone was reeling from Stu's death yesterday or the rumour mill had spread that I didn't go to debrief, I wasn't sure, but I was left alone. I got my new radio from Stores without a single complaint, and the briefing for our next job went without me being pulled aside to ask how I was feeling or would I like to talk to anyone.

The team was quiet, no joking around, no banter. Just a methodical, quiet approach to that day's operation. We'd lost another member of our small family. I was starting to wonder if I was prepared to put my wife and son through the heartache of me not being around any more. What I did was important, I saved lives and I was good at it. But I wasn't the only one who could do this and I could be replaced. I would kill to live on a remote farm with my family right now, no evil cunts to chase and no more carnage.

Chapter Fourteen

I felt the first hand grabbing the back of my T-shirt from behind my passenger seat. It was only then that I realized they had smashed the back window of our car. We had to force our way out of here, but we risked killing innocent bystanders. My team leader quickly made the decision as I started to get pulled towards the rear of the car and hit the accelerator. As we hit the first car the crowd scattered. Piling on the power, we continued to push the car in front of us out of the way, hitting the second car that had trapped us in, my team leader creating enough of a gap to squeeze through. No one else gave chase, but we had to keep the speed up back to the Operations Centre. This operation was too big to sit around and cry about being attacked. We had to change the car and get hold of the targets.

This operation had been going on for months, and, while nearly all our operations have an international element to them, this wasn't just your run-of-the-mill tourist-spot attack. This was the biggest operation I've ever been involved in. A highly planned attack that aimed to kill tens of thousands of people, both here in the UK and in New York City. The terrorist cell was directed by their command in Pakistan, all the major players were difficult to keep hold of, and the investigation into them really ramped when our team saw one of them watching a video of the Twin Towers attacks on his mobile phone while he was travelling on a bus.

That was one of their planned targets. The anniversary of the Twin Towers: their plan was to explode several car bombs in the area where people gathered to remember their loved ones who were lost on that tragic day, September 11th 2001.

The second part of their plan, while they also discussed bringing down a transatlantic passenger plane, was to blow up a shopping centre in Manchester during Easter weekend. We estimated the casualty numbers could top 20,000 dead and triple that in injuries. These two attacks, though months apart, would have been catastrophic. I didn't have time to dwell on the fact that I was nearly lynched for no known reason.

We screeched into a regional Operations Centre garage – the guards had been told we were coming in at pace and had opened the barriers for us so we could fly straight in. One of the ops officers was waiting with two sets of keys to new cars.

'Split up, radios in the cars are ready. We think the police had a team there last week and had a compromise, same make and model as your tracking car.'

Fucking typical, the crowd that were trying to rip me apart earlier thought we were the same police team that they obviously had an issue with. As I walked over to the new car, the team leader was already in his and pulling away, but as I sat in the car I felt a sharp piece of glass in my back. It was the remains of the window. Looking in the mirror, I had bits of glass still in my hair, and one piece must have fallen down my back.

Back out of the car and ruffling the glass out of my hair just roughly enough so I didn't cut my hand, I saw the little chunks of toughened glass hitting the garage floor by my feet. Those fucking pricks wanted blood, and you can't reason with mob mentality. I was dying to know what the police had done to piss the locals off so much that they tried to kill us.

Driving out of the garage, I saw the car we abandoned, which was now being parked up by the ops officer. We'd lost the nearside back passenger window and they had obviously smashed the tail lights and hit the boot with the crowbar too. We were lucky to escape that one, but there was no time to think about it any more. I could hear my team on my radio desperately trying to get hold of one of the main players in this terrorist cell, but without a tracking car locating the GPS in his van the team were struggling. The van was last seen driving south on the M1 motorway. If they went to ground now prior to the attacks people were going to die. I couldn't live with that. In our world people die all the time, but I had to make sure I had done everything humanly possible and made every sacrifice I could to make sure these pricks didn't get to their target endgame.

STEEL BADGE had been in play since we found out the scale of their attack planning and how advanced their logistics capability was. They had already recce'd New York and Manchester and we knew they had capability to get the explosives. This wasn't a Mickey Mouse outfit. They had a plan and a goal, they just had no way to deal with operators like us.

'Charlie Six Four is as far south as Junction 12, nothing seen.'

A motorway stretching the length of the country, and one white van belonging to our target was last seen on this motorway, believed to be travelling south to a lockup where the explosives or detonators could be. The tracking GPS in the target's van had gone into sleep mode and could only be woken up by our tracking car. It doesn't happen very often but it's typical: when you need the tracking devices to work they bloody don't. The entire team was driving as fast as they could up and down the motorway to catch a glimpse of a white van that had the right registration number and our target driving.

We had cars checking the motorway services too, just in case the information didn't come through from our police contacts quickly enough. We left nothing to chance and it was starting to look like we'd never find him.

'WAIT OUT, WAIT OUT, BROKEN LAPTOP is SOUTHBOUND, SOUTHBOUND on the MIKE ONE, one up just past Junction Two Nine, continuing towards Junction Two Eight. Can anyone assist?'

I was a couple of miles out. 'Charlie Nine One, will be there in two minutes, what lane is he in?'

'One of three, passing the roadworks, TC. I'm in front of him so quick as possible please.'

'From Charlie Nine One, I have control, target vehicle is lane one of three, speed six five, seven zero miles per hour MIKE ONE south towards Junction 28.'

'Roger, thanks, TC. I'm pulling ahead now and off at 28, if he continues I'll rejoin behind you and back.'

'Cheers, bud, no change, continuing lane one of three into the countdown markers for Junction 28.'

'Three hundred yards from the exit at 28, still lane one of three, NO indication.'

The rest of the team remained quiet but I knew they would be screaming to get to us as quickly as possible. I was waiting for acknowledgement from the team leader and Base once we got past the junction and we knew BROKEN LAPTOP wasn't leaving the motorway.

'Hundred-yard marker board now, vehicle still lane one of three and that's CONTINUING southbound on the MIKE ONE towards Junction TWO SEVEN, speed SEVEN ZERO SEVEN FIVE.'

'Roger and backing.'

'Roger, thanks, mate.'

'Great work, guys, keep hold of it, team is closing in.'

'Base, permission?'

'Go ahead, no change.'

'From A2A – BROKEN LAPTOP was heard inside a property in Sheffield just off the M1 talking about gate departures. Nothing further.'

We didn't need the ops centre to elaborate. We now knew the likelihood was that we were heading to an airport, either for an attack inside the airport or on board a plane or for escaping the country and committing an attack in the US. Every operator worth their salt would be carrying their passport during a job. Mine was in its usual position in a Tubigrip around my ankle. It doesn't happen very often but sometimes we are required to follow a target on to a ferry, train or plane across borders to keep a surveillance lock. It's unusual because we have a good intelligence relationship with our surrounding neighbours and usually have enough time to pass it through to them that a target needs watching. In this case, though, we didn't know what BROKEN LAPTOP was going to do or even where he was going to go when he got to an airport.

BROKEN LAPTOP was in his late sixties. A devout Muslim, originally from Pakistan, he was rare because it's usually the young, self-radicalized, non-Muslim-born men that carry out attacks in the name of al-Qaeda or Islamic State. The older generation are wiser, less influenced by the propaganda. I was fairly sure he wasn't about to blow an aircraft up or martyr himself in the airport like the Glasgow attack. He was trying to leave the country. It wasn't my job to question why he was leaving, that was down to the wobbly heads back in Thames House wearing suits. My job was simple. Hunt them down, say what I see.

The team had nicknamed this operation Op JENGA after the wooden bricks balancing game. Together the West, with the US and UK at its core, stands strong. Interlocking with each other, passing intelligence and preventing attacks on both sides. We influence other countries' strategies like Australia, New Zealand and Canada, and together we keep the world a much safer place. However, if we or the US pulls the wrong brick out of the tower, the whole thing risks collapse.

Terrorists from Britain blowing up a transatlantic flight or the memorial spot for the Twin Towers would be a huge embarrassment publicly, not to mention the fight behind closed doors as to how we could let something like this happen. We're a tiny island, yet we've an impeccable record at keeping people safe, but if we didn't keep hold of everyone in this cell, the entire tower of bricks would come crashing down with no one wanting to pick up the pieces.

'Red team, permission?'

'Go ahead, Red team, no change, BROKEN LAP-TOP lane one of three still southbound MIKE ONE towards Junction TWO FOUR.'

'Roger, thanks. We have DRAGON CLOUD and HOME FARM under control in the area of Heathrow Airport. White team have SMALL WINDOW under control at Junction ONE FIVE on the MIKE ONE southbound and Blue team have STILL WATER, ROCKY CREEK and HEAVY CARPET under control in the area of Heathrow Airport. Red team OUT.'

That's all seven major players in this cell under control, with Heathrow looking like the destination for BROKEN LAPTOP now. The operations centre would be coordinating the intelligence coming back from the surveillance teams and passing it on to the intelligence officers. At this time of night Thames House would be fairly quiet but every officer involved in this operation would be at their desk, on the ground or working covert agents as hard as they could.

Based on the investigation so far, I wasn't sure the

service had enough evidence to arrest these guys and prosecute them in a secret court.

'TC, are you happy with the follow so far?'

Motorway follows are easy if you stay alert and plan. I had three vehicles in front of me, blocking BROKEN LAPTOP's mirrors from getting a full profile of me. At this time of night, I was using the high tail light of the van to lock on to so I could keep my distance. All the target would see were endless lights behind him.

'Yes, vehicle still lane one of three and I have three for cover. Speed back down to six five, seven zero miles per hour.'

'Roger that. Stations, I want to leave three cars with TC on the follow and get everyone else ahead at the service stations further down the motorway, I'm hoping BROKEN LAPTOP has a weak bladder and we can get close to him and tag his van too.'

This was a smart move, and highlights exactly what is needed from a team leader. As operators we all think ahead, we know exactly what kit to use, when we can push it and when we can't. We don't need organizing at all really, unlike other surveillance teams from non-covert agencies. But things like getting people ahead and being proactive in placing GPS trackers on BROKEN LAPTOP's van are the qualities of a good team leader, plus the ability to manage people like me.

'Just a thought – if he pulls into a services can we check for traces of explosives?'

'Good thinking, TC. Yes, we'll go for that. Charlie Five Three, acknowledge?'

'Charlie Five Three, roger the last and I'm with the follow.'

Another forty minutes of simple motorway driving and the predictions came true; BROKEN LAPTOP pulled into a services.

'That's an OFF, OFF, OFF. Vehicle on to the slip lane towards Newport Pagnell Services, speed down to THREE ZERO, THREE FIVE miles per hour.'

'Charlie Five Three, roger, let me know when he's settled and away from the vehicle, please.'

This was our chance to see if the van contained any explosives or ammunition.

'Roger that, vehicle moving towards the front entrance of the services now, I have control. Stations, hold back if you can.'

Ideally we would see BROKEN LAPTOP go inside the services then at the same time send someone in on foot to find him and watch everything he did including having a piss, while we checked the van in the car park.

'That's a STOP, STOP, STOP. Vehicle is parked just to the right of the entrance. Charlie Five Three for information he's nosey parked facing the motorway but there is a patch of grass directly in front of the van. And that's BROKEN LAPTOP out of the vehicle and walking towards the entrance of the services now, full beige shalwar kameez, I have direct on the exit and the vehicle but can't go with.'

'Charlie Five Three, roger, deploying now.'

'Seven Five is on foot towards the services, I'll give two tones when I have control.'

'Roger, thank you, stations, everyone radio silence until BROKEN LAPTOP back in his vehicle, please.'

It wasn't long before we got the signal that Seven Five had control of the target.

'Roger, Seven Five, you have control of BROKEN LAPTOP, can you give tones when he leaves?'

Another signal for yes.

'Roger, signal heard.'

Seven Five, still unable to talk, sent the urgent signal out on the radio.

'Signal heard – STAND BY, STAND BY.'

'From Charlie Nine One, I have control. BROKEN LAPTOP OUT, OUT and towards the vehicle.'

'Roger and Charlie Five Three is complete, no indication of explosives.'

'Roger, Base acknowledge, lights on.'

'Base, roger.'

'Vehicle is reversing, any station able to take this if he pulls straight on to the motorway?'

'TC, I'm at the garage towards the exit, if he drives straight out without stopping for fuel I can.'

The chances were slim that he was even remotely aware I'd followed him all the way down the M1 at this time of night, there's just a sea of headlights, nothing to stand out, but if he was going to notice something it would be now, when he'd been stationary.

'Roger, thanks, Charlie Four Three, I'll let him run to you if you can see the exit, if you get stuck just let me know.'

'Roger, yeah, I have the exit, no problem.'

'Vehicle now towards the garage and services exit back towards the slip with the MIKE ONE, running free, I'm not with.'

'Charlie Four Three, roger, I have control and that's ON, ON to the MIKE ONE southbound.'

The three of us left behind at the services stayed for nearly five minutes, using the toilet and grabbing what food we could, charging it to our MI5 credit cards. Each of us blanked one another when our paths crossed; the paranoia of not compromising yourself or others was ingrained into us.

As we rejoined the follow down the motorway I was starting to wonder what the goal was here. The van didn't show any signs of explosives or ammunition, I wasn't sure what the other teams had on the rest of the cell in terms of intelligence but if these guys were about to commit a terrorist attack surely executive action would now be in play.

'Base, permission?'

Ah, here we go.

'Go ahead, no change. Vehicle still southbound towards the MIKE TWO FIVE.'

'Stations, it's believed BROKEN LAPTOP will be joining the others at Heathrow Airport, we have Red and White team with Special Branch airside. Once confirmed on their flight to New York, we'll let them run and withdraw. Roger so far, any station?'

The team leader was almost instantaneous with his response.

'So far.'

'FBI and CIA teams will take them on once they hit US soil. Base OUT.'

I didn't like letting these guys run to the States; it was clear they were conducting a recce for the attack over there now. The intelligence officers must have enough evidence from Red and White team on the other targets to know the flight over to New York was going to be safe and they weren't going to try to take the plane down.

When we let targets run free to travel outside the country, we always see them through the border checkpoints, in this case airside. Once they have gone through the security checks and into the departures part of the airport and can't return back to the normal open area of Heathrow Airport, we leave them alone most of the time. If necessary, we're able to quickly get through to airside, as well as using the one-way glass you see at every checkpoint in airports. It comes in extremely handy when we need to confirm targets' identities when they're leaving the country, or arriving.

The rest of the journey down to Heathrow was straight-forward and Red team confirmed BROKEN LAPTOP was through the security gates and airside with the rest of the targets.

'Stations, cease and withdraw back for debrief. Acknowledge down the list, please.'

We were miles away from our starting point in Yorkshire; I knew it would be another night in a hotel tonight, making full use of my grab bag in the boot. It was starting to become a regular feature in my life, stay-ing away from home and living in hotels. The only bonus of this was my wife didn't have to spend as much on the weekly food budget because I was away and I had the service-issue credit card to keep me fed. Our daily food allowance with the service was about £50. That was my family's weekly food budget. What the service gave me to feed myself for a whole day while out on the ground if we had to stay away would feed all of us at home. I needed to be at home with my family. I missed them more and more each time I was away, but the more I was away the better off we would be.

Eventually the whole team reconvened and as the debrief ended we quickly discussed security and tactics before the other teams arrived for their debriefs.

'OK, we need to discuss what happened to me and TC up in Yorkshire near the mosque. As you all know, police undercover teams have been in the area lately cracking down on child grooming. Our friends in Special Branch told the ops room that while trying to find a target the police used a mosque car park to turn around in. While turning around they crashed into a car just as people were leaving the mosque after last prayers.'

'Fucking hell . . .'

Nick summed up our feelings quite well as the team leader continued to tell us the rest.

'I know, the police team didn't stop, they panicked and drove straight out as the crowd tried to close the gates thinking they were under attack from the National Front again. The police team smashed through the gates and drove off. Their car was a grey VW, same as ours. They thought the same police team was back, hence the reason they fucked our car up trying to kill us.'

'How can we stop this happening again?'

The team looked a bit sullen and serious as I asked the question. I didn't want to go through that again and it makes operating in the area incredibly difficult when the place is red hot and everyone is looking for white faces in cars that aren't local.

'Special Branch are setting up a compromise sheet that is internal to the police but which they will pass to us daily on the quiet. It's shit but we have to just be mega aware. Special Branch are dealing with local uniformed police and the community leaders to see what is being said about our incident but in terms of them knowing who we are I think we are OK.'

As we left the briefing room, picking our hotel details up, we exchanged banter with the other teams waiting to come in for their debrief.

'All right, you bunch of pricks! Lost any targets lately?'

'Hahaha! Fuck off, TC, but let us know when you want to join a real team!'

'Yeah, yeah, your fucking mum loves our team!'

As the laughter grew we made our way down to the underground garages, back to the cars to leave towards the hotel, and the other teams filed into the briefing room. I loved the banter between teams and within our own team. It's very military in its sense of humour, and almost any situation can be made better if you take the piss out of someone's mum.

Checking into the hotel a good thirty-minute drive across London, we used our alias names and cover company details and addresses. I was tired now. It didn't seem that long ago that I was inches away from being lynched in Yorkshire and now I was checking into a hotel in London using a false name, and I still hadn't spoken to my family to let them know I wouldn't be home today.

Walking to my hotel room, I made my usual mental note of fire exit routes and quick ways I could leave the building other than the main entrance. As I entered the room, I saw the familiar sight of fresh, clean bed sheets in the dim light. I was exhausted, mentally drained but I knew tonight I couldn't fall asleep. I was afraid, frightened that if I fell asleep I would have another nightmare. They were getting stronger and it was taking longer for me to regain my composure. If I climbed into bed for a proper night's sleep I knew I would plunge into the darkest corners of my mind.

I'm not a hard man, I don't have a reputation for being this urban street fighter, and when people think of me, I know they don't see a muscle-bound ninja. There are people in the world who show their teeth to display their strength and aggression and there are those who cower at the sight of that fierceness. I'm the relentless one, the scruffy runt who despite everything thrown at me remains positive in his mindset that anything can be achieved. When I joined the army I was at the back of the long runs in the hills, but I refused to give up. I weighed just 105 pounds as a boy soldier at the age of sixteen, but I would carry more than half that on my back on exercises and operations.

I wasn't a skinny boy turned Captain America type, I just refused to give up and be looked at as weak. Here I was, former Special Ops with the military, nearly five years' experience working in a Top Secret deniable unit in Northern Ireland and recruited to MI5 as a surveillance officer. And despite all that, I had tucked myself up in the corner of the room, back to the wall with a light purposely aimed in my face to prevent me from falling asleep because I was scared of what lay waiting for me if I closed my eyes.

I was a fucking joke.

Chapter Fifteen

Standing in the corner of our bedroom, it was like we'd been burgled. I was dripping with sweat and completely naked. I saw my wife sitting on the bed, holding her knees to her chest with genuine fear in her eyes, the type of fear I see when I'm operating on the ground.

'Are you OK? What happened?'

As I rushed over to her, she started crying. I now knew what had happened. I'd had another nightmare, but this was something more than a nightmare. I couldn't remember what had just occurred but it was clear I was reliving something and fighting something or someone. As I scrambled to get the bed covers off the floor to stop my wife getting cold, I could see the scrapes and rashes on my knuckles.

'Did I hurt you?'

'No, you just flew out of bed, shouting and hitting everything. We need to get you help. You're not sleeping.'

Putting her hand over my knuckles, I collapsed on to her like a newborn baby. It was only then I noticed my heart rate racing as I tried to switch my focus on to my wife's fingers running through my hair. What the fuck was happening to me? It felt like my mind was running a parallel life to the one I actually thought I was living. For some reason my brain wasn't processing or dealing with something properly. I wasn't hungry or dehydrated, and I was in good health physically. Was it some sort of brain injury or sleeping disorder?? Fuck knows, but one thing I was sure about: this had to stop. Not only were my operating skills on the line if I couldn't function properly, but I didn't want to be that person who scared his family.

We didn't have any internal doors on our house; we had scraped enough money together to buy our house but couldn't afford to finish the refurbishments at that moment so we made do with curtains over the door frames separating the rooms. I went to check on my son who I was praying had slept through all this. Picking my path to walk out of the room over the clothes, plugs and glasses of water I'd knocked over during my sleeping fight for survival, I pulled the curtain slightly to the side to see my son fast asleep on his back, mouth wide open, snoring as usual. Thank God for that.

'He's asleep. I'm so sorry. It was a nightmare. I'll ask for some help from a doctor in the morning.'

'You're meant to be deploying tomorrow afternoon, aren't you??'

My wife was right, and it stopped me in my tracks climbing back into bed. I could hide this from my team and try to crack on, but if this got any worse I risked hurting my family emotionally. No, fuck it. I wouldn't become that person who put their work before their loved ones. My wife believed in me, and I needed to get this sorted out. Anything, as long as it gave peace of mind to her. But I knew it would mean having to talk to a professional at some point, and God knows what they were going to say or diagnose me with. I just hoped there wasn't anything physically wrong with my brain.

That morning, sitting with my son downstairs while he watched cartoons, slowly starting to wake up, I thought about how I was going to approach this with the service. If there is a general medical problem, like you have food poisoning or tonsillitis, then we're allowed to see our normal family doctor. But, if our illness relates in any way to our work for MI5 then we have to see medical professionals in house who have Top Secret clearance so we can talk openly about our reasons for seeing them. Nurses, doctors, physios – basically anyone who service employees may need help from.

I knew I couldn't go to my team leader with this. We were meant to be deploying against Irish targets again and I'd nearly always end up in a pub drinking all day, keeping control of the targets while the rest of the team waited outside, ready to pick them up when they left. We had a welfare department within Thames House but I'd never thought I would be asking for their help. In true public-sector style, though, the service wanted to make sure it was seen to be looking after its employees, so the welfare people had a fair amount of power when protecting someone who needed help for whatever reason, whether that be financial or medical.

While Lucy was putting my son's cereal out, I went upstairs to make the phone call. The bedroom was tidy, all evidence of me freaking out in the night now gone, apart from the broken skin on my knuckles and my dented pride.

'Switchboard.'

I only had an extension number for the welfare team so I had to ring the main number for Thames House. It's manned twenty-four hours a day but the people answering the phone are specially trained not to give details away about the building, or which organization the telephone number belongs to, hence the 'Switchboard' welcome. Once you give an extension number that matches, they will ask for a name of whomever you want to speak to within that extension.

'869497.'

'Who are you trying to speak to?'

'Welfare.'

'One moment, please.'

I knew the call would be recorded; everything going in or out of Thames House or its regional operating centres is monitored and stored electronically.

'Sue speaking, how can I help?'

'My names TC, I'm A4 . . .'

I couldn't get past the opening line, my words just wouldn't leave my mouth and after a few seconds they wouldn't even form in my mind. I didn't know what to say.

'TC, do you need to talk?'

'Yeah, but I don't know . . .'

Fuck me, I was shit at this, I must have sounded like a right twat on the phone.

'Are you supposed to be deploying operationally today?'

The welfare team were well trained, and they knew virtually every department, its roles and the demands they faced. She knew if I was meant to be on the ground today I was at risk if something was on my mind.

'Yeah, I am. Nightmares. Having nightmares.'

'OK, don't worry, TC. Listen, I will speak to your group leader, let them know you can't come in today.'

Cutting her off, this panicked me massively. I hated the idea of letting my team down and, perhaps even more, I didn't want to miss out on the operation.

'No, I can go in, it's fine. I shouldn't have called.'

'TC, it's fine. Look, no one else will know. I'll make up a cover story for you and tell your group leader that a family member is ill and you need the day. That's OK, isn't it?'

In true typical spy style, we lie to our own to facilitate our goals. It was a story my group leader and team would buy easily, so I softened to her approach, and it gave me confidence that making this call was the right thing to do.

'OK, so now what? I need to get some sleep but I'm not sure what's happening.'

'Well, why don't you come in to talk at our offsite office? Have you got a team car?'

'Yeah, I've got a car with me.'

'Great, I'll text the address to your service mobile and when you get here press the intercom, and I'll come and get you. No one from A4 or A Branch as a whole is in this building so you won't be seen.'

278

Sue wanted to reassure me that this was in complete confidence. She gave the impression she'd dealt with operational staff before, and she knew that my primary concern was being seen talking to welfare by anyone in my team or A4. I'd done some questionable things in their eyes over the years, and it would be the nail in the coffin for me if I was spotted talking to welfare.

As I ended the call, Lucy walked into the bedroom with our son, typically upbeat and positive. I felt incredibly lucky to have a family like this.

'Not going on the ground today, just driving down to speak to welfare. Just to see if they can get me sleeping through. Hopefully won't be long.'

'That's good, just text me on your way back and we can have tea in the garden this evening, it's meant to be quite nice all day.'

Driving towards the offsite location to meet Sue, I felt weird. Really uncomfortable without my operational kit on, no covert radio, no passport and spare radio battery strapped to my ankle. I actually used the car's normal radio to listen to music on the way in. I'd never used this car's normal radio before because I'd usually be focused on the team's transmissions. This is what normal people must do when they drive to and from work.

I parked the car at a multi-storey roughly ten minutes' walk from Sue's building, I didn't want to risk anyone from A4 recognizing a team car, and if I was meant to be with a family member in hospital as part of this cover story I needed to make sure I didn't leave any loose threads. As I left the car park I walked a big loop around the streets, taking natural look-backs on my route at traffic lights. I had no problem walking into the most dangerous situations in the world with known killers, but put me en route to talk about personal shit and I become one of my jumpy targets, paranoid as fuck.

The text message from Sue said to press the buzzer marked number 5. This covert facility on a normal street in the centre of London was either hiding in plain sight with the number '5' on the intercom buzzer or it was simply how the numbers fell for welfare and I was drawing conclusions that out of the seven buzzer numbers on the intercom the one I needed was marked with a 5. Jesus, I needed to get a life.

'Hi, I'll be down in a few seconds.'

Obviously Sue had seen me on the semi-covert dome cameras above the large doors, which was a relief because I really didn't want to say who I was or what I was doing stood on the steps to this impressive old building.

I heard several locks being moved, then the door opened and I was met with a smile, the kind of motherly smile the other kids used to get at school. Sue ushered me in without any arrogance or the clinical manner I'd expected from something like this. Walking towards the next set of sealed bomb-proof doors, she scanned her pass and entered her pin code to give us access to the main stairs that led up to the fifth floor.

'Do you want some water or juice?'

'No, I'm good, thanks.'

So far, so good. I had answered a gentle question without clamming up, so maybe this wouldn't be as bad as I thought. Hopefully they would give me something to help me sleep and I could reset my brain activity to allow me to have normal dreams.

'OK, so you're going to be seeing a lady called Pam, she's lovely and has worked for the office a long time. She's cleared to talk to you; actually her husband used to be in G Branch and has a good understanding of A4.'

Waiting on the comfy chairs outside a group of small offices, this place felt a world away from Thames House but had gentle reminders that this was still very much a building hiding secrets. Every door had key-coded locks, no Security Service information on the walls about the purpose of its employees inside, all the stand-ard stuff you'd expect when inside offsite facilities. It didn't take long before a door opened and Pam wel-comed me with another smile, asking me to come into her office.

Now, usually when meeting someone for the first time professionally you'd be met with 'How can I help?' or 'This is what I do here and I can help you by . . . ' Not here. I was met with Pam sitting down in a chair about three feet away from me, smiling. Fucking smiling, noth-ing else, no words, no gesture for me to talk, nothing. I wasn't the one needing help, this crazy fucker was the one needing her head seeing to.

As Pam continued to look at me, smiling, saying noth-ing, I briefly avoided eye contact with her to take in my surroundings. Clocks absolutely everywhere, at least twelve behind her, all set to the same time but of differ-ing sizes and shapes. No digital clocks, which I found strange given the sheer amount in this small office, also how the fuck did she manage to keep them all in sync with each other; she must check them daily. I was starting to profile mad Pam, imagining her having 900 cats at home and switching the lights off and on twenty times before she could leave the room. There had to be something causing her to smile this way.

Five more minutes ticked by, and it felt like a lifetime, then I caught Pam's eyes still looking at me, smiling. It was like a switch had been flicked and I felt my bottom lip twitch; was I about to start crying? No way, I wasn't upset. The twitching got stronger as Pam continued her gaze. Was she some sort of Jedi, mind-fucking me into submission? I had to regain control, I didn't like this feeling of insecurity at all.

'What's with all the fucking clocks?'

Nothing, not even a flinch in her smile. Actually, thinking about it, she wasn't staring at me but I hadn't seen her blink for the entire time I was here. Ah, fuck me, she was a psychiatrist, she wanted me to talk first. Bollocks, welfare had made the link between me not sleeping and being an operator and decided to see if I was suffering mentally. I needed to front this out; if the service thought I was mentally unstable I would never get back out on the ground, and I wasn't ready to be retired yet.

'Have I wasted my time coming down here or what? You've brought me in to smile at me while I count how many clocks you have? Fuck this, I'm going. Shove your smiles up your arse.'

Standing up to leave, I pushed my chair back too aggressively and hit a bookshelf behind me.

'Shit, sorry.'

'Why are you pretending to be angry?'

The Jedi finally spoke and called me out straight away; she knew I was fronting this out to cover up the fact I'd got emotional. She must have seen my lip quivering. Tilting her head, she started her probing.

'You can either tell me why you're wearing a mask and pretending to get through this so you can get back to your team or you can talk to me here and we can get you some sleep.'

Adjusting the chair, I sat down, feeling emasculated. Pam had recognized what I was trying to do and, perhaps more importantly, she knew I needed help. I still don't know how she unlocked that emotion in me but it wasn't long before that upset feeling came flooding back tenfold.

'I, er, I'm having nightmares. It's scaring my wife.'

'What are they about?'

'I've no idea, I can't remember them. But, well, they're getting worse.'

Noticing the fading grazes on my knuckles, she nodded towards my hands.

'Are you lashing out during the nightmares?'

'I think so, yeah. Last night I just came to in the corner of the room, I can't remember the nightmare, though.'

'Tom—'

I interrupted her, I didn't want to be called by my proper name. It was too official. I was an operator, not a patient.

'It's TC, please. TC.'

'Sorry, TC. How long have you been known as that?'

'Since Ireland. I used to be in the army, Special Operations with the service over there. It's where I was recruited from.'

'You were recruited?'

'Yeah.'

'Wow, OK. Most people in A4 went through the application process. Not many are actually hand-picked now. Great. How did that make you feel?'

Oh, fuck's sake, here we go. This wasn't a normal chat to break the ice, I was being analysed here. I didn't trust her; she was clearly smarter than I was. Obviously no operational experience, but she'd got inside my head and triggered emotions I didn't even know I had. I was here, though, and if I didn't play this right I would never rejoin my team.

'How did it make me feel? Erm, not sure. I worked for the service unofficially and then I got given the opportunity to get officially badged as a surveillance officer, so jumped at it.'

'Who recruited you, maybe I know them?'

'Ian. Ian Grey.'

'Ah, I don't know that name. Most of the people I mix with are G Branch. Is he A Branch, I presume?'

She didn't know Ian was dead, she wasn't lying or pretending. If she was hiding the fact that she didn't recognize the name, Pam was extremely good at this game.

'Ian GREY, he died? Found dead in Northern Ireland? IAN GREY?'

My lip went again, and this time my eyes filled up with tears. I couldn't hide this or front it out any more. I couldn't stop giving answers either, because Pam the mad Jedi had somehow managed to pull on little strands within me, knowing which one would give her a specific response.

'Have you been having nightmares about Ian?'

My voice broke while I desperately tried to regain emotional control.

'No, I don't know. I can't remember them.'

'Tell me about the work in your team, anything that happened that has been particularly frightening.'

'Our worlds are totally different, you live in fancy London, the sun hits your face as you walk from the coffee shop into this office checking your clocks. You have no idea what my world is like.'

Sensing my armour going back up and me trying to deflect any more probing, Pam interrupted me.

'Tell me about your world, please.'

Her smiling stopped, her hooks were in now. I was frightened of what she was going to say at the end of the meeting.

'I'm going back to my team, aren't I?'

'TC, no, you're not. But this isn't the end of the world for you. Whatever has happened to you is affecting your personal life. Soon it could affect how you operate, which means you are a risk to yourself and your team.'

'I'm fine, I just need a decent night's sleep. Honestly, I'm fine.'

'OK, so say we put a plaster over this little cut. Maybe it heals and you don't have any more nightmares. But what if that cut becomes infected and you become seriously ill? Let's fix this now and get you sorted. I'll make sure your pay isn't affected.'

I would never see my team again. I knew they would carry on as if I didn't exist because they still had a job to do. I felt deflated, like I was shrinking. I'd lost my identity. Working in counter-terrorism was all I knew. The majority of my adult life up till this point had been stopping people doing evil things. I couldn't do anything else; I had no education or qualifications. I was drowning in debt and had a family to provide for.

'So I can't go back to my team because of nightmares? This is bollocks!'

'Have you heard of PTSD?'

'Of course I have, it's what you guys are calling shell shock or Gulf War syndrome. I don't have that.'

'Then you won't have a problem talking to the leading expert in PTSD, will you?'

'Let's make a deal, I talk to this expert and they say I don't have PTSD then I can go back to my team and we treat this as lack of sleep?'

I needed to get her onside and quick; if this went any further my career would be gone and I'd be kicked out of the service.

'OK, if the professor says it's not PTSD then we'll look at other treatment. But you have to be honest with him. He's a high-ranking officer within the military but he's one of the best psychiatrists in the country. No one in the world knows more about post-traumatic stress disorder than him. He's also vetted, so you can talk to him in this office.'

I felt like I'd shot myself in the foot asking for help. Having PTSD attached to me would officially mean I couldn't go on the ground or operate with any other agency again. Bigger than that, though, it meant admitting there was something wrong with me mentally.

'But while you're here, let's see if by talking you can figure out what's upsetting you, shall we?'

'Fine.'

Pam knew I was pissed off; I lacked the will to hide it from my face. I knew I couldn't trust her.

'Tell me about growing up, only child?'

Funny how when asked about my childhood people assume I was an only child. I must emit some sort of signal that suggests I had to fend for myself as a kid.

'Typical broken home, scruffy kid. Never bullied, the usual.'

'TC, if this is going to work you need to talk to us. You want to get back to your team? Then you have to convince us, without lying, that you're able to return.'

I waited for her to ask questions, but she was right. I had to make them believe I was good to go again. This was going to be hard, opening up to someone I didn't know. I'd spent decades cementing feelings and experiences away to protect those around me. Removing that armour plating completely would be difficult, maybe impossible but if I didn't do this I could potentially lose the most important thing in the world – my family.

'So, tell me about your parents.'

'My dad was in the army. He and my mum were in Hong Kong when my sister was born. I wasn't looked after that well. My sister is a lot older than me and moved out as soon as she could. Sometimes I'd go and stay with her in squats.'

Waiting for some sort of response on Pam's face to gauge whether or not this was what she needed to hear, I waited for the next question,

'Did you join the army following your father's footsteps?'

Fucking hell, this was going to be a long day, but I was here and fighting for my career. Pam would sense if I was lying, so I needed to be honest and bare all. Fuck.

'I suppose so, in a way. Really I just wanted to belong to a family. Be around people who thought the same as me and looked after each other. I pretty much raised myself from an early age. My dad drank a lot.'

'And what about your mother?'

'I don't know the reason, maybe because of the way my dad got when he was pissed or because she had to work to bring in enough money to put food in the cupboards, but she didn't pay much attention to me. As soon as I could join up, I did.'

Her body positioning changed as she hooked her ankles underneath her bum sat on her chair, as if she was enjoying listening to me.

'How old were you when you joined the army?'

'Sixteen, straight from school.'

'Your father, was he ever violent towards you?'

'Not really. Plenty of telling me to fuck off and abandoning me on the street so he could go to the pub, but he never hit me.'

'OK, tell me about your time with A4, how did you find the training?'

'Training was easy, it's just a case of learning the terminology and how the methods and tactics differ from the military.'

I could sense Pam was about to pull on another loose strand here.

'Must be hard to switch off, being trained to such a high level of observation?'

'Erm, I suppose so. But I've always been like that for as long as I can remember.'

'During your training you're given hyper-vigilance, a skill that allows you to do an incredibly important job keeping this country safe. However, unless you have a way of switching that off, your brain becomes tired and struggles to cope. During sleep, your brain will file away memories, that's what your dreams are.'

She was starting to make a lot of sense, and I was guilty of not talking about things or taking time out to switch off. Truth is, I didn't have time to take up a hobby or go out with the family. I was always working.

'Yeah, I get that. The pace of operations at the minute is horrendous. We just don't get time.'

'Can you remember any traumatic events you might have experienced?'

'Traumatic? Not to me, but plenty of other people would class as frightening, but we all have different levels of awareness. Something I find normal could well scare the shit out of the local shopkeeper, couldn't it?'

'You're right, TC, we do have differing thresholds. But if someone finds they go through a traumatic experience, the natural reaction may be to cry, scream or shout and then talk about it. That way the brain can process it all. People who tend to lock it all away and bound onto the next traumatic experience can end up with PTSD. At that point the brain no longer recognizes what is real and what isn't. A nightmare becomes very real because the memory banks can remember something similar actually happening.'

The Jedi was back and she waited for me to say something. She knew exactly how to control me, and I felt impossibly weak and unable to deflect her questions any more. I could feel the tears streaming down my face but only realized snot was coming out of my nose when Pam handed me a fistful of tissues.

'OK, TC. Take as long as you want. I'm going to speak to Sue and sort it out so you can go home. Don't worry about pay, we'll make sure it's not affected. When you're ready, go home and we'll post you a letter out with a date to meet the professor to talk some more, OK?'

I was desperately trying to compose myself, but I couldn't stop crying. Whatever she'd unlocked in my head, it was working, but I didn't want it to. I needed this to stop so I could get back out on the ground with my team. I was fighting for my professional and personal mental freedom, but I was losing this fight; I didn't know if I had what it took to defeat whatever this was, or whether I really had PTSD or not. I didn't want to admit I had a mental health problem.

Chapter Sixteen

Driving home back to my family, I felt numb and vulnerable. I'd let someone in MI5 see my emotional state, a weakness I didn't know I had. The problem was that person was a psychiatrist and, despite her lack of operational experience protecting this country, she was one of the most powerful people in the service. One quick phone call and a few signatures from her would remove me from operational duty and ensure I would never walk through the security tubes at Thames House again.

I couldn't seem to compose myself. It was this strange mix of anger and sadness, I was constantly fighting back the tears but ready to scream and shout at a driver in front of me if they didn't react to the green traffic light quick enough. I was given a prescription of diazepam, which I was immediately suspicious of; with our routine drug testing something like this would almost certainly mean I'd never return to operational work.

When I explained to Lucy that night what had happened, she saw this as a positive step. I knew she was right, of course; our family and health comes first before anything and it was that positivity that I held on to as I desperately tried to focus on beating this. I refused to research PTSD. Its symptoms and the restrictions it had over people didn't interest me. I believed if I focused on something I would attract that thing, and if I focused on being who I was and staying strong and fit I'd be exactly that. Focusing on negativity would ensure I'd crumble.

I was shit at taking medication. I've never been able to swallow tablets. During my time in the military we had to take anti-malaria tablets in the desert. I stopped trying to take mine three days into an eight-month tour. I would rather risk getting malaria than take the tablets. I just couldn't swallow them, until Lucy showed me a really easy simple method. That brief moment of simplicity was golden. She told me to place the tablet in between my front teeth while clenching my back teeth together, then to drink some water, and the tablet slid down with ease. All these years of running around the world with guns, hunting mass murderers and terrorist leaders, and it was only now that my wife with the gentlest of touches showed me how to beat a tablet half the size of a Tic Tac.

'You fucking spaz!'

I nearly spat the tablet back out with laughing. It was exactly what I needed to hear; I couldn't bear it if I was treated like a victim, and after all I still didn't know what was up with me, but having my wife take the piss and make fun of me was exactly the therapy I needed right then.

I'd never done drugs before, which for someone who grew up the way I did was a miracle. I was surrounded by people taking drugs at school, even dealing on the playground. I would watch as the older kids passed wraps of cannabis to each other when they asked for a 'Henry'. I didn't tell the teachers it was happening. I didn't do anything, just watched.

It didn't take long before the diazepam kicked in. I suddenly felt drowsy,

'I'm going to bed.'

Standing up to walk up the stairs, my body felt drunk and tired but my mind still sharp. It was like my body had been shut down but not my brain. I made it to the bed and collapsed in a heap, too heavy to even cover myself up, and my muscles continued to fail me as they completely relaxed. What the fuck was happening? I thought this medication was designed to help me sleep, not lock me in some sort of ridiculous torture.

I could barely move, eyes slammed shut and for all intents and purposes this body was asleep. My brain wasn't, though, and instead of being sharp to the environment around me I could only see my memories as the different parts of my brain tried to process everything. I remembered Pam talking about this and started to repeat what she had said, this was normal. The images I could see now in this dreamlike state were exactly what I had to do to heal.

I hated this, hours and hours of the window of the car smashing, turning my head to see the Special Branch officer's face when I dislocated his elbow as I smashed his head against the windscreen; he morphed into the director telling me of Ian's death, and casting my gaze out of the broken windscreen I see Stu's bike on the floor leaking oil and other fluids, except it's not oil, it's Stu's blood filling the street in front of me. It goes on and on in a loop, I can't fight it or force myself to get up to stop the memories. It's like a horror film happening with me as the main character, except some of the events aren't happening in the right way and starting to merge into others. Suddenly I'm outside the mosque as the riot police close in, I turn to run and all the players from the operation we nicknamed Op JENGA are standing in front of me, laughing. A huge bomb goes off, leaving a massive crater in the ground, and as the smoke and debris settle I see the Russian, DIRTY BOOT, talking to SHARP PENCIL, discussing how they were going to kill me.

I wake up to the sound of the front door closing. My wife was on the school run. I had a massive headache, and the bedsheets were soaked with my sweat. Severe dehydration from a combination of the diazepam and losing about 800 litres of sweat in the night was causing the throbbing pain in my head. As I hauled my body out of bed I heard the crinkle of paper under my elbow. It was a note left by my wife. 'Be back soon, then we'll go for a walk. Love ya.'

Showered and changed, I was still clumsy, like I'd been drinking all night and in that middle ground of not hungover but not yet sober. Except I hadn't been drinking, I'd been heavily sedated because I was fucking mental. I made the decision there and then not to take any more prescription tablets until I'd seen this professor. I needed to be sure what this was so I could fight it myself, not artificially.

It didn't take long before the letter came through with the appointment details, same building but this time meeting the professor. He wasn't MI5, but he was a high-ranking officer within the military. He was widely known as a leading expert on post-traumatic stress and the impact dangerous work has on the mind. It was only a couple of days' wait until I got an independent verdict on what the fuck was wrong with me but I refused to take any more medication, it was like being in a horror-filled coma.

The next two nights' sleep went relatively peacefully; I was jumping and twitching a lot apparently but not thrashing or shouting in my sleep. Maybe the worst was over and I would be able to rejoin my team after all. I was going to fight my case as hard as I could with the professor and make sure he knew I was mentally strong enough to return to operations again.

Sue met me as I pressed the number 5 on the intercom just like last time. I sat outside a different door this time as Pam's office was closed. I presumed it was empty, apart from the millions of clocks all ticking in sync. I was greeted by the professor as he opened the door to his office.

'TC, is it?'

Shaking his hand firmly, I replied with a smile, 'Yeah, nice to meet you.'

I was determined to show no weakness. We sat down in his makeshift office, closing the door, nothing in the room but two chairs and his bag. Not a clock in sight, thank fuck.

'So, let me first introduce myself. I'm not a member of the Security Service. I'm an officer in the Royal Navy. I deal a lot with traumatic stress injuries primarily in the military, but occasionally with members of the intelligence agencies. I have no influence over your career. My aim today is to talk to you and discuss anything that might be troubling you or causing you not to sleep. Sound good?'

'Yeah, no problem, quicker we get done the sooner I can get to my team.'

'Yeah. TC, I want you to be completely honest with me during this visit. Welfare have passed me the notes from your previous session with Pam, and they have cross-referenced that with your group leader and the operations you have been involved with. The more we talk, the better the report I submit and the better chance you have. If you hide anything or try to front it out, it will be reflected on this report. If I say, "TC couldn't open up properly", then it shuts that particular door. See what I'm trying to say?'

I was backed into a corner here. The senior guys in A4 and welfare had obviously been talking and passed each other information about my operations, things that might have been particularly frightening. The service wasn't trying to burn me, they were trying to help, I knew that. But I was caught slap bang in the middle between opening up and risking God knows what pouring out of me or trying to play the game and tell them some bullshit in the hope they bought it so I could return to my team.

The professor gave me a minute to think about things as he went to get some water before he started with his questions. Getting back on the ground was all I wanted, but if I did manage to fool these guys into thinking I was operationally fit, would that really be the best outcome here? Last time I trashed the bedroom and frightened the shit out of my wife, and then there was the night in the hotel during the Russian job, hiding in a corner because my brain was playing tricks on me. All that could become worse if I didn't let these guys do their job. But would helping the professor do his job properly put mine at risk?

He walked back in the room with two bottles of water.

'We good to go, then?'

He wanted an unofficial nod from me that I was going to tell him the truth.

'Yeah, let's go.'

Giving me a smile that suggested he wasn't expecting that from me, he started taking notes as we went over my family history and role with Special Operations in Northern Ireland. We skipped over that quite quickly; he knew what events to ask questions about and he was looking for reaction. I made the decision to be completely honest to him, and whatever happened now was out of my control. I was an operator, I hunted on the streets for people who want to do us harm and it was all I knew. But at home I had a family that loved me despite me being away all the time; they loved the real me. It's about time I found out who that person really was.

'Tell me about your nightmares, in fact first, before we go into that, does the diazepam help at all?'

'Not really, no, it switches my body off but my mind stays alert. It feels like I'm trapped wide awake in a dead body. All my nightmares start happening like I'm watching a film but my eyes are closed. If that makes sense?'

'Absolutely makes sense, it's your brain's way of

shifting all the information it's taken in through your senses and filing it away so it can recall it at a later date.'

He started to explain how the different parts of the brain work and why traumatic events are sometimes misconstrued by the brain leading to PTSD, but to be honest he mentioned two really big words and I switched off immediately. I didn't want a lesson in Latin, I wanted fucking fixing.

'Tell me a bit more about that nightmare film, because up to date you haven't been able to remember, is that right?'

'Yeah, I never remember them usually. It starts off with one event then it morphs into another, sometimes certain people or targets would be in a different situation, like these cunts from a job we did ages ago, a cell planning to blow up a shopping centre in Manchester, they also wanted to blow up the gathering at the 9/11 anniversary in New York, in my nightmare they ended up laughing to a Russian we stopped stealing some tech.'

'And have you been on operations recently with any of these targets? Reason I ask is your memory could be trying to file it all away neatly but might be struggling if you're still involved with seeing them?'

'Yeah, no. The cell was arrested and some deported to the States, the Russian we kicked back to Moscow so I've not worked against them since.'

'And during those operations, TC, did anything happen that may have caused you some stress or anxiety, maybe even subconsciously?'

The professor knew about us getting attacked in the

car on Op JENGA. Bastard. My team leader must have filled a report when the car was repaired or the ops centre passed it up the chain, describing how a police fuck-up nearly got me pulled out of the car when that mob in Yorkshire smashed the window. Pausing for a moment, I tried to think through my response. The professor beat me to it.

'TC, listen, mate. You've been in the military, you know how to play the game. In my experience with the intelligence agencies, you need to be honest. If something frightened you, then say so. What is it you guys say? Something about a secret only staying a secret . . .?'

'If more than one person knows a secret, it is no longer a secret.'

'That's it. TC, your group leader has gone through your operational file with the welfare team here. Pam and Sue have passed me the key events they think may be stressors. I'm not here to end you. If you are suffering with PTSD, trust me, you need my help.'

I struggled to swallow as I took a swig of water, my lip twitching again like some pathetic schoolboy. How the fuck did these cunts do it? He knew, just as Pam did, what questions to ask to trigger a response from me; a response I didn't even know I was capable of. My nose started to run as tears slowly crept to the corners of my eyes, and the professor made one last gentle nudge.

'Having a group of angry men trying to kill you can't be easy to deal with, especially when you didn't have time to talk about it?'

I couldn't talk now. Head in my hands, the tears were

in full force. Completely uncontrollable. I tried to regain some dignity as I cleared my throat, straightening up and looking him in the eye before he hit me again.

'Did you talk to anyone when you heard about Ian's suicide?'

Shooting out of my chair, I felt the blood in my veins about to burst out. I could snap this fucker in half, fear and sadness instantly swapped for aggression and destruction.

'He didn't kill himself!'

'And then there's Stu the biker . . . How did that make you feel?'

I didn't even realize I was losing my footing as I stumbled backwards and hit the office wall. Sliding down, my thigh hit the edge of the metal bin that was in the corner of the room, and the room started to spin as I sat surrounded by waste paper from the bin, the chair I was in now upturned on the floor in front of me. I felt weak and could feel that I was losing the strength to hold my head up. I was passing out. The professor knelt down next to me, but I could only just hear his words, like I was underwater. He put his hands on my chest and right shoulder, and it was then I noticed how fast my breathing was. I was hyperventilating.

After a few minutes I came to with the professor holding an oxygen mask over my face and Sue from the welfare team in the office.

'Tom – Carl – Marcus, can you hear my voice?'

Nodding and pulling the mask away from my face, I tried to stand up. 'Yeah, not sure what happened.'

'That, my friend, was a classic, although extremely violent, anxiety attack.'

As Sue left the office the professor pulled my chair upright and sat me down.

'I deliberately pushed a few buttons there, I'm sorry. But I needed to see what your body did when it remembered certain events. One more question, and it's an important one. Do you ever see or hear things that aren't there? Visual or audio intrusion?'

I flinched as I thought about the hotel room, hearing what I thought was a transmission in my ear when it was the TV, and later that night waking up to fight the invisible hand I thought was attacking me. I didn't need to say anything, my small but very telling reaction did the talking for me.

'OK, I'll take that as a yes.'

Kneeling down in front of me, the professor adjusted himself to get a lock on my gaze; he wanted to make sure this message sank in.

'TC, you have all the symptoms of PTSD. Your group leader has told us you're hyper-vigilant, which for a surveillance officer in MI5 is crucial, I suppose, but it means you see absolutely everything and when that happens you start to see things that aren't there, because your brain is filling in gaps from previous experiences. You're having nightmares based on traumatic events that you haven't had time to deal with. You need treatment and a lot of it.'

I was done, this was it. No more belonging. This was a fucked-up world, dark, dangerous and totally unforgiving, but it was my world. I didn't want to leave it, but the professor wasn't quite finished yet.

'We need to treat you with medication and cognitively with therapy like EMDR through a specialist local to you. TC, this is going to get a LOT worse before it can get better. As the treatment starts to let your brain do its job and work things out it will unlock more and more that you've been hiding away from.'

Imagining I was about to be carted off in a straitjacket to some mental asylum, I wanted the ground to swallow me up. In fact, no, that's bollocks, I wanted a magic pill to make all this mental health shit to go away so I could be normal again. I wished I had never asked for help now. If I had just found some way of coping with the nightmares I could have avoided all this shit and the bollocks that was to come as a result of whatever therapy these experts were going to throw at me.

I felt ashamed. I'd let my family and the team down. I wasn't a complex guy, intense maybe but not complex. I wanted to do two simple things, provide for my family and protect them. I was starting to struggle to be able to provide properly for them and the vines of debt had taken a stranglehold around me, tightening ever more every month, and now I was about to lose the ability to protect them.

I started working in counter-terrorism by accident. I never fitted into the mainstream; even in the military I was always labelled as the 'keen' one. During my time with Special Operations I came top of my selection course despite being the youngest. I didn't really fit in there either because yet again I was 'too serious'. The operations I was involved in, for my part anyway, went without a hitch. Even my weapons work on the ranges was considered an example of 'how to do it'. I wasn't some sort of super soldier warrior, I just loved this work and being part of this world. It's all I knew and for some reason my brain had decided to have a fucking fit. I couldn't do anything else, I didn't want to.

'TC, I can see by your body positioning that you hate me, but I want to be honest with you. The operational experience you have and doing this sort of work from such a young age is, well . . .'

I didn't want a pep-talk or praise for jobs I've been involved in. The professor was looking for words to pick me up before he sent me on my way, but I wasn't in the mood.

'Listen, if I wanted fucking medals I'd have joined the SAS. I don't want your sympathy, this is complete bollocks and you know it is. I have a few nightmares. Who the fuck wouldn't spaz out a few times dealing with this every day?'

'OK, so you're free to go home. I will of course send you a copy of my report and I'm presuming the ladies here will find and send you details of the specialist to see locally soon.'

As the professor stood up to shake my hand, I turned my back on him and walked straight out of that office. He was a professional and an expert in his field, but the people in this welfare department had absolutely no idea what it takes to keep the country safe fighting people who sometimes want to die in order to achieve their goals. As I walked straight past Sue, she made some remark suggesting she was there for me if I needed anything, but, ignoring her, I continued to the security doors. I was fucking done with this place. I'd given everything to ensure the very people in this building and the country as a whole stayed safe, and when my armour showed signs of becoming brittle I was retired without a second thought.

Explaining the whole situation to Lucy that night, I was fuming, and my core temperature was through the roof as I struggled to keep my voice down while my son lay asleep upstairs. My wife instantly brought me back down to earth and made me realize that actually this could be a good thing.

'But they are going to help you with someone close to here? And keep your pay while you get better?'

'Yeah, but I won't be able to go back to the service after this!'

'So fucking what?!? Listen, you can do ANYTHING! You've done your share, get better and let's move on. You're NOT surveillance, you're NOT MI5, you're a great husband and an even better dad. You can do ANYTHING.'

Lucy was right, I could do anything. But what? Can't be much call at the job centre for spies who've been trained by Special Forces to kill people.

'But what?? All I know is this stuff.'

'We'll figure that out, use this therapy whatever it is, and then we'll make a plan, OK?'

She was right, she's always right. I had to swallow my pride and go through the motions with this therapy. If it worked then maybe I'd become a better person. Family mattered more to me than anything. The next morning I got a phone call from the unarmed combat instructor from the SAS who had witnessed me taking out the Special Branch officer in the car during situation awareness training. After we exchanged brief pleasantries he offered his support.

'Listen, I heard about you taking some personal leave from the teams. Everything OK, mucker?'

'Yeah, erm, sort of. Not been sleeping great, got to see a specialist.'

'Mucker, PTSD is a fucking lottery. I know the strongest men in the world, some absolute monsters. There is nothing you can do, it's like a stray bullet. You can be in a thousand contacts and never get hit, then out of nowhere you take a round and you hit the deck. No shame in it, it's a fucking minefield, the longer you're in it the bigger the chance of getting hit.'

He summed it up perfectly, and it gave me a sense of self-preservation. It took some of the blame I was imposing on to myself away too, but I still had one huge hurdle to get over. My 'illness' was a mental one, something people couldn't see. In the military if you have your legs blown off saving someone's life then you'll be a hero and honoured accordingly with medals and thanks. But work undercover on the streets in Top Secret operations and develop post-traumatic stress disorder as a result of your work, and you get nothing. No medals, no thanks. The only thing you do get is suspicion from people who question whether you are actually 'ill' or not.

Just like the appointment with the professor, it only took a few days to get an appointment letter through for the specialist, with the warning that I wasn't allowed to disclose who I worked for or what I actually did for the service, which was going to make it nearly impossible to use the treatment to any effect. My wife took me to my first session with him, which was about a ten-minute drive away from our house. I was starting to panic. My meetings with Pam and the professor had resulted in me either crying or needing oxygen. This specialist was trained to unlock my memories so I could deal with them properly. I didn't want that. Whatever I wasn't remembering, I was sure there was a reason for it. I'd ring-fenced those experiences for a reason.

Thankfully, though, this time, unlike my assessment with Pam, the meeting with the mental trauma expert went as it should do when people meet for the first time professionally, although I had some explaining to do.

'Tom, I specialize in helping people with traumatic events. Before this I was a police officer; I've helped people deal with seeing murders, rape, abuse, right the way through to a car crash. So there isn't much I haven't heard or helped people cope with.'

'OK, great, I take it my employer has paid you already and it's all sorted?'

'Yes, all sorted out, paid very quickly. Just a question about your employer. The woman I spoke to on the phone about you, Sue, was reluctant to give me any information about the treatment you need, the trauma you have experienced or in fact your full name.'

Waiting for a response from me, David already suspected who I was. He was an ex-copper so being cagey about simple things like my name and what I do obviously piqued his interest.

'Did she tell you who my employer was?'

'Only that you work for the government.'

Sensing I was retreating even further into myself, he offered some reassurances.

'Tom, I don't care about what you did, who you worked for. But I do need to know your trauma, I want to treat you properly. I can't do that unless you tell me exactly what's happening. The more honest you are, the better results we will get and the faster you recover.'

Taking a glance around the room, I notice his phone next to him, and a computer that was switched off. Crucially I was looking for anything that could be recording this conversation.

'Are you recording this session?'

'No, Tom, sometimes I send people back into a meditative state to their trauma and I record what they say to play it back to the patient, but I would always ask permission first and it doesn't go outside this room.'

'David, what I'm about to say can NOT be repeated and I'm only telling you so I can get better, I NEED to get better.'

'Of course, Tom. All I want is for you to get back to who you are.'

'OK, I, er . . . This is difficult for me to say because I've never had to tell anyone before.'

Patiently waiting for me to untangle my tongue and say who I was and what I did, David looked on as I saw one of his many mental health professional certificates behind him among all the books on complicated subjects I'd never even heard of. I made the decision there and then that if I was ever going to move on with my life and find out who I really was I would have to shed this cloak of secrecy. I had to tell him.

'I'm MI5, Security Service.'

David may have been a leading expert in treating mental trauma but he wasn't that good at hiding his thoughts; his eyes widened. He was clearly shocked.

'Surveillance officer, to be exact. I've been having nightmares, I've been seen by two people already and they have mentioned PTSD and hyper-vigilance or something.'

'Thank you for being honest with me. I've never met someone in MI5 before, not that I know of anyway!'

Trying to lighten the mood and make me laugh, he continued with his initial assessment of me before deciding what the best course of treatment would be.

'Hyper-vigilance is somewhat at the core of PTSD, but there are varying degrees of the disorder, depending on whether you are suffering with one single event or a culmination of a lot of events.'

I twitched in reaction to the suggestion of a series of traumatic events, and David picked up on it straight away.

'I'm guessing by your reaction then it's a series of events. If you wouldn't mind I'd like to get a handle on your hyper-vigilance and what exactly you're looking for. Would that be OK?'

I reluctantly agreed. I had to go with whatever he suggested now.

'All I want to do is walk around the block here, it takes about fifteen minutes and it's a lovely day. While we walk around I want you to describe to me what you can see. That's it. No tricks, just be honest.'

Fifteen minutes of walking, I could do that. Piece of piss, this therapy, I just hoped he gave me the all-clear quickly so I could tell Thames House I wasn't mental any more and stayed in with a chance of keeping my job.

We walked back outside; this area was very affluent. I'd love to be able to afford to live here one day.

'Right, Tom, let's walk and just talk to me as if I was a close friend of yours. I won't interrupt. What can you see?'

'OK, I know from the map study before I arrived that we are walking north-east on May Lane. Visibility is good. Street is clear, no pedestrians on foot, no one in the vehicles ahead. Bus stop twenty metres away, which is five metres prior to the next junction. House to our right, number 54, has window open on the top floor, no lights on.'

This was incredibly easy. David continued to listen and we walked round and we probably had another five minutes before we were back at the starting point of this big loop.

'One unidentified male standing at the bus stop on the west side, forty-five to fifty years old, chubby build, blue suit jacket, blue jeans, five foot eight to five foot ten white male, no threat. We have a black Mercedes, VRN YANKEE FOUR THREE ONE MIKE OSCAR TANGO, tinted windows, parked up on the east side facing north, engine running, driver's window slightly open, possible threat.'

I didn't like this car being here, it stood out. Quiet posh neighbourhood like this, it looked like a drug dealer's car to me. David wasn't in the best of shape given his age so I positioned myself between him and the car and took half a pace in front to deal with anything that might come from the car.

'Five metres from the vehicle now, smoke coming from the driver's window.'

As we walked past I could see through the dark tint of the window just enough to see the driver was a woman smoking and looking at Facebook on her iPhone. We continued to our starting point and finished our walk.

As we sat back down in David's office he was slightly out of breath. Composing himself, he went on to give me his thoughts on our walk. 'Tom, great day, isn't it ? About time we had some sunshine!'

Smiling, I couldn't agree more; the British weather had really been on form lately so it was nice to be outside without getting piss wet through for once.

'What's obvious to me is that you see everything as if you're working. The detail you see and how quickly you absorb your surroundings is incredible. You were pointing out things I didn't even notice, even in the police I couldn't give that much information out. But, and this is an important point, your perception of what's happening is on a whole other level.'

Pulling a pen out of his drawer, he started to draw on a paper flip chart behind him.

'OK, simple graph: number one at the bottom is someone just waking up, nice and relaxed and still a bit dopey. In the middle at number five is someone walking into a surprise birthday party and the lights flicking on everyone shouting "Happy Birthday!" Adrenaline rushing and shock, but a happy shock.'

I knew where he was going with this but I certainly didn't like what I thought was coming.

'And at the top is number ten, the seconds prior to and immediately after someone having a near-miss crash, the wheels lock up and they narrowly avoid having an accident. Adrenaline focusing the mind and making them extremely aware of their surroundings as the body enters fight or flight mode. This can only be sustained for a few seconds. The impact on the body is too high to sustain.'

Pausing to look at me briefly, he takes his pen back to the paper and makes his point.

'Tom, you're up here at eleven, but ALL the time.'

David sat down and changed the tone of his voice. He wanted to reassure me I was in the right place to get proper treatment.

'When I take people who've experienced incredibly traumatic events around here doing exactly the same thing, they all give similar descriptions. It's a sunny day, it's warm, the pavements are clean, it's very quiet, the flowers are in full bloom.'

David was trying to make me smile but I couldn't help feeling worse, like I was some sort of freak.

'You didn't mention any of that. You gave me a full breakdown as if you were working. Is that how you talk in MI5?'

'When I'm with my team we let each other know everything we need to, constantly. You see something and question it; what's missing that should be here, what's here that shouldn't be. Everything we need to know to do our job.'

'What concerns me is you're like this all the time? Tell me about the security of your family, how do you protect them while you're away, alarms, stuff like that?'

'Yeah, obviously doing the job I do I need to make sure they are safe while I'm away so: alarms, son goes to nursery with a GPS tracker sewn into his pocket, cameras at home and another tracker in his sleeping bag at night. My wife and I have a sentence we use if something is wrong and she will meet me at a prearranged location. Standard stuff.'

David was lost for words. He didn't know how to respond to what I'd just described.

'If your family is in real danger when you're away or because of what you do then surely you need to find a different profession?'

'It's not that they are in danger, but prevention is better than cure, isn't it? I'd rather if something did happen

313

we had things in place to stop it happening or react to it quickly.'

As the session ended, David left me with a metaphor to think about until next week's session.

'You won't find a zebra with PTSD. Think about how a zebra goes about its business having to think about lions hunting it. It'll still go to that watering hole, and carry on its normal zebra stuff. Some will have escaped incredibly violent attacks from predators, and some if not all zebras will have seen family members eaten by packs of lions. But, they will still go about their business, always aware of the threat, but they won't see it everywhere they trot. Human beings have something called imagination, not shared by other animals. It allows us to create machines, to dream about building spaceships landing on the moon, but it also imagines threats based on our past experiences, raising someone's threat perception far too high.'

My emotionless face probably said it all. I didn't want to be told I was imagining things, because being the way I am kept people like David alive.

'Your work probably needs you to be like this, but when you're walking around in the sun in a nice neighbourhood you don't need to be remembering vehicles or people at the bus stop and definitely don't need to be protecting me from a parked-up car. See what I'm saying?'

Walking out the door with my appointment slip for next week, I gave him a quick one-liner and left.

'Let me think about it.'

As well as seeing David once a week, I had to see two

doctors within the NHS too. I was under heavy medication to allow my brain to switch off and to let me sleep a bit better, but as the weeks went on and my sessions with David unlocked more memories my PTSD got worse. Walking into town to see the NHS consultant who was in charge of my medication, I was starting to withdraw drastically from the outside world. The audio and visual intrusions were, as the professor predicted, getting worse by the day.

'STAND BY, STAND BY!'

The noise from my radio was deafening as I desperately tried to turn it off before I got another transmission. People walking beside me must have thought I'd been stung by a wasp or something, because my body folded under the pain. Except there was no radio, no transmission. I was hearing things again. A flashback, but just audio this time.

I was having visual flashbacks a lot. My wife knew when I was having one because I would start to dissociate from my surroundings and not look at what everyone else was focusing on. It happened for the third time that day in front of the consultant who was trialling my medication, trying to get the best results for me, after I had told him that taking diazepam in such high dosages was shutting my body down but not my mind.

'Tom, what's wrong? Tom can you hear me OK?'

Apparently he'd been trying to gently rouse me for a few minutes before I responded sharply, 'What, what do you want?'

'Tom, what did you just see?'

'Briefing officer sat in the chair, couldn't work out what she was saying.'

'How many visions or sounds are you getting a day now?'

'Had one on the way in, thought I had my radio on, this one just then and one this morning. Feel like it's getting worse.'

I was exhausted, my eyes were tired and my brain felt like it was running on empty. I couldn't see an end to this and needed it all to stop. I felt like I was starting to become reliant on medication, addicted. The consultant wrote another prescription slip out for me, increasing the dosage again.

'Tom, the dosage I'm giving you now will mean your body will become dependent on them. But we'll reduce the dosage gradually over the next six months once we start getting results and your flashbacks and nightmares ease off.'

As the months rolled by I was sleeping less and less and wouldn't leave the house. I couldn't drive through having too many flashbacks. I had lost any will or motivation to believe in myself.

Standing in the clinic waiting for the latest bag of tablets, I was surrounded by sick people, coughing and sniffing. I'd had enough, no more. I wasn't going to use chemicals to force my brain to get better. I was the key to recovery not those tiny fucking tablets. I walked out of the clinic, leaving my prescription of strong sedatives behind.

I'd been having treatment for over a year, and now I'd

finally decided if I was going to beat this I would do it the way I always did things. My way. I felt aggressive, angry at the world, at myself for letting PTSD take over my life. I was putting my trainers on, and my wife saw how quickly I was moving as I was about to head out the door.

'This will be good for you, run as hard as you fucking can.'

Putting my headphones on, I was determined to reset my brain and body on this run. I was always a fairly quick runner even with weight on my back, despite my small frame. I was an endurance runner in the military and although I was only going to run three miles now, I was determined to run at such a pace that I would be sick, if not pass out.

Pressing 'Play', the music pounding through the headphones, I set off running, no warm-up. I wanted my body to hurt, to push myself to such a level that I physically couldn't take another step. If I had to hospitalize myself I would. Fitness was the key to beating PTSD, I knew it; just like joining the army at sixteen years old, I had a point to prove.

Reaching the top of the first hill, I could feel the lactic acid building in my legs already because of the pace I'd set off at, then the audio flashbacks started creeping in under the music. I could hear Stu making jokes but couldn't quite make out what he was saying. I didn't want to know. Turning the music even louder, I found another gear and quickened my pace, up the next hill, my heart now thumping and lungs stinging as they struggled to feed my muscles with enough oxygen to keep this speed up. I stared at my path in front of me. Straight across every road junction, not looking for cars. I didn't care, nothing was going to slow me down on this run, my body and brain were going to pay for this. No more medication, no more therapy. I would beat my body into submission.

Getting to the halfway point of my run, I stopped and turned around without taking even a second's rest. Powering back on my route back home, I looked at my watch. I'd done my first 1.5 miles in seven minutes thirty-two seconds, which was a similar sort of standard to when I went on Special Operations selection. This was fast – not fast enough, though. I hadn't been sick or passed out yet. Finding another gear from somewhere, I turned my music up full blast. It now wouldn't go any higher and was distorting slightly.

No more audio flashbacks. Staring ahead, I felt like my lungs were on fire, I couldn't breathe quick enough. No excuse, the oxygen was there, don't slow down, you fucker. Run faster, you prick, find another gear in your legs, punish yourself and realize you are strong. Increasing the pace again, I didn't stop until I got home and that's when it hit me. Steadying myself on the door of the house, my vision started to blur as I went light-headed. Feeling the water from earlier surge up through my throat, I was violently sick as I stumbled to keep my footing. Job done.

Talking to my wife after the run, we both agreed physical activity was going to help me recover from PTSD faster than any drugs or therapy would. Over the next few months I trained every day, the nightmares eased off first, then the flashbacks. Ultimately my symptoms subsided but Thames House still had the final word.

My team leader and Sue arranged to come and see me. I already knew at this point that I was getting the sack. I'd become content with the fact I was no longer in MI5. Sitting around the kitchen table in my half-decorated house, I was asked to sign several bits of paperwork, Section One of the Official Secrets Act being the main one. My team leader asked for my radio kit and Security Service ID badge and the pass that used to get me into Thames House, as Sue went on to explain the final piece of paper I had to sign.

'In recognition of your service and the sacrifice you've made, the office have decided to award you a pension because you are unable to operate effectively. It's not much but you'll get it every month.'

I wasn't expecting this at all, and Sue was right, it wasn't a lot, but if I managed to secure another job it would go towards paying the mortgage at least. As they both left out the door, Sue remembered she had to give me another piece of paper.

'Oh, Director B says he needs you to read this: it's a list of countries you're not allowed to visit. Ever.'

Closing the door, I looked at the list of locations. They were hardly the normal holiday destinations at the top of our family list. Countries like Russia, North Korea, Syria, Iraq, Egypt, among nearly thirty others. I'll always be under the threat of foreign intelligence agencies for the rest of my life.

I was officially unemployed, having been medically

retired from the Security Service. Over a ten-year period I'd protected this country in covert counter-terrorism. All of it in a Top Secret role. What the fuck did I do now? How did someone like me fit into mainstream society?

Over the next couple of years I bounced around from job to job, from working in a call centre to flipping burgers at a drive-through. I couldn't tell anyone about my background so it looked like I was hiding something, which meant I could only get basic, low-skilled jobs. This was perhaps just as tough as dealing with PTSD. I was willing to do anything to earn money and give my family a positive role model to follow but because of the secrecy that shrouded my previous career I couldn't get anything that paid well, unless I was willing to take the many offers of work overseas in Iraq and Afghanistan. But for me no amount of money was worth my family seeing me being beheaded on a cellar floor if I got caught out there.

As one mundane job rolled into another, it must have looked from anyone else's perspective like I wasn't committed to seeing a new career through, like I was some sort of waster. But I slowly started to realize that how I earned money didn't define who I actually was as a person; it would be my actions that told my story. I once heard an agent handler in Thames House talking about family and it's something that has always stuck with me.

'A man is only a man if he puts his family first. If he puts the needs of his wife and children before anything else, then he can be called a man.'

*

This is just the beginning.

Watching the news, you could be fooled into thinking the world is descending into chaos. Radicals using religion to create genocide. Mass murderers using the name of God to kill innocent people. Countries flexing their military might in each other's airspace. Let me set that straight: you are safe. Go about your lives loving those close to you, be aware of your surroundings, but don't live in fear.

There are people working night and day in the shadows all around the world surrounding you with an iron curtain, stopping those who wish to cause you harm. Fear is a profitable business, and a shocking event will receive wider publicity than a happy one, which is why the press will always talk about a bombing rather than something positive.

I was in the counter-terrorism world for a long time. I've stopped some of the most catastrophic events from happening, alongside the teams. I was a tiny little cog in a massive machine, and there are thousands of people like me out there protecting you. Unfortunately, the IRA put it best when they said, 'You [the government] have to be lucky 100 per cent of the time; we only have to be lucky once.' It's true. People who wish to harm us will take the opportunity to strike when they get the rare chance, but I don't want anyone focusing on the attacks that have slipped through the net. I want people to focus on the hundreds if not thousands of attacks, over the decades worldwide, that we have prevented.

I very nearly paid the ultimate price when PTSD took

over as I desperately clawed my way out of that dark place. I was extremely lucky to get the help I needed to recover, focused on getting my body fit and allowing my mind to regain its strength. As I move into a new chapter of my life, blindfolded as to what the normal world has to offer, I will take the same relentless drive into anything I do to show my family that anything is possible.

I am a soldier and a spy, our enemy's worst nightmare and the country's darkest asset. This is a word of warning to those who wish to hurt us: our nation is strong and united; that strength has been built on thousands of years of hardship, and if you even think about trying to hurt us, my friends will find you, and fucking destroy you.

Semper Vigilat.

Acknowledgements

Thank you to those who have made this book possible: Luigi, Rowland, Louise and the incredible team at Michael Joseph. All of you have become extremely important to me.

I also want to thank everyone at the Security Service in Thames House, especially my old team, for giving me the help I needed, when I needed it.